"In this elegantly written and extremely well-researched book, Dyson. . . helps to illuminate the internal struggles of Tupac that were manifested in such spectacular fashion. It is a sympathetic, but not sentimental, look at a young man who although only 25 years old when murdered left a legacy. . . that will undoubtedly live on for a lifetime."
    —*Detroit Free Press*

". . . paints a nuanced picture of his subject while illuminating the effect hip-hop has had on America."
    —*The New Yorker*

"*Holler If You Hear Me* not only analyzes the conflicted workings of a young man gone too soon but considers how Shakur's life and spirit, in ways good and bad, continue to challenge popular culture and inform the world he left behind."
    —*Boston Globe*

"[Dyson] makes a distinctly substantial contribution to deconstructing the mystique of Tupac Shakur. . . . By focusing sincere academic attention on significant aspects of Tupac Shakur's life and art, Dyson has provided an indispensable text for the university courses on Pac that have already cropped up nationwide."
    —*The Village Voice*

"An earnest attempt to explain the ever-growing appeal of 'the black Elvis' to fans' parents, and even more so, to cultural critics and academics. . . . It is worth reading."
    —*Atlanta Journal and Constitution*

"'Though castigated as a shameless promoter of thug life, Tupac appealed to a large and surprisingly diverse audience. Dyson tells us why they listened and why this dead rapper still matters."
    —*Quarterly Black Review*

"Fascinating and provocative. . . Dyson deftly and convincingly shows the contradictions that divided Tupac's soul. . . . He writes passionately and knowingly but not uncritically about Tupac and the rap and hip-hop culture."
    —*San Antonio Express-News*

"Dyson swapped life in the Detroit ghetto for a Ph.D. from Princeton University and a position as one of the nation's premier critical thinkers. . . . Through sociological examination, he explores Tupac as both revolutionary and thug while shedding new light on American culture and hip-hop itself."
    —*Philadelphia City Paper*

Michael Eric Dyson

Basic Civitas Books
A Member of the Perseus Books Group

HOLLER IF YOU HEAR ME

Searching for

Tupac Shakur

Copyright © 2001 by Michael Eric Dyson
Published by Basic *Civitas* Books,
A Member of the Perseus Books Group

First paperback printing by Basic Books in 2003.
Second paperback printing by Basic Books in 2006.

Designed by Lovedog Studio

A CIP catalog record for this book is available
from the Library of Congress.

ISBN 0-465-01755-X (hc); 0-465-01756-8 (pbk)
2nd pbk: ISBN-13: 978-0-465-01728-7;
ISBN-10: 0-465-01728-2

10 9 8 7

Photo Credits: Joel Levinson / Corbis-Sygma, page
9 • James Bevins / Globe, page 32 • Danny Clinch /
Corbis-Outline, pages 56, 214, 237 • Hulton /
Archive by Getty Images, page 83 • Raymond Boyd
/ MichaelOchsArchives.com, page 121 • Al Pereira
/ MichaelOchsArchives.com, page 122 • Michael
Benabib / Retna, page 155 • Ernie Paniccioli /
Retna, page 156 •Helayne Seidman / Getty Im-
ages, page 194 • John Spellman / Retna, page 213
• Jeffrey Newbury / Corbis-Outline, page 222
• Andrew Lichtenstein / Corbis-Sygma, page 259

DEDICATED TO THE WOMEN TUPAC LOVED

Afeni Shakur

Jada Pinkett Smith

Leila Steinberg

Danyel Smith

Cassandra Butcher

Jasmine Guy

Tracy Robinson

Kidada Jones

AND TO THE SISTERS WHO FEARLESSLY LOVE OUR YOUTH

Maxine Waters

Nikki Giovanni

Sonia Sanchez

Ingrid Saunders Jones

Ruth J. Simmons

Susan L. Taylor

Toni Morrison

Also by Michael Eric Dyson

I MAY NOT GET THERE WITH YOU

RACE RULES

BETWEEN GOD AND GANGSTA RAP

MAKING MALCOLM

REFLECTING BLACK

CONTENTS

ACKNOWLEDGMENTS

As usual, I thank my wonderful, brilliant, and gifted editor, Liz Maguire. She has shared my vision almost from the beginning of my writing career, and I am indebted to her for nurturing and inspiring my gift. Love you, Liz. I also thank William Morrison, Stephen Bottum, Christine Marra, and Jane Raese, for their expert transformation of this manuscript into a book.

I thank the following people for sharing their precious time and granting me interviews: George Duke (a gifted musician); Todd Boyd ("my Detroit nigga" and a hell of a professor and writer); Karen Lee (a good sister and sweet soul); Atron Gregory (who took my many calls); Mos Def (an extraordinary young artist of incomparable gifts); Eric Meza (who made smart comments); Connie Bruck (who took time from her wedding preparations to help me with last-minute research); Larenz Tate (a great actor and good brother); Anna Marie Horsford (my beautiful chocolate diva; I'm her number-one fan); Big Boy (a humorous personality); Ray J (a sharp young brother); Warren G (for his on-the-spot insight); Big Tray Dee (for true sharing from the heart); Matthew McDaniel (for the words in between filming); Congresswoman Maxine Waters (fearless warrior, my beautiful, brilliant role model and hero); Preston Holmes (for his sincerity and generous time); Vivica Fox (for her beauty and brilliant craft); Reverend Willie Wilson (an awesome preacher and pathbreaking Christian); Vanesse Lloyd-Sqambati (a brilliant and resourceful public relations person); LaTanya Richardson (a beautiful treasure); Quincy

Jones (still the man, a great genius); C. Delores Tucker (who was so generous with her time); Geronimo Pratt (an old-school warrior and strong black man); Allison Samuels (a gifted journalist who was extremely helpful with contacts); Keith Harrison (a sharp young professor and good brother); Bill Maher (the politically incorrect guru of late-night television); Arvand Elihu (a sharp young physician-poet–Tupac expert); John Singleton (a singular director with mad skills who squeezed me in); Jada Pinkett Smith (a wonderful artist and a true gem of a woman who took time from *Matrix II*); Samuel Jackson (there's only one of this brother); Takashi Buford (for granting me time); Rose Katherine (my beautiful Princeton homie); Vondie Curtis Hall (a wonderful artist, gifted director, and my homeboy); Cassandra Butcher (a sweet, talented, and generous sister); Peggy Lipton (a warm woman who's still bright and mod as all get-out); Reginald Hudlin (a dazzling raconteur and intellectual); Everett Dyson-Bey (my big little brother who drops mad science); Reverend Al Sharpton (who keeps witnessing for the truth); Kim Fields (a bright and gifted thespian); Common (a lyrically ferocious emcee and ingenious poet); Shawn Chapman (a wonderful attorney and kind sister); Bishop T. D. Jakes (an enormously talented preacher); Yanko Dambaulev (a great poet, philosopher, and brother); Khephra Burns (an immensely gifted writer and my brother); Talib Kweli (a supremely moving wordsmith of enormous gifts); Johnnie Cochran (who hooks up all the brothas in trouble); Robin D. G. Kelley (an intellectual giant); Sonia Sanchez (a great poetess, both profoundly intelligent and generous); Stanley Crouch (a stunningly smart critic who defines the Renaissance man); Charles Ogletree (an amazing professor, excellent jurist, and good brother); Danyel Smith (my sweet, beautiful, and brilliant friend and an amazing writer); Vijay Prashad (for the thug science); Toni Morrison (for her genius, her generosity of spirit, and her plain old soulfulness); Big Syke (a soulful, wonderful, and magnanimous brother who mentored Tupac in important ways); Tracy Robinson (for her extraordinary open-heartedness, wonderful and guileless spirit, and stewardship of Pac's projects); Leila Steinberg (for the amazing drive to keep Pac's spirit alive and for her own remarkable spirit and love); and especially Afeni Shakur (the woman without whom there would be no Tupac Shakur, for her beautiful, bold, and brave spirit; her commitment to fulfilling her son's work; and her giving soul).

I also want to thank the following folk for tending to my heart, body, mind, and spirit: Stanley and Barbara Perkins (amazing and wonderful friends with tremendous spirits— and unbelievable food); Al Colon and Linda Malone-Colon (precious friends who opened hearth and home); Valentine Burroughs (my wonderful friend, big brother, and healer); Carolyn Moore-Assem (a sweet-souled sister with magic in her mouth); Veronica Mallett (my beautiful homegirl and a gracious, generous professional); and my sweet, brilliant, giving friend Deborah Langford ("You know what I'm saying, mofo?"). I am grateful as well to Mia Stokes and Kim Ransom for their efficient and solid research as well as Paige McIntosh for her assistance and dedication. And a special shout out to the inimitable D. Soyini Madison, brilliant critic, my soul's most precious friend, spiritual warrior, and a great woman. Profound gratitude to my wonderful family, Freda, Frederick, and Dr. Sampson (my true hero and role model).

Finally, I want to thank my family: the memory of my father, Everett Dyson Sr. (gone for twenty years); my mother, Addie Mae Dyson; my brothers, Anthony, Everett, Gregory, and Brian, as well as their children; and my own wonderful children: Michael Eric Dyson (who sweetly said to me when Tupac was murdered, "Dad, I think if you had met Tupac he wouldn't have died"); Maisha Dyson (a terrific actress who is blazing her path to artistic excellence); and Mwata Dyson (a physician whose commitment to holistic healing is exemplary); and my lovely Jennifer and my wonderful Virgil. Finally, I am grateful to my wonderful and amazingly loyal wife, Rev. Marcia L. Dyson, who took time from her novel *Don't Call Me Angel* to give me extraordinary assistance in every phase of this book.

Introduction to the 2006 Edition: Holy Ghost

A full decade after his death, Tupac Shakur has the culture in a headlock. He has released nearly twice as many albums dead—eight—than the five albums he released when he was alive. His posthumous releases often outsell the efforts of living artists and debut at the top of the music charts. As recently as 2004, Tupac's posthumous album *Loyal to the Game* bested the release of R&B songstress Ashanti's third LP, *Concrete Rose*, and was top in sales the week it debuted. (Interestingly enough, a collection of Tupac's adolescent verse, *The Rose That Grew from Concrete*, was posthumously published in 1999.) When he drew breath and spit venom, Tupac sold nearly 10 million discs; in death, he has sold at least 25 million more. In 2003, through the miracle of technology, Tupac was the lone star of a successful and moving documentary on his art and life. In *Tupac: Resurrection*, Tupac nearly topped Moses's feat in the Bible of discussing his death in a work of art created after his demise. Tupac was the subject in 2004 of a scholarly conference sponsored by the Hip Hop Archive at Harvard that strained to explain his enduring appeal. In 2001, Tupac's life and death were explored in a play that debuted in New York's East Village entitled *Up Against the Wind*. He regularly appears on lists of the top money earners among dead artists, alongside Elvis Presley, Marilyn Monroe, and Bob Marley. Tupac is widely regarded as the most influential rapper ever—"I put Tupac beyond Shakespeare" says legendary rapper Nas—and one of the most important figures in music history.

Anticipating his legacy, Tupac once boasted to his early benefactor Leila Steinberg—who permitted the fledgling rapper to temporarily live with her family and who served as his first manager—that future generations would analyze his raps the way they do Shakespeare's plays. Tupac's words would prove more prophetic than anyone could have guessed; starting with a class at the University of California, Berkeley, in 1998, a slew of college courses dedicated to studying Tupac's body of work cropped up after his death. In the classroom, students probe every nook and cranny of his storied and controversial existence.

One of the reasons Tupac still resonates in the culture is his outsized literary ambition. When it came to the themes of his music, Tupac thought big, and often in stark binaries: life and death ("Life Goes On"); love and hate ("Hail Mary"); judgment and forgiveness ("I Ain't Mad at Cha"); joy and pain ("To Live and Die in L.A."); and heaven and hell ("I Wonder if Heaven's Got a Ghetto"). He fearlessly, and poetically, explored dimensions of the male psyche neglected by his rap peers. (None of them had before dared to as tenderly, or publicly, praise his mother as Tupac did in "Dear Mama.") Tupac squeezed the various vulnerabilities of black life into verse without smothering its defiant hope. In "Unconditional Love," for instance, the narrator acknowledges the "urge to die" but reminds his listeners that "tomorrow comes after the dark/So you will always be in my heart, with unconditional love."

His language was inflamed with love for the desperately poor; Tupac was a ghetto Dickens who explained the plight of the downtrodden in rebellious rhyme. But like the unconventional literary masters he brought to mind—think Jean Genet meets Sylvia Plath—Tupac was often smeared by critics and pundits who took his words literally. The vibrant imagination that fueled Tupac's gift was often dismissed, perhaps because it was too dark, too dangerous.

Like so many of the "troublesome" artists who preceded him, it was Tupac's tolerance for life's grey ones that provided a constant problem for both his critics and those seeking to interpret his work. While he often decried racism and spoke about blacks and whites, Tupac rarely thought in black and white terms. His eager embrace of ethical ambivalence came off to critics as mere hypocrisy. After all, how could the same artist—or, given the unwilling suspension of disbelief, the same man—encourage women to keep their heads up one moment and then quickly pelt them with harsh epithets? How could he proclaim peace while carrying a sword? Obviously his critics weren't too familiar with the harsh personalities and dualities of the Old Testament. To be sure, Tupac leaned in his lyrics toward that epic tradition. It's clear that his moral codes and conflicts—and, yes, his self-destructive contradictions too—were strictly biblical.

Tupac was enamored of literary creators and characters—from Sun Tzu to Maya Angelou, from Richard Wright's *Native Son* to Niccolo Machiavelli's *The Prince*. They flashed regularly in his titles, lyrics, ideas, and allusions. For example, *Still I Rise*, a posthumous album Tupac recorded with his protégés The Outlawz, pinched its title from Angelou's poem. Legions of Tupac's fans devoured her poetry after they gave their idol's record a listen. Tupac's first posthumous album, *Makavelli: The 7 Day Theory*, borrowed Machiavelli's name for its protagonist's artistic alter ego. It also compelled millions to scour the Italian political theorist's revered work *The Prince* for signs of how Tupac might have faked his death to bolster his influence. Tupac not only got young folk to read; he got them to read classics that educational critics thought they ought to be absorbing. And they read them for the reasons anybody should read anything—to enhance the pleasures and thrills of learning, and to put their knowledge to good use in the real world. By referencing great works of literature, Tupac created the hip hop version of Oprah's book club.

Tupac read books because he was deeply curious about the world around him. He agreed with Socrates that an unexamined life isn't worth living. His mother, a Black Panther, taught him to be skeptical about truth claims, especially where politics is concerned. Tupac's budding erudition only strengthened his suspicion of authority. It makes sense that when he chose to be a rebel not just any kind of rebellion would do. Tupac didn't just become a thug—he became a metaphysical thug. He was a thinking man's verbal outlaw. It might be hard out here for a pimp, but it's even harder for a gangsta with a brain and half a conscience. In our day, the rapper Nas, arguably, has best carried forth Tupac's restless quest for broad literacy.

Of course, those who admire Tupac don't always understand him the first, or second, or even the third go-round. Many of them surely *felt* him before they *grasped* him. They didn't get all the references he spit in his charged soliloquies. But neither do readers of William Butler Yeats or

Rita Dove. That may be precisely the reason Tupac remains alive—his future is utterly literary and knowledge intensive. The more you learn, the more you get what Tupac is up to. That's an inspiration to keep listening in order to keep hearing what Tupac keeps saying. It spurs repeat listeners to revel in decoding esoteric allusions. (Did a generation weaned on crack and *The Cosby Show* immediately get the reference to murdered Panther Bobby Hutton on *Ghetto Gospel*?)

Of course, such an endeavor includes a self-congratulating gesture: because Tupac is so smart, the more you know about what he's saying, the smarter it must mean you are. The feeling that they are brimming with knowledge dares Tupac's audience to raise their game even more and to learn as much as they can. But in an era when prominent political figures parade their ignorance like a Thanksgiving Day float, the odds are that such learning is neither illusory, nor exaggerated, nor irrelevant. The same black youth culture that is frowned on for allegedly glamorizing dull thought—an allegation not hard to prove in the sort of hip hop obsessed with materialism, machismo, and misogyny—has also made a hero out of a fallen poet who made deep thinking sexy. His calling card consisted of politics, history, and race as much as it did raunchy boudoir talk. And given the sheer volume of Tupac's posthumous output, and the growing catalog of books about him—there are already more than a dozen in the marketplace ranging from pictorials to academic treatises—Tupac's lyrical and literary immortality are secure.

But it's not just the volume of Tupac's work that makes him irresistible. Tupac's magnificent obsession (what it means to be young, black, male, and poor in America) guarantees that his eloquent fury is as up to date as, say, the *New York Times* report in early 2006 that argues that—a drum roll should be inserted here, or better yet a funky drum machine rhythm that is a staple of hip hop's sonic force—black males are in crisis! That wasn't news to Tupac's fans. For a while, it was almost the only story they'd been hearing in one guise or another from their beloved griot. While the academic studies cited in the *Times* article argue that trends in the economy left black males behind even when others prospered, Tupac in 1991's "If My Homie Calls" put his lungs on one source of suffering: low-wage work without benefits. "My homies is making it elsewhere/Striving, working nine to five with no health care." Tupac took note in 1995 of the rabid incarceration of black men when he lamented in "F*** the World" the plight of "tha young black male/Tryin' to stack bail/And stay away from the packed jails." Though Pac often assailed racism—"Why do they keep calling me nigger?" he queried in "White Man'z World"—he could be clear-eyed and pitiless in examining the black roots of black ruin. "And they say it's the white man I should fear/But it's my own kind doin' all the killin' here," he rapped in "Only God Can Judge Me Now."

Besides racism and the crisis of black males, Tupac addressed a myriad of problems that have tragically gone nowhere: economic inequality, police brutality, racial profiling, teenage motherhood, absentee fathers, false prophets, failed political leadership, and state-sponsored violence. Because the issues he embraced are still around, so is the need for Tupac's biting commentary, a role few other rappers have, or can, fulfill. Pac spoke of how the government found cash for war but not for the economically strapped, a claim often associated with the war in Iraq and the lack of response following the devastation of Hurricane Katrina. "You know its funny when it rains it pours/They got money for wars, but can't feed the poor," Tupac declared in "Keep Ya Head Up." And while he could howl in deplorable misogyny, Tupac wasn't an uncomplicated sexist. He wavered between paeans to black women and ugly justifications of their degraded standing—or between "Baby Don't Cry" and "Wonder Why They Call You Bytch." As Tupac saluted and scolded black women, he channeled warring tendencies in black life that have hardly subsided. Even his flaws have traction and the potential to instruct. They are, after all, the flaws of the larger society and not just the fleeting preoccupations of a lone man.

Perhaps it is Tupac's ability to reach a broad audience within and beyond hip hop that separates him from most of his peers. Tupac is the consummate all-purpose rapper; he appeals to backpackers and thugs, to the roughnecks and the ladies, and to those who like to party and those who hunger for political relevance. Only Kanye West has even begun to attract such competing constituencies within hip hop. When he declared that George Bush's fatally slow response to the victims of Hurricane Katrina proved he didn't care about black people, Kanye accepted Tupac's mantle of fearless truth telling. And while Tupac reveled in extravagant toys and sexual trysts in his raps, he resisted through a Herculean work ethic the tyranny of commercial rap's holy trinity: broads, bling, and booze. He relished all three, but he subordinated their pleasures to an artistic demon that drove him to feverish creation.

The reason there's so much to say about Tupac is that there are so many parts of Tupac to say something about. His raps are endlessly recombinant; mix tapes, bootlegs, and a seemingly unquenchable flow of new configurations of Tupac's lyrics testify to his seminal soulfulness. *2Pac: Rap Phenomenon II* features some of Tupac's best-known lyrics over updated beats from more recent rap hits. Most of the songs feature an original verse from current rap stars like Busta Rhymes and 50 Cent. These pairings allow contemporary rap stars to associate themselves with Tupac's enduring legacy even as they assure that Tupac's canon is both classic and contemporary. Tupac's music can be readily copped on street corners or in corporate music stores—and on rural routes and distant shores—around the globe. He is a peerless ambassador of hip hop to the world.

There are a lot of reasons why Tupac continues to be even more popular in death than he was in life: his thug-revolutionary-artiste persona that resonates in our occasionally barren pop artistic epoch; his extraordinary handsomeness and perfectly sculpted physique that embody his youthfulness and our vain adoration and envy of it; his diligent martyrdom, one that he predicted, and thus, in part, precipitated, setting him apart from other fallen stars like Notorious B.I.G., who, despite his lyrics, fought it like the plague; and his translation of epic religious ideas into secular eulogies and cautionary tales. Tupac even exacted a revenge of sorts on all those critics who charged him with pathology but who lauded the genius of a rapper who has carried Tupac's urgent and contradictory moral vision into the next generation: Eminem. As gifted novelist Zadie Smith argues in her 2002 *Vibe magazine profile of the rapper*, Eminem's "music shares Tupac's obsession with truthfully representing a group of disenfranchised people." But for Eminem, as for Tupac, "being the truth-telling prophet to a generation is troublesome" because, as Smith contends, some "truths are hard and self-destructive" while other truths "are conflicting to the point of schizophrenia."

But what ultimately makes Tupac a legend is the way he made the music he made, and the way he made it easy for others—producers, DJs, and rappers—to make something of the poetry he left behind. Even that may not satisfactorily explain his enduring appeal. Perhaps it is because he spoke straight from the heart that we recognized that a troubled prophet had risen to articulate a truth that we couldn't possibly live without. While that is certainly not true for all of us, perhaps not even for most of us, it is true for enough of us. For those folk, Tupac's searing voice is a siren of sanity.

The success of *Holler If You Hear Me*—*Publisher's Weekly* kindly cited it, along with Tupac's book of poems, for helping to "establish the notion that hip-hop books were marketable"—is further proof that Tupac continues to command attention in the culture and in the academy. Tupac is not likely to fade from cultural view anytime soon; the persistence of the problems he brilliantly addressed, and sometimes painfully embodied, make his urban prophecy even more relevant. Those problems include racial and economic inequality, the burgeoning prison-industrial complex, institutionalized misogyny—and the president's dipping deeply into the domestic pot to fund the war machine and divert resources from the socially vulnerable. Tupac's legacy is bound up with the fate of this country. As long as the ghetto poor continue to suffer, there will be a shelf in the record shop devoted to Tupac. In a great twist of irony, the only way that Tupac could lose his relevance would be if this country got its affairs in order. If urban poverty were eliminated and young black males were given their rightful place in society, then Tupac's music might quickly become a historical artifact from a dark national nightmare. As things stand, Tupac's riveting art, and the problems he rapped about, are all here to stay.

"i Always Wanted to Make a Book Out of My Life"

In Search of Tupac

This past March I made my way to the warehouse district of Los Angeles on a warm Sunday afternoon in hopes of talking to Snoop Dogg about his late friend and sometime collaborator Tupac Shakur. The famed rapper and his cohorts Warren G and Nate Dogg were set to perform at a small, private promotional concert arranged by the recreational footwear company for whom he endorses shoes. I climbed the stairs of the converted warehouse that serves as the company's headquarters and found the third-floor makeshift "green room" where the artists and media would gather before the show. I mingled with the other writers and made small talk with the few celebrities and artists who streamed through, awaiting Snoop's arrival. I caught a few minutes with Big Boy, the L.A. radio personality who spent time with Tupac on the road when Big Boy was a bodyguard for the West Coast hip-hop group The Pharcyde.

"You know, what I liked about the dude," Big Boy told me as we huddled in a corner as an intimate crowd of over fifty people milled about the room. "He loved everyone, but he always knew that he was a strong black man. And he wasn't afraid to say a lot of stuff that other people wouldn't say. Others would say, 'I can't say that.' Not Pac. If I want to get everybody's attention, I can't just sit here and say, 'Hey. . . .'"

Without warning, Big Boy finished his sentence by cupping his hands around his mouth and screaming at the top of his lungs, startling me and the other folk in the room.

"You've got to say, 'HEY!'"

After I recovered from his unanticipated sonic blast, my brow furrowed and my eyes slightly bucked, he continued, laughing at my response and the way the crowd momentarily froze.

"Sometimes you've got to scream. You've got to snatch their attention. And that's why his music lives on, that's why people care—because he made such an impact. It wasn't that Pac became a star after he passed. Pac was a star from my first handshake with him; he was a star from the get-go. He *always* commanded attention."

Our impromptu session over, I scanned the room for other folk that might have known the rapper. I chanced upon Ray J, a star, with his sister Brandy, of the television series *Moesha* and a recording artist as well.

"I just recorded a new song with Tupac," the young artist told me.

Uh-oh, I thought to myself. Although he's talented, this is obviously a young brother who believes that Tupac is still alive. But then I remembered that Tupac's posthumous recordings are already legendary and that many artists have gone into the studio to supply music and vocals for the hundreds of tracks he laid down. I'm relieved.

"It's called 'Unborn Child,' and it's coming out on the second release of his double CD. Nobody has heard it before."

Ray J was excited about recording with Tupac. I remembered as I spoke to him that the new technologies ensure that very few living artists even record together in the same place at the same time. So in a way the method of recording was nothing new. But his enthused expression made it apparent that the opportunity to partner with Tupac was still thrilling.

"Tupac is one of the greatest poets out there right now," Ray J told me. I took note of his present tense, since Tupac's continually unfolding artistry, in books, in movies, and in compact discs, makes it difficult to speak of him in the past.

"The brother just went into the studio and did songs that a lot of people can relate to and learn from before he went out. Like he said, he's just a thug who has a lot of money. But on the other hand, he's a thug that is giving positive messages to kids so they can be like him."

Besides noting the persistent present tense in his speech,

which was slightly jarring—done without irony and fully passionate to boot—I was curious about how a thug, even a poetic one, came off as positive to a young man noted for his clean lyrics and wholesome demeanor. So I asked him.

"He taught us that we can make a living for ourselves and become rich and become entrepreneurs in the game."

His press person whisked him away to his next appointment, and I was left to ponder just how many young people like Ray J were affected by Tupac's message and music, how many generations would continue to admire him and keep his memory alive. Just then I spotted the ferociously gifted actor Larenz Tate, known for his agile, adept, and brooding performances in the Hughes brothers' films *Menace II Society* and *Dead Presidents*. But it was clear that he was, as the hip-hop phrase states it, "on the down-low," very low-key and unassuming and hence unnoticeable, or at least he hoped. After we exchanged pleasantries and mutual admiration, he led me out of the room and down the hallway for maximum privacy—and to relieve other scribes of the hope of pressing him for his thoughts. He was studied, altogether genial and affable, and quietly reflective.

"For most of his core fans and people who knew him, he was a prophet," Tate calmly expounded in a near whisper. "It's really weird how a person can predict things the way he did. When he passed away, everything he had talked about before he died actually happened."

Tate gets a bit of a spark with his next comment, his intense eyes brightening as he states a parallel that's been made time and again but whose repetition is no hindrance to the truth it means to convey.

"I think he is the hip-hop version of Elvis Presley," Tate declared. "People are claiming Tupac sightings everywhere." I couldn't help but think to myself, as he spoke of Tupac and Elvis, that it's about time. White folk are always spotting Elvis or JFK or Marilyn Monroe, which is a great thing if your icons and heroes were only apparently gone but in truth were hanging out on a deserted island, living beyond their legend in the solitude of old age. I've asked myself through the years why nobody has ever spotted, say, Sam Cooke or Otis Redding or Billie Holiday or even Donny Hathaway, cooling out in the shade of a palm tree, content that their tragic, storied pasts are a world away. Black mythologies and legends are hard to create, even harder to sustain.

"He has definitely etched a mark in hip-hop culture." Tate's words brought me back from my momentary reverie. "But he was also able to transcend the hip-hop culture into the pop world, to film and television and all kinds of media. For him to still be just as big now as he was when he was alive is amazing." Since Tate is such a talented thespian, I asked him about Tupac's cinematic aura.

"Your goal as a performer is to give something that's the truth or something that is real. In the context of real-life stories—and he was usually in films that reflected real street life—he was able to draw from his experience with the streets." The notion of truth, of authenticity, of the real, is a recurring theme in the narratives that swirl around Tupac and that he spun for himself. "Keeping it real," is the mantra that Tupac lived to its devastating, perhaps even lethal, limits. Tate reflected on his brief encounters with

Tupac, the promise they held, and the promise they left un-fulfilled.

"I didn't spend as much time with Tupac as I wish I would have," Tate lamented. "A lot of people who knew Tupac and who knew me said it would be great if we really sat down and had a meeting of the minds, because he needed to hear more positive things. Unfortunately, that didn't happen." Unfortunate indeed, since too often the love and inspiration black men need to stay alive is only a brother away. The thought that Tate might have made a real difference in Tupac's life is a missed opportunity that bathes us in a moment of silent musing. We break by giving each other a black male hug—right hands entwined in a friend-ship clasp as our right arms clench and draw us forward to better grasp each other on the back with our left arms. Tupac is the bridge that brought us this close, but we don't need to acknowledge it with anything more than an implicit recognition we glimpse in each other's eyes.

Just as we parted, I heard the long-awaited caravan of buses pulling up in front of the warehouse. They were only a couple of hours late, not bad in CP time—no, not colored people's time but chillin' posse's time. Since Snoop took his name from the canine, I suppose it was only right that we had all aged in dog years awaiting his arrival. As I emerged into the sunlight from the building's cavernous spaces, I was greeted by a gaggle of camera crews and reporters seeking to get a piece of Snoop as he made his way from the bus to the private room reserved for him—and it wasn't the green room in which many of us had waited. The shoe company executives were there, of course, as well as a slew of handlers and other personnel intent on escorting Snoop to his temporary digs. I grew more uncomfortable by the minute. I knew this was no way to get a serious interview with Snoop, even though I'd tried to reach him through more traditional—and less dicey—channels. But when all else failed, I embraced serendipity when a behind-the-scenes executive working with the concert recognized me in the hotel from television and my books and offered me a backstage and green-room pass when I told him about my desire to speak to Snoop for my book on Tupac. Hugging corners and waiting on celebrity entertainers while beating back crowds was not my métier. I simply wanted to grab some time with a man I thought would be helpful to my cause.

Moreover, I had done enough reading and writing about hip-hop, enough attending concerts and shows and club promotions to know that nothing offends the machismo of the rapper more than male groupies. There is a distinct genre of the dis in hip-hop that pours venom and disdain on the heads of guys who outwardly display their love of hip-hop or its stars by showing up backstage to seek an autograph or give praise. In the misogynist lingo of the culture, that was the job of the "ho," or the "bitch," and I wasn't about to subject myself to the hateful stare or acerbic rebuff of youth no older than the students I teach at the university. That is, not until I realized that I would have little time to get to Snoop if I waited for the crush around him to collapse upstairs as he entered his secluded domain. So there I was, in the line of reporters and hangers-on who were granted fleeting access by the heavy security to the area where the bus had lodged to deposit the rap stars. I

managed to perch right at the bus's door as it opened and a
cloud of smoke greeted the small clutch of onlookers. I
recognized the face of Warren G, like Snoop a southern-
cadenced rapper whose melodies were often enhanced by
the dulcet tones of gangsta crooner and preacher's kid Nate
Dogg. I figured I had better press my case immediately,
since the competition was almost as thick as the weed
smoke that filled the air around us.

"Brother Warren G, I'm writing a book on Tupac, and I'd
love to get your opinion about him." I felt silly in saying it
so quickly, so publicly, and, yes, so desperately. My pride was
aching something awful, and my resentment at having to go
this route was sweeping fast. I suppose I was the hip-hop
equivalent of the anxious white liberal—I didn't mind giving all kinds of support to the culture, but when it came
time to put my body and ego on the line, well, that was another matter. Plus, my self-aware status was rubbing against
the unfolding drama: "I am a figure, an intellectual, a person
who writes books and appears on television and has a following of people who think I'm important. This is no place
for me to be, no way for me to behave. I should just leave."
But since I'd come this far, I figured it might not hurt to
stay a little longer. That's when Warren G opened his
mouth.

"Damn, you gon' hit me right here, huh?" he said in
amusement, gently laughing and ambushed by a tape-
recorder-wielding, geriatric (by hip-hop standards) scribe
wanting to know about a fallen comrade. But he was a good
sport, a far better one, I was soon to find out, than his
speechifying peers.

"Well, I've got to be ready, man," I shot back.

"What do you want to know?" he asked.

"I want to know why, five years after his death, Tupac is still a significant figure."

Warren leaned back on the stairs and took hold of the door handles to steady himself as he spoke.

"He laid down a real message that you can feel from the heart—you know what I'm saying?" he said. "I did a lot of work with him, but we never kicked it major on the personal side, but we kicked it enough to where we had major love for each other. When he did 'Definition of a Thug,' that was one of the times when I was going through some stuff, and he was going through some stuff, so we chatted at each other and really got an understanding about each other." When I asked him to tell me something about Tupac that the world didn't know, he spoke of his work ethic.

"In the studio he was amazing," Warren G said. "He handled his business. Once you shook hands and you talked for a minute, then he would go and he would grab that pad. Damn. Doing his stuff. And that's when it all came together."

I thanked Warren G as he stepped out of the bus and slowly made his way to the warehouse. He was replaced in the doorway by Nate Dogg, the smooth-voiced crooner, gangsta rap's Frank Sinatra, who has made guest appearances on countless rap recordings. When I asked Nate about Tupac, he was more withdrawn and tight, insular in a self-protective fashion. It was obvious that I had struck a nerve, and he gently brushed me off by telling me he'd speak to me upstairs. "Let me speak to my people first, then I'll talk to you." But I knew the chances were slim to none.

By the time Snoop emerged from the bus, black sunglasses on, hair plaited in two big braids that drooped to either side of his face, I knew it would be next to impossible to reach him. So I thought I would call it a day, when I spotted Big Tray Dee, the Eastsidaz rapper who had also appeared with Tupac on the soundtrack for *Gridlock'd,* a film directed by Vondie Curtis Hall. I decided to head upstairs and to mill around in the kitchen where food had been prepared for the artists and their guests. I sat at the table where Big Tray Dee had found a place. His beautiful little daughter sat next to him, her braided and barretted hair a stylish complement to the Gerri-curls that peeked out from Big Tray Dee's cap, a true West Coast player with a 1980s vibe. It was immediately apparent that Big Tray Dee had a warm spirit and that the hard reputation of the gangsta rapper found dramatic relief in the care he showed for his precious child. I asked Big Tray Dee about Tupac, and between licking from his fingers the tasty barbecue sauce that splashed the ribs he consumed, he opened his heart.

"I knew he was a workaholic," he said, echoing Warren G's observation. "He would write three or four songs a day. If he was really into it, and his boys was ready, he might do six or seven songs in one day. He was phenomenal to watch." After he discussed Tupac's style, his method of working up a song, the themes of his work, and the response it evoked in Big Tray Dee, the rapper touched on Tupac's legacy.

"Everybody knows he was taken from us too soon," Big Tray Dee said. "He didn't have a chance to reach his full potential, like Donald Trump or Howard Hughes or Michael Jackson, somebody who is going to live out their years to see all the fame. He's not going to enjoy seeing how the music he made is going to be remembered and the statues of him that will be made. Do you know what I'm saying? People feel for him; he was a great person. We feel his loss."

I was moved as this freckle-faced soldier, whose ghetto war scars were invisible but palpable, recalled in touching terms the moments of creativity and brotherhood that he shared with Tupac. But what happened next was even more remarkable; it was both heartwarming and heartbreaking. As Big Tray Dee finished his comments and I thanked him for his time, he began to cry. Silently, without sobs, but steadily, for twenty minutes. The stream of tears that creased his cheeks reddened his eyes. His daughter held onto her father's right arm tightly, glowering at me as if I had harmed her daddy. I offered him several napkins, and he poured his wordless anguish into them without fear of hurting his reputation or losing his manhood. When I saw that he had finished, I thanked him and made my way out. But I will never forget his crying image as a powerful metaphor for the agony many have over the loss of Tupac's unspeakable gift—a gift that nevertheless continues to speak to millions around the globe.

Although I didn't come away that day with what I had gone for—an interview with Snoop Dogg—I got so much more. I gained a richer appreciation for the complexity of Tupac's life, for the contending identities that defined him, for the competing passions that claimed his attention, and for the contradictory forces that shaped his art and career. Tupac is perhaps the representative figure of his generation. In his haunting voice can be heard the buoyant hopefulness and the desperate hopelessness that mark the outer perimeters of the hip-hop culture he eagerly embraced, as well as the lives of the millions of youth who admired and adored him. But as his legend grows, Tupac recedes further from historical view and is trapped in the ruthless play of images that outline his myth in the culture. All the themes that surfaced in the conversations I had when I went to the warehouse are important: his strong black masculinity, his willingness to speak up, his thirst for attention, his powerful poetry, his thug image, his entrepreneurial exploits, his prophetic stances, his role as a pop icon, his search for the authentic black experience, his heartfelt messages to the urban poor, his incredible work ethic, his unfulfilled potential, his ascension to Elvis-like status, and the grief that was provoked by his premature death. These themes, and many others, are the ones I explore in this book.

In the first part of the book, "Childhood Chains, Adolescent Aspirations," I explore Tupac's childhood experiences and adolescent influences. His mother, Afeni, looms large in Tupacian lore; she was elevated in his beautiful "Dear Mama" but subject to public criticism by her son for her drug addiction and domestic instability before its release. Like her son, Afeni Shakur is a remarkable human being. As a black revolutionary, she fought for black liberation. As a mother, she raised two children without help from their fathers. And as a woman who descended into addiction, she risked her home to feed her habit. I explore the dual legacy Afeni gave to Tupac, as black revolutionary and as an addicted mother. I first tackle the effect Afeni's addiction had on Tupac, how it deprived him of a stable home in his adolescence, how it shaped his view of himself as a maturing teen, and how his art reflected the existential agonies he encountered as a result of her troubles.

I also probe Tupac's postrevolutionary childhood, seeking to discover how a child who has been reared to combat white supremacy fares in a world where such lessons must be adapted because the times have changed. I look at the themes that Tupac learned as a second-generation Black Panther, and how he both absorbed and resisted the messages he received. Since so much of his appeal rested on the divide in his mind and soul between his revolutionary pedigree and his thug persona, this is a crucial dimension of Tupac's background. I am also interested in the intellectual influences that shaped the growing boy and budding rapper. Tupac was a remarkably bright and gifted child. His acting gifts were encouraged by his participation in an acting ensemble in Harlem and, later, at Baltimore's School for Performing Arts. He was as well a voracious reader who had an insatiable intellectual appetite for an impressive range of books. Although he dropped out of high school, he continued to read a huge amount of literature until the day he died. I examine Tupac's views of school and his conceptions of learning, while also tracking down the kinds of books he cherished.

In the second part, "Portraits of an Artist," I take up Tupac's artistic vocation, since his first and lasting fame derives from his rap career. He was by no measure the greatest rapper of all time, but he is perhaps the genre's most influential star. I explore Tupac's role in rap, especially his lightning-rod status as rap's most renowned and controversial artist. Although his exploits away from the studio garnered huge headlines, Tupac's powerful, prophetic—and too often, self-destructive—work is the final basis of how we can judge his artistic achievements. But his preoccupation with being a "real nigga" looms over nearly everything he did. The question of black authenticity haunts the culture; within hip-hop it is especially vicious, with artists often adopting a stance as a thug or gangsta to prove their bona fides and their ability to represent the street. Perhaps more than any other rapper, Tupac tried to live the life he rapped about, which had spectacular results in the studio but disastrous results in the world. Tupac was in constant trouble with the law and in relentless conflict with peers, pretenders, and rivals, conflicts that sometimes spilled over into the recording studio. The infamous East Coast–West Coast beef owes its origins to Tupac's ingenious fury and outsized agonistic rantings.

In the third part of the book, "Bodies and Beliefs," I look at how Tupac dealt with huge themes in his art—such as gender, death, religion, suffering, compassion—and the status of the black body in his craft and career. I tackle hip-hop's especially harsh and misogynistic beliefs, as well as Tupac's own complex gender views—particularly in light of the sexual abuse for which he was convicted, though few believe he was guilty—through the prism of what I term *femiphobia,* the cruel attack on women that grows in the ghetto and beyond. I explore how Tupac's relationship to his mother affected his views and how his early experiences with girls left an imprint on his gender philosophy. I look at the influence of cultural cues and social history on how females are viewed not only in the ghetto but also in the larger culture. I try to grasp hold of Tupac's religious views and spiritual beliefs as they developed over his youth and his young adulthood. Tupac had strong views on God, suffering, and compassion, which I probe. He seemed to recklessly embrace his own death, even as he meditated on the nature of death extensively in his work, a subject I briefly consider. Finally, I explore the ways that Tupac viewed his body as a text, as the ink of the tattoo artist bled all over his torso. I examine as well how Tupac viewed his own body, not only as a work of art but as an object of scorn and as a vehicle for addictive pleasures and, in the end, as a temple of contagiously gloomy self-destruction.

In the epilogue, "Posthumous Presences," I examine the impact of Tupac's death on his evolving legend, especially the notion that he is not dead but alive in an undisclosed location. I explore how he has been cast as an urban legend, as what I term a "posthumous persona," as a martyr and a ghetto saint. I analyze the social uses of proclaiming that Tupac is any of these things, above all to the adherents and followers who have elevated him. One of the effects of claiming that Tupac, thug persona and all, is an important figure, a legend even, is to funnel critique of the society that made him believe that was the only way to survive. Tupac's ascent to ghetto sainthood is both a reflection of the desperation of the youth who proclaim him and a society that has had too few saints that could speak to the hopeless in our communities.

Tupac Amaru Shakur is one of the most important and contradictory artists to have spoken in and to our culture. Our adoration of him—and our disdain for his image—says as much about us as it does about him. This book is an attempt to take measure of both impulses and, in the process, to say something meaningful about urban black existence in the last quarter of the twentieth century and the beginning of the twenty-first.

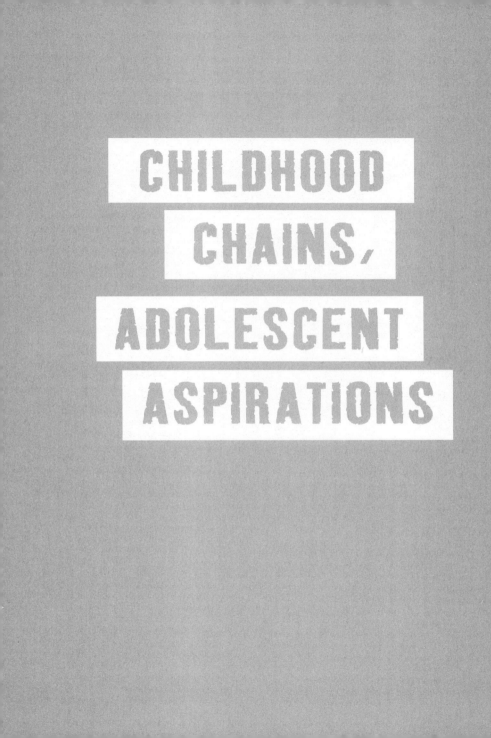

CHILDHOOD CHAINS, CHAINS, ADOLESCENT ASPIRATIONS

CHAPTER 1

"Dear Mama"

Motherhood and
a Hood's Mother

In black America mother love is second only to the love of
God—but just slightly. No one emblematizes this truth
more than Tupac Shakur, whose relationship to his mother,
Afeni Shakur, was as devoted as it was turbulent. In a rarely
seen interview videotaped when Tupac was imprisoned for
sexual abuse in 1995, he speaks movingly of his mother.
"My moms is my homey," Tupac insists.[1] "We went through
[several] stages. You know, where first it was mother and
son. Then it was like drill sergeant and cadet. . . . Then it
was like dictator [and] little country," he contends, broadly
smiling. Tupac says that he moved out on his own and then
"came back, like the prodigal son," noting that his mother
now "respects me as a man and I respect her as a mother
for all the sacrifices she made." Tupac suggests that he is
not alone in his adoration of his mother. "I think all young
black males and all Hispanic males, all males period, but es-

pecially from the ghetto . . . we have a deep love for our mothers, because they usually raised us by themselves. So you always feel closer to your mom. Even back in the day, 'I always loved my mama.'"

Bonds like Tupac's tie to his mama run through black culture. Mother's Day is a genuine holy day for African Americans, a time when otherwise stoic men break into song or tears recalling the nurturing love of their maternal root. Grown children salute their mothers when they recall their extraordinary sacrifices and the adolescent terrors and cruelties these women endured. Nearly every recording group has paid homage to the black mother, although the 1970s, when Tupac was a child, seemed to be an especially ripe period of mother love. The Intruders' rhythmically pulsating "I'll Always Love My Mama" surged onto radio waves in 1973, and a year later the Spinners' hauntingly melodic "Sadie" became an instant classic. It is now common to see long-limbed basketball players accompanied by mothers who are the heart of their peripatetic posses, as their gridiron counterparts mouth "Hi, Mom" to pursuing cameras after a spectacular score. The black mother even receives negative praise as the symbolic core of "playing the dozens," the game of verbal improvisation that pits one black youth against another in a competition to draw laughs by an elaborate exchange of gibes starting with the phrase "Yo mama."[2]

If the mother is central in black life, she is also made a scapegoat for the social disintegration of black culture. Single black mothers who are poor have been maligned in the media for cruelly misshaping their offspring, with some critics claiming they are at least partly responsible for absent black fathers. The logic of mother attack—often dressed as masculine uplift at the expense of female put-down—has seeped into black popular culture even as mother love gushes. The seepage is the result of a paradoxical but predictable trend among young black males: loving *my* mama while loathing my *baby's* mama. When mama is also lover, she draws the wrath of her male peers.

The sharp juxtaposition of maternal acknowledgment and disparagement is a characteristic symptom of rap music's artists. Tupac is surely unexceptional in this regard, but he represents an intriguing twist: He is capable of both embracing and chiding his mother in a single artistic gesture. In his almost elegiac "Dear Mama," Tupac declares his love in a moment of unsparing criticism: "And even as a crack fiend, Mama / You always was a Black Queen, Mama." Tupac's maturity allows him to value his mother's love even as he names her affliction. His refusal to lie as he praises her is all too revealing. What kind of woman raised a child who could have such pitiless mercy in loving his mother? What kind of relationship did Tupac have with his mother, and how did it shape his life and career?

Afeni Shakur has become a cultural force in her own right. As Nobel laureate Toni Morrison told me, Afeni is a "courageous, creative woman." As her son's influence has grown, so has her stature as a skilled adjudicator of competing images in his outsized mythology. The bare outlines of her story are both captivating and brutal, much like the charged racial desperation and generational conflict her son bore on his similarly slight frame. Afeni burst on the hori-

zon of black history with blazing elegance, at least as measured by the times in which she came of political age. In the
immediate aftermath of the civil rights movement's precipi-
tous decline, she did her part in helping black militancy gain
currency through forceful gestures of social rebellion. First,
as Alice Faye Williams, she was a twenty-one-year-old emer-
gency substitute teacher caught up in the bitter racial politics of New York in the 1960s. When the infamous Ocean
Hill–Brownsville teachers' strike flared in 1968—pitting
United Federation Teachers, who were mostly white and
Jewish, against poor black and Puerto Rican parents in the
struggle for community control of schools—Alice was re-
cruited to instruct because she was aunt to one of the children in the community. Her initial baptism in the waters of
racial unrest plunged her deeper into the ocean of black resistance. Alice revoked her "slave name" and was reborn as
Afeni Shakur, member of the Black Panthers. Along with
Panther organizer Lumumba, her new beau, Afeni quickly
became part of the now legendary New York 21, the Black
Panther contingent that was arrested and charged with con-
spiring to bomb several New York department stores, police stations, and commuter railways.

When she got out on bail, Afeni got pregnant, but not by
Lumumba. The two men who were the candidates for fatherhood embodied the choices that Tupac would confront
in deciding what image would shape his life and career. Billy
Garland was a Black Panther, whereas local hood "Legs"
was a disciple of notorious Harlem gangster Nicky Barnes.
After two of her male codefendants took flight, Afeni returned to jail to nurture her baby—"my embryo was in

prison," Tupac said years later in the taped prison interview—and to defend the New York 21 with an astonishing display of mother wit and oratorical skill. Serving as her own lawyer turned out to be Afeni's saving grace. Later her unborn child, delivered a month after she won acquittal for her revolutionary coterie, proved to be her black prince and his generation's defining voice. She renamed him Tupac Amaru (he was born Lesane Parish Crooks), after an eighteenth-century Incan chief and revolutionary who was killed when Spanish conquistadors tore his body apart with horses. Shakur, a common name adopted by the New York Panther clan, is Arabic for "thankful to God." The rest, of course, is history, but a history increasingly colored by revisionist myths that cloud the true story. Her son's legend has assured Afeni's public adoration as a revolutionary-turned-mother. But that same spotlight has fixed on her personal and political flaws as the intelligible explanation for her son's hieroglyphic rage and self-destruction. That interpretation may skirt dangerously close to a sexist blame-the-female logic, one that is all too familiar in the press, in hip-hop, and in social science's often dim view of black home life. But paying attention to Afeni's struggles may shed light on the conflicting ideological and existential trances that bewitched Tupac the artist and man.[3]

Afeni was born in 1947 in Lumberton, North Carolina. In one of those mysteries that mark the tides of black fate—its risings and fallings forever calculated in rough synchronization with the emergence and eclipse of iconic figures and those near to them—Lumberton is also where basketball star Michael Jordan's father was murdered three years before Tupac was killed. Thus, this little-known southern geography is the ground of durable—and literally *relative*—black mythologies by association: The parents of two icons were reared or ruined on its soil. Afeni's family, including her mother, father, and sister, lived in Norfolk, Virginia, but she was born in Lumberton when her pregnant mother paid a visit to Afeni's sick grandmother. Afeni divided much of her childhood between Virginia and North Carolina. Her father's family boasted nurses and air force careers, although Afeni had no contact with them. Her mother's family was far less fortunate. "On my mother's side, my family went from slave to sharecropper to domestic worker to factory worker," Afeni tells me, underscoring the working poor caste of her clan. She grew up under Jim Crow's vicious wing, enduring racial epithets hurled at her by neighboring whites on North Carolina's highways. She lived inside the brutal contradictions of southern apartheid, observing its hateful manifestations even as she witnessed its self-defeating logic up close. Her grandmother married a mixed man—half white and half Indian—who was disowned by his family and dragged by them through town tied to a wagon, an object lesson for others who committed miscegenation. But it was in Lumberton that Afeni also learned to fight back. After the Ku Klux Klan imposed a ten o'clock curfew on the black and Indian communities, the Indians soundly thrashed the Klan, liberating the blacks from their fear of white supremacy.

Afeni moved to New York when she was eleven. She says that she was "very bright" but also "very ill equipped."

"I was a street child," Afeni admits. "I was more comfortable there." Afeni, like her son after her, attended a performing arts high school, attracted as Tupac would be to acting classes, which were the only ones she attended. Otherwise she hung out and got high on Thunderbird. She was also president of the Disciple Debs, the female version of the infamous New York street gang. During the late 1960s, when the black power movement took root in New York, Afeni was exposed to the burgeoning black militant elite. "I saw Eldridge Cleaver at Mt. Morris Park," Afeni remembers. "And then I saw Bobby Seale on 125th Street and Seventh Avenue, the first time he came there." By the time of Seale's arrival, there was already a strong "contingent of New York people in the party." Afeni was "awestruck by the men in the Black Panther Party," and through her relationship with Lumumba, the lieutenant of the Harlem branch, she began attending meetings at Long Island University in the summer and fall of 1968. By April 2, 1969, "the police were in a coordinated raid around twenty-one houses in New York City, and I was arrested at 5 in the morning along with many other people." Afeni asks me, first as a verbal tic but then as a real question, "Do you understand?" "Yes, ma'am," I respond. Even though I'm only twelve years her junior, I feel, I suppose, the weight of her natural aristocracy and the immensity of her suffering and loss in her urgent inquiry. "That's really who I am," she insists. But her self-assertion is not based in the belief that she was a pivotal player in black politics. On the contrary, she feels that revisionism and nostalgia are predictably concomitant. "You know in history, you look back and you say kindly, 'We're smart and we're great.' No!" she gently mouths. "Really all I was was that."[4]

When her mother came to visit Afeni in prison, she could barely acknowledge her daughter's new identity. "She couldn't even say my name to the [prison] guard," Afeni recalls. "She would be so reduced [because of] the humiliation and shame I put my mother through. But that's who I was." The scene conjures the generational gulf of an earlier era, when some blacks embraced quietism out of fear of white reprisal and fear for their dangerously uppity children, whose unruly speech and actions, their parents believed, would bring the wrath of white folk down on all of their heads. But Afeni understood her mother's plight, even shared it somehow, perhaps not as much then as she would when she confronted the prospect of seeing her revolutionary life in harsher terms through the eyes of her equally petulant son. If Afeni rates mother love now, it's perhaps because she gave mother love then. Afeni's destiny as a single black mother was already patterned after her mother's experience. "My mother had two children, two daughters," Afeni says. "And as you know with [many] colored, poor women in the South, there's no husband, and it doesn't matter. My mother was fiercely protective of her daughters. No matter what our situation was, it was always me and my mother and my sister in the world." Years later her son would adopt a creed that at once reflected his fractured home life and affirmed his essential aloneness and his combativeness with the universe he inherited, a stance that captured the domestic alienation of millions of other black youth in his song "Me Against the World."

Afeni's significant role in determining the fate of the New York 21 was glimpsed when she was bailed out of jail after eleven months, an eerie foreshadowing of the exact time her son would spend in prison for sexual abuse before he managed bail. A group of women who had been active in the labor movement in the 1930s and 1940s raised her bail money largely through church fundraisers. "I was the first member of the New York 21 bailed out of jail," she says. "The reason I was bailed out is because it was my responsibility to speak and to raise money and to help get my comrades out." Later, Michael Tabor, Richard "Dhuruba" Moore, and Joan Bird were also released on bail. Newly free, Afeni faced the formidable task of raising consciousness and cash for the cause.

Perhaps most famously, a group of celebrities including Leonard Bernstein and Jane Fonda drummed up $10,000 for the New York 21 at a fundraiser at Bernstein's Park Avenue duplex, earning them writer Tom Wolfe's acerbic critique for displaying "radical chic." It is true that there was a convergence between black revolutionary resistance and deep-pocketed white radicalism that mocked the very solidarity it sought to effect. The result was an uncomfortable compromise for both parties: Black militancy was reduced to style and performance, whereas white patronage became a superfluous tour of black suffering through checkbook rebellion. Black resistance became a commodity for the cultured classes to consume at the metaphoric black market, which was all the more attractive since it traveled beyond its racial haunts to downtown whites. But it is also true that white backlash against black protest in the 1970s meant that potential revolutionaries had to seek support beyond traditional liberal circles. If the struggle for black liberation had grown to openly embrace self-determining nationalists, sources of support had likewise enlarged to include the white left.

When Afeni became pregnant, she hoped that her sister would raise her child, since she and her comrades faced 352 years in prison on 156 counts and assumed they would be convicted. "I had never been able to carry a child past three months of pregnancy," Afeni says. "But in the midst of this, this child stayed." It was similar to the case of Italian singer Enrico Caruso, whose mother miscarried many children before she had the great tenor. Secure in the knowledge that her child would remain, Afeni discovered that she and codefendant Joan Bird would be returned to jail because two of their male comrades had skipped town. Afeni says she had to "get a court order so that I could have one egg and one glass of milk every morning." Despite the poor nutritional value of her jail meals—"you don't get real eggs in jail"—Afeni says that she "had overdosed on vitamins and minerals, and that's a good thing, because then when I went into jail again, my body had something to eat." Tupac's birth signified a new stage in Afeni's life. The Panther 21 had fired off a missive to the Oakland headquarters accusing the West Coast branch of "tripping out, pseudo-machoism, arrogance, myrmidonism, dogmatism, regionalism, regimentation, and fear." It anticipated the East Coast–

West Coast rap rivalries that Tupac helped to foment. Unsurprisingly, the West Coast headquarters dismissed the New York 21 from the party, a gesture that typified the hubris and intramural carnage that often afflicted revolutionary groups.[5]

Afeni worked as a legal assistant, a chocolate Erin Brockovich who drew on her skilled self-defense to do her job. Tupac's father, Billy Garland, abandoned his seed and left Afeni to raise him alone. (Garland would not see his son regularly until years later, when Tupac was recuperating in the hospital from his first shooting and woke up to see his own spitting image staring straight at him.) Afeni sought to give her son a sense of racial pride and personal security. As a baby she sang him lullabies, including songs by soul music icon Roberta Flack. "What I played on my box all the time as the mantra was the Main Ingredients' 'Black Seeds Keep on Growing,'" Afeni says. "I knew, my gut knew, something about this child: that he wasn't supposed to be here. And he was! And he was strong and he was beautifully spirited and just the prettiest smile in the world. What a wonderful, wonderful spirit this child was right from the beginning." Afeni gave Tupac love as a growing child, but they suffered greatly. She had a daughter, Sekyiwa, in 1975 with Mutulu Shakur, a fellow revolutionary who was eventually imprisoned on robbery and murder charges. Often homeless, out of work, and plainly destitute, Afeni shuttled with her brood between Harlem and the Bronx. Although it has been reported that the family sometimes lived in shelters, Afeni demurs. "Black people don't do shelters," she says. "Black people live with other black people." But when the

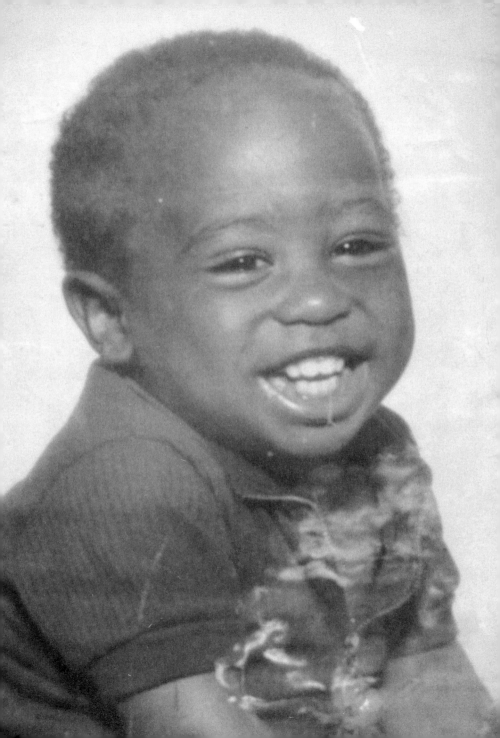

family went to White Plains, New York, they got public help. "Right after Tupac was thirteen, like days after that, we went up to White Plains and a friend of ours got us into the White Plains homeless system," Afeni remembers. "[White Plains] is different from New York, and they put us in a hotel, and they gave us money to buy [things], and that's ultimately what we used to leave New York."

Afeni used her stipend to move the family from New York in 1986, when Tupac was fifteen, but not before he appeared as Travis in Lorraine Hansberry's *Raisin in the Sun* during a 1984 Apollo Theater fundraiser for Jesse Jackson's presidential run, a harbinger of his future cinematic achievements. Relocating to Baltimore's tough ghetto, Tupac simply found another space to feel alienated and out of sorts. By the time the family had made its next move to California's Marin County, Tupac was near his majority. He was a poor, often homeless child whose growing conflicts with his mother were driven by her past and present choices: to be a black revolutionary—and thus to risk totalizing governmental repression and the vicious indifference, even ingratitude, of the black bourgeoisie—and to anesthetize the pain of her postrevolutionary life, and its attendant rejections, self-destructions, and eruptions, with crack cocaine. I later examine Afeni's revolutionary politics and what that legacy meant for her son, but first I want to explore how Afeni's addiction affected Tupac's youth and career. At the very least, her habits may have set the stage for his own self-medicated response to his chaotic postadolescence.

In the rolling annals of popular black history—the informal knot of narratives floating through black communities that draw on conspiracy theory, defensive suspicion, keen observation, and autodidactic rumination to critique racism and its effects (not to be confused with black popular history, which is a critical examination by intellectuals of the forces that shape black society at grassroots levels)—the force and function of crack cocaine in black life in the 1980s were devastating. To a large extent, cocaine addiction can be seen as the logical outcome of the "culture of narcissism" articulated by Christopher Lasch that symbolized the 1970s, with its themes of self-deification and its rituals of self-pleasuring in tow. But aspects and moments of the 1970s also disabled political obligation to one's neighbor and delegitimized countercultural dissent as a means to viable citizenship. This was glimpsed in the backlash against anti–Vietnam War activity (despite its subsequent vindication) and the eventual absorption of political rebellion into the stylistic idiosyncrasies of mass-cultural responses to generational anomie, such as the marketing, merchandising, and mediations of Woodstock.

For black communities, the 1970s set up the prerequisites for devastation in the 1980s: economic restructuring, social dislocation, and urban regentrification. Through incipient globalization, deregulation, and loosened trade restrictions, there was the loss of manufacturing jobs, especially automobile and steel labor that paid the bills. The sprawling suburbs outside the ghetto were open only to the well-to-do blacks whose black track to the suburbs mimicked earlier white flight and emptied ghetto communities of the middle class and viable aboveground economies. Perhaps worst of all, social suffering increased the thriving underground economies and the gang warfare that riddled black urban spaces. And it instigated the rise of crack addictions, economies, and crimes.[6]

Crack addiction resulted from crack economies and lead to crack crimes. The political organization of crack first directed the transformation of cocaine from powdered to rocklike substance for its mass marketing and distribution. Drug pushers secured networks of distribution through violent occupation of ghettos, especially abandoned houses and neglected neighborhoods. Drug gangs developed to exploit middle-management opportunities for the distribution of crack cocaine, regulating its import into ghetto districts through the law of predatory capitalism and rational choice theory. It has been argued, largely through popular black history but also in a famous series in the *San Jose Mercury News,* that the government looked the other way, first, as the exploitation of black and brown populations through crack addiction was established by permitting huge amounts of the drug to drench our domestic terrain and, second, as officials directed the profits of exploited populations to finance the illegal disruption of foreign governments in the name of guerrilla democracy. Whether that's true or not, it is sufficiently clear that crack economies were well established in black and brown ghettos.[7]

Moreover, it is clear that the high of crack appealed to those on the lowest spot on the economic totem pole. Crack addiction soared. And in a disingenuous and cynical gesture, the government claimed to base its harsh sentencing of folk caught with crack cocaine—as opposed to those who abused powdered cocaine, who were overwhelmingly white and rich—on the premise that it was so much more immediately and fatally addictive. White powder, white power—the two were barely distinguishable. The addiction to crack destroyed families by separating users from nonusers. Thus, crack addiction created or exploited the desire by users to steal from kin and friend alike to support their habits. It led to mothers and fathers forsaking familial ties and parental responsibilities in deference to crack's uncoordinated but almost total domination of life. Crack addiction, along with gang activity, fed the rise of the juvenocracy: the shift in economic and social authority from the older to younger members of the family and neighborhood. If you are paying the cable bill, buying disposable diapers for the baby, and stocking the food pantry, in patriarchal terms you are "the man." Of all the crimes that crack exploited—the drive-by, the purse snatch, the television steal, the body sale—one of the most heinous was child abandonment, whether literal or figurative. This was Afeni's Achilles' heel. There is dispute as to when Afeni's addiction disrupted her family life—she claims it was in Tupac's later adolescence, when he was seventeen, whereas Tupac claimed it was earlier, when he was twelve or thirteen years old. No matter, the effects of poverty and homelessness were severe enough. Her refuge in alcohol and the pipe lit a powder keg that exploded on her entire family in a crippling addiction.[8]

Afeni now faces her addiction soberly, admitting that it harmed her children, especially her man-child. "I know what harm I brought him," she says, "so really what I did was to prepare him to be able to live through the harm."

With a tear in her voice, she laments the job she did yet avoids self-pity. "I didn't do a great job of it, or a good job of it," she says, "or maybe he would be here. But you never know." I feel her struggle to illuminate the thought with honest confrontation of her trials. "I'm not saying this to put harm upon myself," she says, "but I'm a recovering addict. So it's very important for me to look and examine each horrible thing, with my eyes open and not lying to myself." It was that same penchant for truth that characterized Afeni's relationship with her son. Perhaps because she grew up with him, maturing as he matured, growing as he grew, learning as he learned, she refused to tell him lies.

Afeni's claim is supported by comments Tupac made when he was seventeen. Tupac was captured on videotape in a remarkable interview conducted in 1988 when he was a high school student in Marin City, California, a recent transplant from Baltimore. Tupac had sacrificed his bright future at the Baltimore School for the Arts to escape his mother's addiction, her foul treatment at the hands of a violent boyfriend, and the trauma of moving from home to home. In this never-released interview, Tupac's fresh-faced innocence suffuses his precocious observations. Tupac portrays his mother as a valiant role model who countered the corrupted narratives of official society and history, an inclination she acquired as a member of the Black Panthers in the 1970s. "The way my mother brought me up is no lies," Tupac says, his toothy smile brightening his youthful brown face and confirming his mother's domestic pedagogy.[9] "You know the total truth. Everything is real in this society. If something is going on wrong, then I know everything." But with that knowledge comes tremendous responsibility, although Tupac hints that the responsibility was too much for one so young. "It was like I was given responsibility before I wanted it, and so now I can't really differentiate what great responsibility is because I've had it for so long."

Still, Tupac spies advantage in his mother's insistence that he shoulder his own load in life. "I'm going to be a little more ready than someone who's grown up in Disney World," with the belief that "Santa Claus is coming." The budding rapper believed that his upbringing would prepare him to cope with life far better than the pampered youth who were spared hardship and struggle. Afeni's life—its heartbreaks, setbacks, failures, contradictions, tragedies, and triumphs—was placed before Tupac as road map and object lesson. In some child-rearing manuals, such parental disclosure is considered irresponsible. In fact, knowledge foreclosure is the rule. According to this logic, Afeni's renunciation of the epistemological gap between parent and child shredded the myth of adult omniscience, a crucial pillar in the developing ego leading to trust and faith in humanity. But for ghetto cosmologies—and in revolutionary worldviews where knowledge was either disclosed or withheld by the government for devious purposes—much of the logic is reversed: What you don't know can kill you.

"I used to write poems for him," Afeni says of her young son. "And I wrote this poem for him, that went: 'Where are you going brown man? / Little brown man / Where are you going, little brown man of mine?'" In Afeni's mind the poem was her attempt to warn her five-year-old son of the perils of ignorance and the strength of self-knowledge and self-determination, themes she borrowed from her politics and applied to her personal life. "This poem was saying to him, 'I don't know where you're going or what things you're going to do or what kind of decisions you're going to make,'" Afeni recalls. "'But I know I can't make them for you. I just want to go with you.' I basically wanted him to be able to make his own decisions, understanding that I would much prefer him to make his own informed decisions than for him to follow what I said all the time, because that could end up killing him. He wasn't in a position where he could not use his brain." There's no question that Tupac used his brain early and vigorously to question his surroundings and to challenge his mother.

Tupac at seventeen may have been cheery for the camera, praising his mother for her virtues—such as allowing his friends to call Afeni by her first name, making them feel "they can just come in the house" and talk about issues— but more severe problems were brewing. In the tape Tupac admits that he and Afeni occasionally argued—especially when he came home at 2:30 one morning. He also says, "She'll be wrong a lot," though they "can talk about it." Understandably, there is little discussion about her drug woes or the emotional distress it caused him. Interestingly, Tupac says that he can ask Afeni "anything and bring it up . . . and I can say . . . 'I'm really curious about this drug,' and she'll go, 'I did it, and this is what happened, and I don't think you should [try it].'" But Afeni lacked the will or encouragement to resist the pipe.

Elmer "Geronimo" Pratt, the legendary Black Panther who spent twenty-seven years in prison for the murder of a schoolteacher during a robbery in Santa Monica in 1968 until his conviction was overturned in 1997, learned in prison of Afeni's descent into addiction. "[Afeni and her children] were staying at my wife's house with my two children," says Pratt, who was Tupac's godfather. The home of his wife, Linda, was one of many places to which Afeni and her children retreated in their serial domesticity in California. "And it was pandemonium. Because there was no man over there, it was just madness." A good deal of the madness involved Tupac's living at Linda Pratt's home while Afeni "was around the corner" doing drugs. Pratt says that Tupac was especially hard hit. "He was the oldest one around, and his mother was on crack. . . . There was a lot of weight on that young brother's shoulders." Because of the chaos at home, Pratt instructed his comrades occasionally to check on the children, who were sometimes left alone. Now and then his colleagues would "stay with them at night. They would be literally abandoned." It was an abandonment that deeply affected Tupac, spurring him to create brilliant art and to cry out for attention with his own brand of chaotic, self-destructive behavior.[10]

Long before Tupac's abandonment in Marin City, he had faced domestic difficulties in Baltimore. Tupac formed a close friendship at Baltimore's School for the Arts with a diminutive beauty whose self-confessed volatility matched Tupac's stormy persona. "We were a lot alike in a lot of ways," recalls famed actress Jada Pinkett Smith. "Very opinionated, very passionate. And just basically wanting 'our way or no way.'" Smith says that she and Tupac "bumped heads a lot" because they both "had mothers who were using at the time, and that was a real difficult struggle for us both." Smith says it brought out "a lot of insecurities on both of our parts." Much of Tupac's insecurity related to his extreme impoverishment as a result of his mother's erratic life. "He was poor," Smith says. "I mean, when I met Tupac, and this is not an exaggeration, he owned two pairs of pants, and two sweaters. Okay? He slept on a mattress with no sheets when I went into his room, and it took me a long time to get into his house because he was embarrassed. He didn't know where his meals were coming from." Smith says that because of "his relationship with his mother," he didn't have a good opinion of himself. "Your mother is your pulse to the world. And if that pulse ain't right, ain't much else going to be right. I don't think he ever reconciled [that] within himself. His sense of himself and his self-worth started with his mother." But Smith's next sentence reveals the modus vivendi Tupac adopted in the face of his gargantuan maternal conflicts: "And he is just not a forgiving person." Smith says that Tupac was "really rough on Afeni. And you know, he took every opportunity to punish anybody who he felt didn't do right by him, by his standards. That came from his relationship with Afeni." Smith acknowledges that Afeni's addiction fundamentally harmed Tupac and that it hurt his relations with others as well. "We all paid the price for her drug addiction."

That's a painful truth that Afeni continues to face. But her unflinching candor about how her self-destruction brutally impacted her children is consistent with how she raised them. "I taught my kids—and you have to do what you teach them, you know—'If you shit in the middle of the street, go to the middle of the street, and stand next to it, and claim it,'" she insists. "If you can't do that, don't shit in the middle of the street. Bottom line." Afeni believes that such honesty can actually help young people deal with their inevitable failures. "Every young person is going to make an awful error," Afeni says now. "We can teach them that you really can recover from an error. You really can do better. If we can't teach them that, then forget algebra, because what good is it going to do them?" If algebra is mastered by repeated practice, by erasing mistakes and postulating successful formulas, then Afeni is the recovering soul's mathematician. Standing in for all parents, Afeni argues that children won't know that they can overcome their problems "until they know that I did ugly things first." She evokes the language of faith to underscore her belief in the redeeming lessons that may be learned from suffering. "They say in church, 'How [else] will people know your blessings? If you can't go down in the garbage can and tell them about the garbage, how are they going to know where God brought you from?' They ain't going to know your deliverance. You've got to know something. I am a living testament!"

Unlike some in the recovery movement, Afeni doesn't excuse her abusive practices by cavalierly cleansing her failures in the light that freshly bathes her. Nor does she possess that alchemical amnesia that magically dismisses the harm done to others in the name of self-aggrandizing self-reconstruction. Although Afeni has been in recovery for ten years, she candidly recalls believing, even naively expecting, that Tupac would immediately applaud her pilgrimage to enlightenment and health. On the first anniversary of her liberation from chemical addiction, right as Tupac was scorching the screens in *Juice,* his film debut, he burned her hopes. "After I had been in recovery for a year, I was very proud of myself," Afeni recalls. She felt that her remarkable progress would wipe out her children's painful memories of her addictions. Her daughter, Sekyiwa, embraced her with open arms. Tupac, in contrast, wrote Afeni a nine-page letter on a plane ride and handed it to her when he landed. "In that nine pages, he explained as honestly as my son could do how he hoped that I really was going to stay clean," she remembers. But he admonished her that "'you cannot erase every single thing that you've done. You cannot expect me to believe that you can change simply because you said so.'" Afeni recalls her sponsor's telling her that Tupac's letter was a healthy gesture. "So I came through recovery understanding how important it was for my children to have the space that they needed to deal with the damage that I did in the way that they needed to do it, not in the way that is convenient for me. What he said was really true, though. How 'bout that? He challenged me every day. I thank him for that. I taught him that. What am I going to tell him—it's a lie? He always helped me to stay honest."

It was still difficult for Afeni to endure her son's public exposure of her addiction, although she sees a benefit in the ordeal. "I really find that the worst things that people know about me . . . make me stronger . . . because people are unable to blackmail me with anything, because I will tell you things about myself worse than what you think you are going to tell somebody." Afeni's mixture of defiance and bone-cutting honesty is the sort of fusion that made her son so compelling as a young artist flashing his demons to the world. In fact Afeni says she encouraged Tupac "to get as much of that poison out as possible, you know, because only when it's been fully explored can you have that peace."

To an extent, the 1995 song "Dear Mama" represents Tupac's public peace with his mother's painful past. The song's haunting eloquence consists in Tupac's forgiving Afeni her drug addiction, her domestic inconstancy, and her eviction of her only son. Tupac highlighted instead the difficulties that confront poor, single mothers. He expressed gratitude for Afeni's heroic persistence in the face of both her self-destruction and the obstacles thrown in her way by a callous society. Above all he praised her unsparing honesty: "You never kept a secret / always stayed real." Lasting peace, however, seemed to elude Tupac. The more he poured his soul into his lyrics, the more he voiced the stinging lack of self-worth that made him believe he didn't deserve the adoration he received. "His deepest feeling about himself is that he didn't feel he was shit," Smith sadly remarks. She feels that Tupac spurned the light and clung willfully to his own darkness later in life because he didn't believe that "people who were in the light would . . . embrace him." Smith tried to convince him otherwise. "I knew that the people of the light were just waiting for him. I knew that because that was the journey I was on. And studying my path, I saw that I was worthy of the love, and I was smart enough, and I was good enough, despite what my past might have been. And he never believed that."

Actress LaTanya Richardson, who appeared with Tupac in *Juice,* agrees. "I don't think [Tupac] in any instance was

comfortable being good," she says. "It was like psychologically maybe he knew that he was not looked at in that light.
Or it wasn't expected of him, and he didn't want to disap-
point [those who had that image]." So Tupac played up his
image of being tough and fatally tethered to badness. "But
really I think that given a different time and a different
space, he could have just gone off and acted and made music and been happy. If we had raised him." Her coda is most
telling of all, rooted, perhaps, in the African proverb borrowed by Hillary Rodham Clinton: "It takes a village to
raise a child." Richardson removes from Afeni's shoulders
the exclusive responsibility for raising Tupac and places it
squarely on the black village that benefited from his gifts
and feared his almost unavoidable undoing. "He was one of
the ones we just let fly by," she notes. "And I think we're all
held accountable for that."

CHAPTER 2

"The Son of a Panther"

A Postrevolutionary Childhood

The scene irresistibly evokes Tupac's revolutionary roots: When he was a few days old, Tupac was taken to his first political speech, given by Minister Louis Farrakhan at the 168th Street Armory in New York. "That was the first time I saw him," says Karen Lee, then a black militant who, in another twist of fate, served as Tupac's publicist nearly twenty years later. "He was a little baby with big eyes. They were the first things you could see." Those big eyes and the world they envisioned made Tupac the hip-hop James Baldwin: an excruciatingly conscientious scribe whose narratives flamed with moral outrage at black suffering. Tupac imbibed his disdain for racial oppression from his mother's revolutionary womb. As Tupac's godfather, Black Panther

Elmer "Geronimo" Pratt remarks, the artist "was born into the movement."

That birthright of black nationalism hung over Tupac's head as both promise and judgment. Some saw him as the benighted successor to Huey, Eldridge, Bobby, and other bright stars of black subversion. In this light Tupac's career was best imagined in strictly political terms: Rapping was race war by other means. Others see the Black Panthers as a strident symbol of political destruction turned inward. This would mean that Tupac's violent lyrics and wild behavior suggest the ethical poverty of romantic nationalism. Tupac initially embraced the former view, though he quickly wearied of the aesthetic and economic imperatives it imposed. As he won fame and money, he brooked no ideological limits on what he could say and how he could live. But even as he exchanged revolutionary self-seriousness for the thug life, he never embraced the notion that the Panthers were emblematic of political self-destruction. To be sure, Tupac saw thug life extending Panther beliefs in self-defense and class rebellion. But he never balked at Panther ideals. The practices, as we shall see shortly, were another matter.[1]

The boosters and critics of the Panthers alike agree that Tupac was problematic. It is an agreement, however, stamped in irony. Each side finds Tupac unacceptable for the same reasons they find each other's views intolerable, even reprehensible. Panther purists claim that Tupac's extravagant materialism and defiant hedonism are the death knell of political conscience, the ultimate sellout of revolutionary ideals. Critics of the movement contend that Tupac's thug fantasies fulfilled the submerged logic of

Panther gangsterism, what with its sexual abuse of women, financial malfeasance, and brutal factionalism. In either case Tupac is the conflicted metaphor of black revolution's large aspirations and failed agendas. Early in his short life he sought to conform practical survival to revolutionary idealism. Later he reversed the trend.

To borrow W. E. B. DuBois's notion of dual consciousness, in Tupac two warring ideals were (w)rapped in one dark body. The question to ask now is: Could Tupac's dogged strength alone have kept him from being torn asunder? In hindsight a negative answer seems certain, though perhaps disingenuous. It was perilous enough for old heads to try to reconcile competing views of black insurgence, as proved by figures as different as Malcolm X and Huey Newton. How much wisdom could one expect from an artist who barely lived beyond his twenty-fifth birthday, even though he was hugely talented and precocious to a fault? It is a testament to his gargantuan gifts—and to our desperate need, which after all, screams so loudly because of our failure to find suitable answers—that the expectation existed at all. Our best chance of understanding Tupac's dilemmas, and his failures and triumphs, too, rests in probing the ideals with which he was reared and that shaped his life for better and for worse. What did it mean to be a child of the Black Panthers, to have a postrevolutionary childhood?[2]

In explaining his ministerial vocation, Martin Luther King Jr. remarked that his father, grandfather, and great-grandfather were preachers. "I didn't have much choice, I guess," he humorously concluded. Although Tupac's revolutionary lineage is not as long, it is equally populous and perhaps more storied. He was surrounded by figures that lived and died the struggle for black freedom. Afeni and her lovers Lumumba and Billy Garland were Black Panthers. Tupac's stepfather, Mutulu Shakur, an acupuncturist and black revolutionary, was sentenced in 1988 to sixty years in prison for conspiracy to commit armed robbery and murder. He was also found guilty of attempting to break Tupac's "aunt" Joanne Chesimard, later known as Assata Shakur, out of prison, where she was sent in 1977 after being convicted of murdering a New Jersey state trooper. And Tupac's godfather, Geronimo Pratt, loomed large as a heroic figure. From the very beginning, Tupac was, as Pratt says, "fascinated with the history of that which he was born into."

In the haunting footage of Tupac at school at age seventeen, he confirms Pratt's impression. "My mother was a Black Panther, and she was really involved in the movement," Tupac says. "Just black people bettering themselves and things like that." And from the start, Afeni's role in the movement was costly, limiting, in Tupac's mind, the time she spent with him. "At first I rebelled against her because she was in a movement and we never spent time together because she was always speaking and going to colleges and everything," Tupac says. But after a period of intense movement activity, Tupac and his mother bonded. "And then after that was over, it was more time spent with me and [I was] just like, 'You're my mother,' and she was like, 'You're my son.' . . . So then she was really close with me and really strict on me."[3]

Even as a youth, Tupac discerned the price paid for revolutionary principles, especially when one had little money. "Being poor and having this philosophy is worse," Tupac says. But he brilliantly analyzes the difference between financial and moral wealth. "Because you know if money was nothing, if there was no money and everything depended on your moral standards and the way that you behaved and the way you treated people, we'd be millionaires. We'd be rich." Ever the realist, Tupac presciently sizes up his family's situation, especially the cost of critical thinking spurred by revolutionary beliefs. "But since it's not like that, then we're stone broke. We're just poor because our ideals always get in the way, 'cause we're not 'yup-yup' people." Tupac knows that taking critical inventory of one's surroundings does not make for job security, though he admits that he's bitter about being poor for his principles, since he missed "out on a lot of things" and because "I can't always have what I want or even things that I think I need." That does not keep him from dissecting the futility of many wealthy people's lives. "But I know rich people, or people just well-off, who are lost, who are lost." For that reason, his mother's sacrificial choices really have paid off. "She could have [chosen] to go to college and get a degree in something and right now [could have] been well-off. But she chose to analyze society and fight and do things better. So this is the payoff. And she always tells me that the payoff to her is that me and my sister grew up good and we have good minds and . . . we're ready for society."

Tupac's revolutionary sensibilities even shaped his inclination to protest injustice with grand gestures. To begin with, on tape Tupac compares himself to his mother by claiming they are both arrogant. His self-knowledge is bested only by his keen sense of dramatic timing and his ability to enliven the everyday with artistic flourishes. In a gem of a story, Tupac recounts how he got himself free to participate in the interview:

"I just quit my job today, actually, because I wanted to come and do this [interview] and they wouldn't let me. And I thought it was important—a little more important than serving pizza. And we had enough people so I felt like, since I'm an actor, they should understand. They should have let me do it, but they didn't. And then I had a cold, so they were making me work in the freezer, and I'm really not to be disrespected. And I felt like that was disrespectful because I asked to go, you know. So I quit and [my boss] told me I couldn't quit. And that made my hyper. I'm arrogant, so when he told me I couldn't quit, we had all these customers. I chose that time to jump up on the soapbox, grab my leather jacket, light a cigarette in front of him, smoke, and leave in the middle of a rush."

As it turns out, this story is vintage Tupac: glossing his personal story as a reflection of social injustice; showing an impeccable sense of vocational priority; drawing on the stylish machismo of pop culture to make a point; countering authority with dramatic gestures of defiance; linking the question of respect to morality; highlighting, perhaps even exaggerating, the degree of emotional injury to justify rebellion; and transfiguring a blasé occurrence into charged theater through superb thespian instincts. Even here Tupac sees the advantage of his mother's political experience.

Tupac admits that his mother, by having gone "through the sixties," is coolheaded and more inclined to say, "Let me think about this first and then do it, because I know how that happens." But he also recognizes that her noble efforts are often harshly repaid. Tupac claims his family moved from New York "because of my mother's [political] choices. And she couldn't keep her job because of her choices, because it was too much. . . . They figured out who she was and she couldn't keep a job. That should be illegal." It is almost impossible for those who have never been under surveillance by the government or had their families shattered by political harassment to comprehend the veil of suspicion, skepticism, and of course paranoia that hangs between hounded political activists and the rest of the world. We now know that many government agencies covertly and corruptly tried to destroy the black freedom movement, from the Southern Christian Leadership Conference to the Black Panthers.[4]

The Panthers' example inspired Tupac to address racial conflict. Discussing a fight between skinheads and black youth at a party in Marin City, seventeen-year-old Tupac says he and his friends tried to "figure out what to do." Concluding that "this couldn't happen in the sixties" without a response from black activists, Tupac and his friends decided that "we'll start the Black Panthers again." Tupac says that unlike the Panthers of the 1960s, "we're doing it more to fit our views: less violent and more silent." There would be "more knowledge to help" with the restoration of black pride. "I feel like if you can't respect yourself, then you can't respect your race, then you can't respect another's race. . . . It just has to do with respect, like my mother taught me." By starting the Black Panthers again, Tupac and his comrades would not only teach black pride but instill the value of education as a means of self-defense and as a safe-guard against bigotry. By doing this, they would harken back to a turn-of-the-century strategy adopted by DuBois. The revived Black Panthers would function "as a defense mechanism [against] the skinheads, because that's wrong, and I hate to feel helpless," Tupac explains. "And so skinheads hate black people and . . . I have this vision of us just grow-ing, and them decreasing, because that's how knowledge works. It's contagious, you know. And if there [are] war and peace, peace wins out." Tupac says he will "learn from our mistakes. And I'm talking to a lot of the ex-members of the Panthers from the sixties now, because they're less violent. You know, they've learned." Tupac is quick, however, to un-derscore their virtues. "They did a lot of good things in the past, and we can do a lot of good things. . . . My mother was an ex-Panther, and [we'll be] talking to Geronimo Pratt, and a lot of ex-ministers of defense. So we're going to do a lot of good."

Contrary to the caustic criticism he later received, Tupac was not drawn to the Panthers because of their stylized vio-lence, their hypermasculinized images, or their alluring so-cial mystique. His attraction to the Black Panthers was a practical attempt to answer racial oppression. The embrace of black pride was not for compensatory or therapeutic ends. Rather, its purpose was, first, self-respect and, then, respect of others. It was self-regarding morality linked to other-regarding social concern. By embracing education as well, Tupac hit on a key point of liberal reform: that enlightened minds help improve social behavior. His pedagogy of race was equal parts Paulo Freire and John Dewey, based in the belief that morally literate citizens can help transform society.[5]

For all of his reveling in Panther racial theories, Tupac was far less enthusiastic about their contradictory practices. Tupac was especially wounded because he felt the party unjustly abandoned his mother at her most needy moments. If Tupac grew bitter about the poverty Afeni's ideals brought about, he was equally bitter about the failure of the Panthers, for whom she sacrificed family and career, to offer help. As they touted anticapitalist beliefs, some of the party's chief icons lived luxuriously, even dissolutely, at the expense of the proletarian rank and file. If such practices appeared distasteful from a distance, up close they were downright ugly. Afeni remembers that her children inherited her sacrificial spirit. "If they had too many [toys], they gave them away," Afeni recalls, "and I was not rich." Their practice reflected her belief that "everything should go to the community." She says that receiving her "training from the movement" made her believe that "'capitalism' was a dirty word." Tupac, however, had different ideas. He "had a logical mind," Afeni says, and thus examined her situation without the ideological trappings that bound her. But according to Afeni, Tupac "really resented the fact" of her betrayal by the party. Afeni remembers that Tupac wanted desperately to argue with godfather Geronimo Pratt, but out of respect he held his tongue. Tupac felt less favorable about other members. "Other people who were in the party,

he really didn't have a lot of respect for," Afeni says. "Because he was a child who was there. He knew what they did and what they didn't do. And I never lied to my kids . . . for better or for worse. That is basically the way we lived our lives, so they knew exactly what was going on in our lives as it was happening. And they knew who wasn't there and who left us and who never bothered to help." Afeni believes that Tupac saw the contradictions, and "he did stand in judgment." But she quickly adds, "He loved the principles. It wasn't the principles that he was mad at." Instead, it "was the lack of courage in the face of" suffering that riled him, especially the hurt it caused the movement's female soldiers.

Many male Panthers chose, or were forced, to leave behind children and women. The government's repressive techniques destroyed many activist black families, often dividing fathers and mothers from their kin. In fact, Tupac was constantly approached at school by FBI agents seeking the whereabouts of his stepfather, Mutulu Shakur. Tupac was grieved by the gruesome pattern of family abandonment he witnessed, perhaps reminding him of his own desperate plight. Afeni says that from the perspective of a child such events were surely painful. "When you talk about the pain that the child felt, especially when you realize that you can't change it, it is hard," she says. "It is such a deep place." A place so deep that it obviously left a permanent scar on his conscience, leaving Tupac with the belief that one could be—in fact, should be—a rich revolutionary. If revolution can't pay the bills—or, more precisely, if those revolutionaries who are the movement's bread and butter can't keep their heads above water—then the revolution has already failed. Afeni says that in Tupac's eyes, "not only was [the] revolution not paying the bills, but it was causing a great deal of disaster for me." Tupac therefore taught Afeni to make peace with money. "I think I am learning how to live in a capitalist society, which I did not know how to do," she says. "But I learned that from Tupac. I didn't know how to do that. I just knew how to be mad with capitalism." Tupac, according to Afeni, learned to rebel and make cash, a lesson she slowly absorbed. "It never occurred to me," she says. "I never gave myself permission to do that. . . . He released me from so much. . . . Tupac would challenge the [things] that I held sacred. He would make me think about them."

If Tupac demanded that his revolutionary forebears consider the consequences of their failed practices, he also challenged artistic communities and the entertainment industry to face up to their equally heinous contradictions. Free from the bruising environment that trumped revolutionary ideology, Tupac appeared free to embrace its worthier elements. It was evident from the start of his fledgling career that Tupac wasn't simply play-acting the part of a revolutionary, even if his excesses sometimes made him appear extreme, even self-destructive. "He made me think," says Danyel Smith, former editor of *Vibe Magazine* who was a twenty-four-year-old struggling writer when she met eighteen-year-old Tupac in Oakland. "Even before he was famous, and even more so after he was famous, and began to really write the kind of songs that were in his heart," Tupac made "you question whatever line you were riding on." Smith says that she would have been happy simply to have a job, whether at Kinko's or the department store, and "Tupac would say, 'Why are you working for the white people?' Now you know, people have said that throughout history to black people: 'We were slaves to the white people; we need to start our businesses; why are you working for the white man?'" But the way Tupac would say it made it appear to Smith like a new, urgent, even inescapable question. "And then I would be sitting there really saying to myself, 'Should I really be working for white people?'" Smith says that Tupac had "an absolute truth for himself, which is appealing in anybody because it's so rare."

Tupac's absolute truths were apparent to his first manager, Atron Gregory. He began working with Tupac before he had a record deal, when he contemplated giving up music altogether to become the leader of a youth program. Tupac's intensity meant that he had a "willingness to take risks, which [also meant] his willingness to fail." Gregory says that Tupac did everything with a real intensity. "It didn't matter what it was he was doing," recalls Gregory. "Whether he was cooking tacos, whether he was doing music, whether he was doing a movie, whether he was in front of a judge arguing his point, or talking about the same thing with a police officer," Tupac was at full bore. "He went to the airport one time in Burbank," Gregory remembers. "He had a chain with a rust-covered gun on it, and I said, 'You can't take that on the plane.' So he almost went to jail behind that." Finally Tupac took the chain off and boarded the plane. "But he didn't understand how he couldn't have a chain that obviously was not a gun around his neck." Almost as a concession to Tupac's rabid insistence on his right to possess a harmless chain, Gregory adds, "Quite honestly, I didn't understand it either." But few would deem that a fight worth fighting. Tupac's indiscriminate intensity would prove fruitful in his art but far less productive outside the recording and acting studios. His inability to distinguish between issues worthy of a scuffle and those deserving a pass would often land him in trouble, sometimes with his colleagues, more often with the law.

As the child of a Panther, and a second-generation revolutionary of sorts, Tupac was all too familiar with the police. There are many who believe that as an outspoken celebrity and the seed of a radical mother, Tupac and other chosen children were singled out for special brutality. Afeni says that when Tupac was arrested on charges of rape and sexual abuse, "they went into that huge hotel in New York, and they took 200 SWAT team members" to arrest her son. "He was dealt with harshly by the police," Afeni says, "more harshly than maybe the next person." Given Tupac's background, it "always got to be just a little bit more, and for him it got to be like a challenge all the time for him to overcome." Afeni raised Tupac "knowing his situation" as a young black male and the son of a Panther. It was the way she passed that proud legacy on to Tupac that deeply affected Cassandra Butcher, a publicist who worked with Tupac on the films *Poetic Justice* and *Above the Rim*. After Tupac was released from jail on his own recognizance when he was charged with sexual abuse, Butcher accompanied him to a relative's home in Harlem. "I walk into this apartment," Butcher remembers, "and I think this is what changed my life in terms of making me conscious of . . .

who I am to this day." Butcher says she saw Black Panther paraphernalia and the sight of a close-knit family enjoying each other's company. It gave her a different picture of Afeni as a revolutionary matriarch whom her son had spoken of in less than glowing terms around her drug addiction. "I just thought, 'Wow, you know, Tupac is always kind of talking about how his mom has been on drugs, and this hard life he's had," Butcher says. "But, my God, if this is a hard life I would rather be from that than what I'm from. All of a sudden I'm just thinking, 'Man, you've got it great, just to have this soulfulness.' And then you kind of saw where he was coming from."

Butcher's palpable sense of Tupac's revolutionary pedigree sheds new light on the singer's comments about how the police harassed Panthers and black revolutionaries. He spoke of how being a child of a Black Panther made different organizations watch their every move and how "naive it was for us to think that because the Black Panthers are not around . . . that they have stopped looking at the children of the Black Panthers." Butcher says Tupac argued that Hoover's FBI had put in place a surveillance and harassment network that was still active. "'And where did those things go?'" she remembers Tupac asked. "'Do you think that they didn't continue to search?'" Butcher recalls that his probing questions made her search herself. "That just brought me into this consciousness of just like, 'Wait a minute, there are some issues'" that need to be seriously addressed. Working with Tupac on *Above the Rim,* she grew close to Afeni, who introduced her to a great Harlem bookstore and neat survival tricks gleaned from her revolutionary past. "Once I started to hang out with Afeni . . . I felt like movies were nothing," Butcher says. "Afeni taught me things," like "not sitting closest to the door" and "wiping my fork again before I eat." Butcher says of Afeni that "this woman had that influence on me over a five- or six-day period," concluding that she was the reason "Tupac is the man that he is. This woman is truly amazing."

Vondie Curtis Hall, who directed Tupac in *Gridlock'd,* one of his last films, also felt the magnetism of his revolutionary roots. "The brother could quote a million muthafuckas you know," Hall says. "He was like that because he was so obviously a young brother who had grown up around intellectual black folks and revolutionary-minded individuals. He had that kind of weight, that education, that kind of earthy consciousness of a brother who grew up like that." It was a consciousness that threaded through Tupac's art, no matter the forms it took or how much it appeared to be sacrificed on the altar of his commercial ambitions. The Reverend Al Sharpton, who twice visited Tupac in prison when he was incarcerated for sexual abuse, noted his struggle between his Panther past and his career. "Tupac was very conflicted," Sharpton told me. He wanted to be honest to his radical past, but "at the same time, he wanted to be commercially successful." Sharpton says that Tupac "never got far away from his commitment because he grew up where people looked at the way [Afeni] had struggled" and reminded him. "So there was always this balance between thug life and revolutionary life. And I see it reflected in his art, in his personality. He was torn . . . and I think that's why he represented so much more than just another hip-hop artist."

That is a sentiment shared by renowned poet Sonia Sanchez, who concedes that she was forced into hip-hop because of her twin sons. "I'm not a revisionist," Sanchez remarks, admitting she didn't like rap at first. She says that her sons had the music "bouncing off the sidewalk outside, and I'd come in and scream, 'Shut that stuff down. It's so loud I can't hear myself thinking.'" But a powerful baritone changed her mind. "One day I came in and they were playing this piece, and I was pouring some water to drink, and I said, 'Who is that?'" Sanchez recalls. "And one of my sons said, 'That's Tupac Shakur,' and I dropped the glass. It shattered on the floor." Startled, her sons asked Sanchez what was wrong. "And I said, 'Shakur? Do you know that all the Shakurs are in jail, dead, or in exile?'" And then she asked a question she didn't mean them to answer, a question that was more for her sake than theirs: "Does that young man know he's at risk?" Sanchez tells me "That's when I sat down and listened to him. . . . Then I started . . . getting his tapes and playing them at night. I'd turn off the light and listen to them, and I had to hear how his mom had raised him." Echoing Tupac's comments to Cassandra Butcher, Sanchez goes even further in ascribing mythical power to certain children of black revolutionaries. "All of these children named what I call these holy names have been identified by this country," she says. "When I heard his name, the first thing I said [is], 'Is someone protecting him?'" Sanchez argues that we "must protect these children who have come through with their parents who have been activists, and who have challenged the country. Because their children have been hurt along the way because [of the parents'] challenge." Sanchez suggests that it is up "to us, the adults, to help heal them," to help "bring them back along the way with all the other children who didn't have to experience any of this" but who are "gathering the goodies from the work of all of these brothers and sisters who have been out here challenging the world and the country and everybody."

It cannot be said that Tupac bore the burden of his heritage with grace. He sported his pedigree in reckless pride. At the same time, he claimed his place in hip-hop in a fashion that seemed to reject the political utility of revolution. Tupac appeared to forgo the traditional meanings of revolution in favor of the thorny ambivalence of thug culture. On the one hand, the thug embraced the same secular teleology that ran through revolutionary rhetoric: Flipping the economic order was the reason for social rebellion. Thugs are a product of unequal social relations. But thugs bring arbitrary correction to the imbalances that revolutionaries seek to redress. It is that arbitrariness that most offends political activists hoping to bring about social justice. On the other hand, thug logic undermines the society the revolution seeks to change. In the case of the thug, class reversals are sought as much through individual assertion as by collective enterprise. Thug ambition is unapologetically predatory, circumventing the fellow feeling and group solidarity demanded of revolutionaries.

Tupac lived the tension between revolutionary ambition and thug passion. Surely part of the madness he reacted to in life, and reflected in his art, had to do with the negotiation of his revolutionary upbringing in a postrevolutionary world. As publicist Karen Lee said, Tupac was split in his allegiance to the Panthers. "There were times when being a second-generation Panther child was a burden to him," she says. "Because he couldn't step out from under it. But there were other times when he wanted to use it to platform himself." The pain he frequently massaged on record grew in part from the tricky effort to integrate conscience into his art. Some critics see Tupac's glamorization of thug life as the logical outcome of disturbing trends that can be traced to the Black Panther Party. Cultural critic Stanley Crouch argues that two influences on black youth have led to the dangerous moment summed up in Tupac's confused revolutionary gangsterism: the Panthers and the book and film *The Godfather*. Crouch argues that thug rap embraces *The Godfather* as its bible. "Interestingly enough," Crouch says, "Huey Newton got all the people around him to read *The Godfather*." Crouch says that when French social scientist Frantz Fanon's influential book *The Wretched of the Earth* was translated to English in the 1960s, it sparked a romantic preoccupation with revolutionary violence. He says that the first long essay in Fanon's book elevated the "fellah" who argued, "Anything that the oppressor says is right . . . is wrong." Crouch believes that "what began to happen in the late sixties with the emergence of the Panthers was the emergence then of the so-called street brother." He argues that once the intellectual framework of *The Wretched of the Earth* was adopted by black folk, it spelled doom for black culture. "Having [Mao's] 'Red Book' in your pocket, a black leather jacket on . . . and possibly a 45 stuck in your belt" made the Black Panthers attractive to middle-class black girls. "It was okay to chase after these knuckleheads because these knuckleheads had a political philosophy."[6]

One need not agree with Crouch's views about the relation between revolution and the regression of the race—after all, the same period sparked the heroic examples of Fred Hampton and Angela Davis—to embrace his tough analysis of the link between black masculine identity and its political consequences. One result of masculinizing the black freedom struggle was to define the interests of the black community as the interests of black men. Thug life, too, is a decidedly masculine affair. But an equally important feature of black nationalist politics is the conservative turn it took in the 1980s, the era during which Tupac politically matured. In historian Robin D. G. Kelley's view, "both the movement that produced [Tupac], and the movement that he was projecting" are "reflective of the era. Tupac is such a 1980s product, where even black nationalism takes on a new twist." Kelley says that conservative black nationalism—which promotes "good capitalism"—always coexisted "with this more radical, revolutionary nationalism." But in the 1980s black nationalism "was certainly more about institution building, participating in mainstream politics, and taking care of your own, more so than trying to rob banks or blow up buildings."[7]

If black nationalism turned inward in the 1980s, seeking to protect its interests rather than destroy the corrupt power structure, its newfound direction also confused many children of 1970s black revolutionaries who still measured their effectiveness by earlier standards. Tupac's split conscience reflected that confusion. Rapper and actor Mos Def empathizes with the dilemma Tupac faced. "What was it like to grow up living underground?" Mos Def asks on behalf of the children of the Panthers. "What was it like to grow up with your parents under siege? What is it like to grow up with your parents under surveillance, or [to] not feel safe or secure?" Mos Def's answer is simple. "You grow up to be like Pac. You grow up in the street. You grow up doing street things, [knowing] there has got to be something better, because you come from something better." Mos Def says that the social repression experienced by the Panthers and their children had devastating consequences. "The whole governmental [harassment] was effective on a whole other level, because it conflicted the youth. It conflicted the children of our generation." Mos Def sees the most lethal consequences in the lack of direction many of the children suffered. "They not only destroyed the movement, or the bewildered children of the movement, but . . . [the children] had to struggle with no guidance. They were out there on their own." Mos Def eloquently argues that it was not the immediate impact of government harassment on the Panthers that was most hurtful. Rather, it was the effect of such action on the second-generation Panthers. He powerfully and succinctly captures the torn legacy that Tupac embodied. "It is not the nuclear holocaust, the dropping of the bomb, that is terrible," Mos Def says. "The fallout is the real bullshit. Tupac represents the fallout generation. That is my generation. Pac represents something that is heroic and tragic, not just for black society but for *American* society."

CHAPTER 3

"No Malcolm X in My History Text"

School, Learning, and Tupac's Books

"What do you know about Winnie Mandela?" a voice called out to Leila Steinberg in November 1988. Steinberg had just cleared a space on the grass in Marin City's ghetto park to read Mandela's *A Part of My Soul Went with Him*. She remembers that she turned to find a slight, caramel-skinned boy with "beautiful eyes" standing over her. He was the youth she had danced with the night before at a club party where her husband had been the DJ.

"What do I know?" she asked in mock defensiveness. "Someone gave me this book [since] I do a lot of reading. I can't tell you what I know until I'm done." Without missing a beat, he quoted her a couple of lines from the book, verbatim.

"Okay, you read this book?" Steinberg asked.

"I read everything I can get my hands on," he replied.

Tupac Shakur was always hungry for knowledge. When he was a boy in Harlem and got out of line, his mother made him read the *New York Times* all the way through. When he hit the road as a rapper and actor, he consumed an endless diet of books and magazines. His interviews and lyrics were littered with learned allusions to ancient philosophy, mystical writings, African and European cultures, health food manuals, black literature, and pop culture. He could quote passages from cherished books and cite lines from favorite films.

"He was very clearly smart," says journalist Allison Samuels. "He could quote Shakespeare." But his knowledge didn't end there.

"You could have a conversation with him about everything," says actress Peggy Lipton, whose daughter, Kidada, Tupac was in love with when he died. She remembers playing classical music and some Kate Bush music one night when he came over. "I remember sitting there saying [to him], 'This is Kate Bush.'"

"I listen to Kate Bush," Tupac replied.

Lipton was surprised, especially since he "carried this heavy-duty" reputation. "He divulged his incredible musical interests. He had wonderful musical taste, and he listened to everybody. Kidada confirmed that with me."

Tupac's lawyer, Shawn Chapman, got a firsthand sense of the variety of Tupac's musical tastes. The first time she defended Tupac occurred on a criminal charge that took them to the Los Angeles Criminal Courts Building. Tupac was accompanied by several acquaintances, who decided after court to dine at Roscoe's, the famous Los Angeles soul food restaurant. Tupac invited Chapman and elected to ride in her car. The lawyer, a fan almost exclusively of rock-and-roll music, had a tape partially lodged in her tape player.

"What tape is this?" Tupac asked.

"You are never going to know who it is," Chapman replied. Tupac grabbed the tape from her deck.

"Oh, Sarah McLachlan," he said as he started singing one of her songs.

"He knew all the lyrics," Chapman remembers in disbelief. Lipton, however, argues that Tupac's interests stretched well beyond music: "You could have a conversation with him about everything. He knew about everything, and he was open to everything." Jada Pinkett Smith agrees. "He was quick to tell me what book I should be reading," says Smith. "He was a well-read brother. And I loved that because he always had something to teach me. And he didn't graduate from high school."

Tupac's high school career was ultimately short-circuited by homelessness, his mother's addiction, fierce parental spats, and a fatherless adolescence. But he gained valuable experiences in school and in the arts community that nurtured his love of learning, even as his family suffered one setback after another. For a short time after her acquittal, Afeni became a minor celebrity on the liberal speaking circuit, garnering invitations to lecture at prominent universities like Yale and Harvard. She was even set up for a while in an apartment on Manhattan's Riverside Drive. Then the tide turned against black radicalism, and her liberal allies fell away. A year after her trial, Afeni's support dried up. And her family suffered, despite her work as a legal assistant at Bronx Legal Services. "Dick Fishbein was the managing attorney there at the time," Afeni says. "He was doing a rent strike for my sister's building, and he knew about me, and he came to see me to try to help me. I had never met him before in my life. He gave me a job at Legal Services, sight unseen, no resume, no job description, no nothing." Times were still tough. Afeni had three mouths to feed with little help from her children's fathers. Eventually, Afeni, Sekyiwa, and Tupac had to go on welfare. By the time Tupac was ready for junior high school, the family had already moved nearly twenty times.[1]

Tupac displayed promise when he began writing plays at the age of six. "When they were kids, Tupac used to stage productions with his cousins," Afeni says. "He wrote plays, and they had to be the actors, and they had to do everything he said, because he would tell them that he was the director," she recalls, laughing at the memory. Tupac's earliest influences as a fledgling playwright were distinctly Asian. "He saw every single karate movie," Afeni says. "We used to travel back and forth to California, so he would go to San

Francisco where they have the Kabuki theater, where they have the real Japanese movies." Inspired by what he saw, Tupac emulated their moves on his makeshift stage. "He made all the props," Afeni remembers, "and the poor people had to act in these productions." Tupac's quick mind and natural talents sometimes kept his early instructors from challenging him. One teacher complimented Afeni when she retrieved four-year-old Tupac from school. "You should be proud; he is so perfect," the teacher said. "He didn't come here to be entertainment for you," Afeni says she replied. "He came here to get an education."

When he was twelve, Tupac found a nurturing community in the West 127th Street Ensemble Company in Harlem. He didn't like his life, but he loved escaping through the characters he played. He fed off of the affirmation he absorbed from his fellow thespians. Realizing that he was homeless, members of the company treated him to a thirteenth birthday party after a company rehearsal. Noted actress Minnie Gentry, a visiting performer with the company, publicly recited Langston Hughes's poem "Mother to Son." Another member presented him with a special gift. "She went and got thirteen brand new one-dollar bills," Afeni recalls with tears. "And [she] rolled them up like a scroll, put a yellow ribbon around each one, the way you would do a diploma, and then she lined up every one of them in a box, and she presented that to him." Tupac was fortunate to have encountered people who loved him and recognized his gifts. "We might have been poor," Afeni says, but there was a "richness [to] the people in Pac's life," especially because "they knew he was gifted," and "what they had, they gave to him. . . . There was no place that didn't happen."

The love flowed as well at the Baltimore School for the Arts after the family moved to the Maryland capital with the promise of a job for Afeni in 1986. Although it's reported that Tupac learned to act in Baltimore, he always took pride in his earlier induction into the acting guild at the age of twelve. "That season [the company] performed for a paying audience in . . . an off-off-off-Broadway theater," Afeni says. "But Tupac was told by those actors and by that director—and he believed it from that day—[that] he was a professional actor. And he went to the Baltimore School of the Arts a *professional* actor." Indeed, many believe that had Tupac lived, he would have become, as Bill Maher told me, "a big movie star." As compelling a hip-hop icon as he was, says Quincy Jones, "he was a better actor than rapper."

In Baltimore Tupac prized the broad arts education he received. His interest in acting and art had already been established, the latter coming when Afeni brought home from the library prints of various artists, including van Gogh, whose *Starry Night* Tupac found particularly captivating. (In fact he also loved singer Don McLean's haunting paean to van Gogh, *Vincent,* which played continuously as he teetered on the brink of death in a Las Vegas hospital years later.) Tupac also delved into Shakespeare, ballet, jazz, and poetry, which he began writing in grammar school. It was easy enough for Tupac to move from poetry to writing raps, which he did with great skill and remarkable speed, features that added to his legend as a rapper. (Rapper

Notorious B.I.G. said that when he once visited Tupac, the latter went to the bathroom, and when he emerged, he had penned two songs.) Though he thrived in school, Tupac's domestic troubles escalated, and Baltimore's mean streets got meaner. At the end of his junior year in school, gang violence claimed the life of a neighborhood boy. The boy's death and Tupac's chaotic home life thrust him onto a bus for a cross-country trek to Marin City, California, and to the equally troubled home of Linda Pratt, wife of Panther Elmer "Geronimo" Pratt.[2]

If Tupac hit his stride in Baltimore, he lost his footing in California. By his own admission, he was an outsider, especially since he couldn't play basketball, he dressed like a hippie, he was a target of street gangs, he wrote poetry, and he secretly loathed himself. When Afeni joined him in California, her drug addiction, which came at the height of the crack epidemic, put her in dangerous proximity to the drug's infamous center of distribution in northern California's black ghettos. Tupac momentarily lived with Afeni, but when she could no longer hold her house together, he left her and his sister and joined a group of boys in an abandoned apartment while working at a pizza parlor. He eventually started hustling crack, but some good friends, like Charles Fuller, who discerned his talent for bigger goals, discouraged him. Tupac enrolled at the affluent Mt. Tamalpais High School, the school in rich Marin County that overlooked the ghetto of Marin City, known as "the Jungle." Tupac gained a reputation for his riveting acting but eventually left school after forming a rap group, the One Nation Emcees, with his roommates.

Before he left school, Tupac's desperate desire for a useful, relevant education loomed large. I had the chance to see this desire dance on his countenance when Leila Steinberg showed me the video of Tupac being interviewed in high school. His handsome brown face was lit by a brightly contagious smile. At seventeen Tupac had not yet shown signs of the alopecia that would cause him to completely shave his locks. His hair was faded on the sides and higher in the top in the style of the late 1980s, with a part in the left and a brownish red tinting splashed across the top. He had a small stud in his right ear. Tupac's look could be called boho— bohemian homeboy—and featured a black tank top with two spindly arms sticking out like spider's legs.[3] His slight arms were capped with three bands on the right wrist and a sky blue watch with an inexpensive band on the left wrist. Steinberg popped the tape in, and I sat, transfixed by this highly articulate young man who spoke gently but animatedly about his views on schools, education, a curriculum rooted in real-world needs, poverty, and his difficult but rewarding upbringing. Long before he found fame, Tupac possessed a sharp intelligence and acutely observed the world around him.

Tupac readily admits that he has goofed off in school, largely because he craved popularity and being social. He gives a precocious analysis of the tension between schooling and education. "I think that we got so caught up in school being a tradition that we stopped using it as a learning tool, which it should be," Tupac says. "I'm learning about the basics, but they're not basic for me. . . . To get us ready for today's world, [the present curriculum] is not helping." Tupac suggests that dull tradition is responsible for the deadening effect of passing on irrelevant knowledge from one generation to another. Seeking an escape from such unimaginative transmission of information, Tupac proclaims the practical source of his knowledge. "That's why the streets have taught me." Discussing the bland repetition of knowledge—"they tend . . . to teach you to read, write, and [do] arithmetic, then teach you reading and writing and arithmetic again, then again, then again"—Tupac suggests that the purpose of such pedagogical routines is "to keep you busy." He offers instead a list of classes he thinks will benefit his peers. "There should be a class on drugs. There should be a class on sex education, a real sex education class, not just pictures and diagrams and illogical terms. . . . There should be a class on scams. There should be a class on religious cults. There should be a class on police brutality. There should be a class on apartheid. There should be a class on racism in America. There should be a class on why people are hungry."

Watching this tape, I'm astounded at the thoughtful engagement displayed by this young man who is on the verge of a wildly successful life that will take him far outside the schoolroom. It is clear that Tupac believes schools should address the pressing social issues of the day, and even more specifically, they should help youth confront the ills that directly affect them. Classes on sex education, scams, and religious cults would explore general problems confronted by youth of all colors. But police brutality, apartheid, and racism are of obvious relevance to poor black and brown youth. Tupac's pedagogical themes are linked to salient so-

cial issues that are rarely explored in rich detail in our nation's educational institutions, especially in high school. For
Tupac, educational relevance is not an index of frivolous or
ephemeral concerns. His list gives pride of place to the
themes that he learned as a child of social protest and radical resistance. Like a good son of the Panthers, Tupac is interested in forging connections between sites of learning
and the communities in which they are located. Schools
should help students negotiate the worlds they occupy.

So he points out that "the things that helped me were the
things that I learned from my mother, from the streets, and
reading." He is grateful to school because it "taught me
reading, which I love." Questioning the relevance of algebra and foreign languages, Tupac makes a forceful criticism
of dishonest political rhetoric that reflects remarks made
decades earlier by George Orwell. "I think [foreign lan-
guages] are important but . . . they should be teaching you
English, and then teaching you how to understand double-
talk. Politics is double-talk." Tupac makes a point that is
neither xenophobic nor jingoistic. Instead, he looks beyond
the abstract good of foreign-language education by questioning its comparative worth in a curriculum that should
be geared to the real lives of poor youth: "When am I going
to Germany? I can't afford to pay my rent in America. How
am I going to Germany?" Although his query may be dismissed as an index of his parochialism, it may just as well
reflect the lack of opportunity open to a desperately poor
youth, even one as bright as Tupac. The real misfortune is
not that Tupac appears provincial; the tragedy is that by
seventeen he has not had the chance, one enjoyed by many

of his wealthy peers, to experience the mind-opening, life-altering effect of foreign travel—or to imagine the international itinerary that would soon dominate his life.

Tupac appeals to traditions of learning that are older than America's, citing "ancient civilizations [that] have survived without going to schools like this." The budding rapper also delivers a stinging judgment of the nostalgia on which he believes American education is built, even as it fails to transmit values that are useful to young people. "We're being taught to deal with this fairyland, which we're not even living in anymore. And it's sad, 'cause *I'm* telling you, and it should not be me telling you. It should be common knowledge." Tupac's disgust with educational officials who overlook social misery and the willful ignorance on which it thrives is apparent. "Aren't they wondering why death rates are going up, and suicide is going up, and drug abuse? Aren't they wondering? Don't they understand that . . . more kids are being handed crack than they're being handed diplomas?" Tupac's insightful criticism of the social circumstances of poor youth suggests a reordering of educational priorities that values survival over repetition. It is also interesting to observe Tupac's relentless efforts to link the economic and racial contexts of learning with the pedagogical and curricular strategies that are most likely to help poor black and Latino students. Tupac's remedy, in part, for such a state of affairs is a Twain-like update on the prince and pauper exchange, a switch meant to right social wrongs by inviting the rich to see life through the eyes of the poor, and vice versa. In Tupac's case it was also the old viewing society through the eyes of youth. He contends that rich folk should trade places with the poor and that adults should go to school again. If his suggestion reflects the naiveté of youth, it also captures a poor bright boy's ardent desire to combat the social ills he observes at home and in his neighborhood.[4]

One of Tupac's most revealing comments about the regulation of the poor comes when he compares the effects of society's control over youth to rats being routed through a maze and their arbitrary trapping for experimental purposes. "They'll let you go as far as you want, but as soon as you start asking too many questions, and you're ready to change, boom, that block will come." He links critical questioning to social regulation, not altogether unexpected in light of his experience as the child of a black revolutionary. "Since I'm living in a slummish area and I'm black, [my block] will come through being a statistic, you know. I'll get caught up in all of this, and one day I'll be with my friends, and they'll go, 'Let's go out partying. We don't have a car; let's steal a car.' . . . We'll steal a car, and I'll go to jail for sixteen years and then come out and be bitter." The math may indeed be fuzzy, but Tupac is depressingly accurate in his prediction that he will serve time and that the experience will have a damaging effect on his outlook on life. Of course what is perhaps most disheartening in Tupac's analysis is to see how already, by the age of seventeen, a poor black youth perceives his expendability. His prescient and disturbing vision of trouble for himself is nonetheless chilling: It reflects the disproportionate incarceration of young black males caught up in the criminal justice system.

In keeping with his yen for an education that is relevant,

Tupac reflects on the relation between politics and class. His hopes for "a better America" were dashed when instead of electing Jesse Jackson or Michael Dukakis to the presidency, the nation chose George Bush. "I couldn't believe it because every time I asked people, 'Who would you have voted for?' . . . They were like, 'Well, Dukakis.' But how did Bush win? I keep wondering." Tupac's question is one that has stumped far more seasoned experts and points to a vexing feature of the electoral landscape: Citizens who are polled often publicly claim to have voted for one candidate but have privately chosen another. Bush's election makes Tupac "rebel more against society because they're supposed to represent the people." Tupac displays his acute political judgment in a withering attack on conservative politics. "I don't want Bush in government. I spent eight years of my seventeen years on this earth under Republicans, under Ronald Reagan, under an ex-actor who lies to the people, who steals money, and who's done nothing at all for me." Tupac links destructive conservative policies to class politics, carefully distinguishing personality from principle. He manages to avoid personal attack while also refusing to confuse interpersonal pleasantness with political compassion. "I don't think Bush is a bad person or a bad president, because for the upper class, he's a perfect president. And that's how society is built."

Tupac brilliantly distinguishes between discourse about politics and the real exercise of political power, a distinction that is driven by class. "The upper class runs [society] while . . . the middle class and lower class, we talk about it. And for the working class, we're just lost; we're going through the motions. We're the worker bees, and they get to live like royalty." Those class distinctions flare up at his school as well, as Tupac carves up social space with an acumen that might have made Karl Marx, Max Weber, and Talcott Parsons equally proud. "There's the lower Marin City class. There's the lower white class. There's the 'middle-class' white class. There's the 'middle-class' black class and . . . there's the upper-class white and the upper-class black. And it's a shame that it has to be cut in so many pieces, because it all boils down to just one piece of money." Zero-sum economics could not have found a better advocate.

Following through with his class analysis, Tupac makes an interesting suggestion: Since there is so much room in the White House, President Ronald Reagan could address a "staggering" homeless problem by opening the White House to displaced indigents. "Why can't he take some of them people off the street and put them in his White House?" Tupac yearns to know. "Because he doesn't want to get dirty. The White House would be a little tainted." Tupac's fangs are admirably flashing, a foretaste of the acerbic criticism he would wield against chosen targets in his rap career. But he displays humanity when he refuses to identify homeless people with their condition. Instead, in the best tradition of enlightened social theory, he argues that their critical importance has not been erased by their unfortunate circumstances. "They haven't been homeless forever. They've done things in society. . . . They've had jobs before. . . . They worked hard."

Tupac's insight into social problems grew from critical reflection on the harsh circumstances of his youth.

Although he obviously had a problem with school, he displayed a deep love of learning. He brought his analytical
skills to bear on his recent upbringing in Baltimore and
Marin City. By his own admission, it makes him "upset to
talk" about Baltimore's horrible conditions. "Baltimore has
the highest rate of teenage pregnancy, the highest rate of
AIDS within the black community"—an awareness that put
Tupac far ahead of most leaders in black communities—
"the highest rate of teens killing teens, the highest rate of
teenage suicide, and the highest rate of blacks killing blacks.
. . . And this is where I chose to live!" Obviously the choice
was his mother's, not his, but Tupac's comprehension of
the clutch of social ills that ganged up on poor ghetto
blacks is remarkable. But he is not willing simply to observe
the pain; he seeks to relieve it, an admirable glimpse into the
social compassion that will stick with him throughout his
life. "So as soon as I got there—being the person I am—I
said 'No, no. I'm changing this.' So I started a stop-the-
killing' campaign and safe sex campaign and AIDS preven-
tion campaign . . . and then I came back, and I felt like I did
a lot of good." The good he did, however, could not stem
the tide of violence that would drown his peers after he left
Baltimore. "The second week I was in California, I got a call
and two of my friends were shot dead in the head, two of
the friends that were working with me at the time . . . and
it's just like, why try? Because this is what happens." In
sharp contrast to his later life, when hopelessness erupted
in him like a volcano, Tupac is able to bounce back. "But I
still try, you know."

Tupac does not miss the irony of his situation: He escaped New York's violence by heading to Baltimore, only to escape its violence by coming to California, where he encountered the violence of racism, which he "can't stand in any form, shape, or color." He also sees death and needless brutality. "I mean, this lady slashed a man's throat because he spit on her kids, and I've seen teenagers fight last night over girls." But he mostly endured the violence of poverty, an experience that, he repeatedly states, has left him bitter. "I loved my childhood, but I hated growing up poor, and it made me very bitter. You know, it's like, all right, now I got a job. I had to quit now. I had a job, and just today I got paid, and I have money in my pocket that I worked for. And that's the greatest feeling, you know, that I worked for it. . . . But I'm still poor. My family is still poor. I still live in a poor neighborhood. . . . I still see poor people."

Haunted by a sight that was invisible to most people, Tupac could no longer pretend school fit his view of the world. Neither could he reconcile the poverty he saw and the useless education he felt he got at Mt. Tamalpais, so he simply stopped going, although he had psychically withdrawn months before. His quest for learning, however, was undiminished. In a delightful twist of fate, he was about to meet someone who would help him reach his goal.

When Tupac came across Leila Steinberg that day in the park, it was a serendipitous meeting that changed both of their lives. Steinberg bridged many cultures, both in her name—"Leila" is Arabic, "Steinberg" Jewish—and in her work as a dancer and teacher who held workshops on poetry and self-expression for poor youth around the city. She was born in Los Angeles in 1960, reared in Watts, and attended all-black schools. "The black community nurtured me, raised me, and gave me a sense of where I stood on the planet," Steinberg, who is white, remembers. "I didn't even understand my North African roots or my Jewish roots, and I ran as far as I could from [them]." Under the influence of black artists in the 1960s, she came to understand "how fucked up we are in our schools, in our healing process, [and] in education." By the time she reached sixth grade, Steinberg found her mission in the arts. "It was the only place that I knew that the truth was told," she says. "You could go 500 years backwards and know what was going on with any people, because artists don't lie." Her mother, who was born in Mexico but whose roots were in the Middle East, was an activist involved in Latin and black politics. She also thrust Leila and her siblings into social protest through marching for the rights of migrant farmworkers. By the time she was twelve, Leila's mother left home to pursue her activist agenda full time. She was raised by her father and influenced by her grandfather, a Latin dance teacher, who introduced her to salsa, Brazilian, and other Latin dance. Leila performed around the city and met teachers who taught her West African dance as well.

When she graduated from high school, Steinberg moved to Central America, researching various music and artists and enrolling in college in Panama. When she returned to the United States a few years later, she moved to northern California, attended college, and started touring with well-known Congolese and Latin artists. She also went on the road with guitarist Carlos Santana's band and the soul group the Neville Brothers. During this time she met and married

Bruce, who was caught up in the L.A. rap scene; had a daughter; and studied sports therapy, with the aim of exploring alternative healing as an athletic trainer, her fallback career in case she needed steady money. Her husband's involvement in rap exposed her to its powerful social critique. "Because I was so involved in African music, [rap] was the first honest voice in a long time that was very fresh." Steinberg juggled several responsibilities: her dance career, her therapy job, raising her daughter, and supporting her husband's efforts as a rap promoter. Steinberg and her family moved to the Bay area and eventually further north as her husband earned a growing reputation as a skilled DJ. When the family moved north, Steinberg began to front her husband's business ventures. As a black male, Bruce faced difficulties in renting facilities to hold rap concerts and club parties. They started promoting shows in California, drawing up to 10,000 kids in a single event.

Along with her burgeoning promotional career, Steinberg got involved in the local schools because of her expanding brood of children. "I didn't want my kids to be subjected to the same stuff that I wasn't okay with," she says. Steinberg began volunteering her time in class and eventually met a woman who ran Young Imaginations, a nonprofit educational agency. The agency focused primarily on getting artists to come into local schools to entertain the students. Steinberg spotted a larger opportunity. She helped the head of the agency reshape her organization into a multicultural arts and education agency that used artists from a variety of races, ethnicities, and cultures to help educate the children about history, culture, and politics. Steinberg began addressing assemblies in the high schools during the day and promoting rap shows with her husband at night. When she witnessed the enthusiastic response to their rap programs, she yearned to bring rap into the curriculum. "I really saw how kids resonated [with us], because we had square dancing coming in the black schools. . . . God, what I would have done to have some rappers and some African artists and rap artists come up and do something." But Young Imaginations was not prepared to make the leap, so Steinberg started her own nonprofit program, joining forces with a woman who had access to "white corporate money."

As Steinberg's program took off in school, her promotional work with Bruce was paying big dividends as well. But tensions flared when her name became almost exclusively associated with efforts that her husband had initiated and when her reputation rose above the artists she helped to promote. "The really messed-up thing is that every time there was success in the black community, there was always a nonblack person that came in and took credit," Steinberg says. "So I was really afraid to have myself on the forefront in an industry that deserved to be credited to what these young black men were doing." Steinberg pulled back on the promotional front and directed much of her energy into her work in the schools of Marin City and Oakland. She wanted to have a program that, "would touch these kids, and . . . [that] would make a difference because we really care." Because she loved language, rap could be a natural ally to her efforts. "I kept saying, 'I need to find somebody who has that political connection and the social connection, but is really ready to also move past . . . a world of . . . black and white."' Although she hadn't found the right person to fulfill her goals, Steinberg continued to hold free after-school workshops—on writing and performance—two days a week. Her reputation grew quickly. "If you want to write a poem or rap, a piece, a monologue; if you want to read the dictionary with me; if you're willing to create and be out of the streets, come on," Steinberg says in explaining her appeal to the more than 300 students who signed up for her workshops in Marin, Nevada, and Sonoma counties. And then her breakthrough came, at least in principle. "One day one of my students, Lawanda Hunter, an amazing young dancer who was also on my team of promotions and [who worked] with my husband . . . came to me and said, 'You know, Leila, you touch and inspire a lot of us, and your commitment to work is great, but I found somebody in Marin who just moved here, who is everything you're look-ing for [in a person to] collaborate with." Discounting her student's glowing recommendation—"everyone wanted to bring me their shining stars"—Steinberg brushed Lawanda off "for a long time." In the meantime Hunter was telling Tupac about Steinberg.

Several weeks later Leila and Bruce held a promotional party at a local club. Bruce was the DJ, Leila the free spirit. "He's deejaying and I'm like the life of the party," Steinberg recalls. "We are doing this thing together, and we are con-verting Sonoma County, [which] is very white, scared to death of rap." As Steinberg danced, "this very beautiful young person made eye contact, [and] jumped on the dance floor and started dancing with me." After their dance,

Steinberg quickly turned her attention to the night's business without the chance of learning her dance partner's name. The next day she had an early afternoon workshop in Marin City and before class headed to the park to read her new book. And then she met Tupac.

"By the way, what's your name?" Tupac asked after giving Steinberg a good ribbing.

"I'm Leila."

"You're shitting me," Tupac gasped. "You're not Leila. I'm Tupac!"

As the two excitedly jumped up and down—because of their dance the night before, because Steinberg was reading a book Tupac had just finished, because of how destiny brought them together—they celebrated their good fortune.

"How old are you?" Steinberg asked.

"Oh, I just turned seventeen," Tupac replied. "Where are you going right now?"

"Well, I have to go teach in Marin City. Don't you have school?"

"I'm not going today."

"Does your mother know you're not going?"

"I raised my mother and sister. I'm taking care of my home. I'm the man. I don't know if you understand that."

"Well, I was the woman, and my dad did his best, but I raised my younger brothers. So I understand what it is to be the parent of your parents and have a house full."

"Would you like to come with me to my class?"

"Yes, I would. I want to talk to you."

As Steinberg did her workshop, Tupac sat silently and observed her every move, squirming in his seat. He made faces and was anxious to speak but refrained from talking since Steinberg asked him not to interrupt her. After class Tupac opened up. "I appreciate what you're doing," he said. "I feel you. But I've got a lot to tell you about what you do." As she was to learn later, this was classic Tupac. "He was very challenging," Steinberg recalls. "Because as brilliant as he was, Tupac would challenge everybody and anything. That was his nature." After her workshop Steinberg phoned home to tell Bruce that she was bringing a guest who would be attending her evening workshop. Tupac went home with her, attended the evening workshop, and almost instantly had a big impact on Steinberg. His aggressive questioning about her pedagogical methods forced her to rethink her approach. "I've been teaching now for the last fourteen years," Steinberg says. "And Pac changed my teaching. He changed who I am as a woman and as a parent, because as Pac entered our group, he took a lot of my infantile thought processes to the next level." At seventeen, Tupac was a for-midable intellectual presence in the life of this formally ed-ucated artist and teacher. If he shook her brain up, he did the same to her household: He moved in with Steinberg's family shortly after meeting her.

Tupac and Steinberg began to tour the schools together. She taught; he rapped. Their success forged a profound bond between the two. Tupac told her almost immediately that he was soon going to be a famous artist selling millions of records and that she was going to be his manager. As it turns out, Tupac was right on both counts, although Steinberg handed Digital Underground manager Atron Gregory the reins to Tupac's career as he was getting started. But she remained a crucial presence in his life. She argued with him about his ideas and career direction. She supported him through his personal and career crises. She listened to his boyish pride in his famous conquests (he once called her with a white female pop star in his bed). She provided unflagging love to an artist she saw rapidly transform from a sweet-faced teen to an internationally recognized rap superstar. But above all she believed in the mythological power of his life and career, a belief that has only enlarged since his tragic death.

Perhaps the most important role Steinberg played in Tupac's life was that of literary soul mate. Steinberg encouraged Tupac's ample literary talents in her workshops. She kept the many efforts he made there, especially his poems, which were published after his death in a volume entitled *The Rose That Grew from Concrete,* a project Steinberg oversaw. But it was as reading partners that Steinberg and Tupac most profoundly shaped each other's lives. They incessantly shared, reflected on, responded to, and argued about the written word. When Steinberg met Tupac, he was already well read. "He could recite sonnets that I couldn't understand how this seventeen-year-old could memorize," she says. "He did a class project that blew me away, where he did his own 1990s version of one of Shakespeare's plays." In fact the Bard played a significant role in Tupac's rapidly expanding self-mythologization. "The way these kids study Shakespeare in class now, they will study my work, too," Tupac told Steinberg. To many observers this may have come off as the delusion of a poor black youth who felt relatively powerless and therefore projected his fame as a means to compensate for his lowly status. But Steinberg quickly became a true believer. "This is why I'm so committed to his work," she says. "Because I knew it was true then. . . . That's why I think we have to study Pac in every university." Steinberg contends that Tupac's poetry and life can be a means to the critical self-reflection that Tupac believed should be taught in the nation's classrooms. "Most of his documenting and his [artistic] process was really an internal process lived out loud, publicly, for you to question everything you do, for you to question . . . how you live, what's right and wrong and who decides it. That's really who he was in all these fragments."

Tupac and Steinberg spent hours reading books at their favorite haunt, L.A.'s Bohdi Tree Bookstore, especially after Tupac moved to Los Angeles in the early 1990s. Located on Melrose Avenue, Bohdi specializes in spiritual literature and revolutionary tomes. "He did it on his own," Steinberg says. "He was totally self-educated." Tupac wanted to get everyone in the country reading. "Oprah got going what Pac wanted to do," Steinberg says. "He was going to use rap to get kids reading again. They were going to analyze and destroy all the great theorists and philosophers." Tupac's literary interests were impressively catholic. He read novelist Kurt Vonnegut and political theorist Mikhail Bakunin. He read books on anarchy and Platonism. He read Teilhard de Chardin's *Phenomenon of Man*. "He loved that book," Steinberg tells me. "We would go in [to Bohdi], and he would want them to refer books to us." But it was Steinberg's teacher Peggy Shackleton who was the primary reference librarian of their growing archive. When Tupac asked Steinberg where she got the books in her library, she told him about Shackleton. "He wanted to talk to Peggy," Steinberg recalls. "He was like, 'Whoever this lady is that's sending you these books [is great]. I know some of those books; I found them on my own.'" Steinberg was impressed, since she hadn't found "Khalil Gibran on my own. . . . So he just had this love affair with this now sixty-five-year-old woman and wanted every book Peggy ever gave me, which was his introduction to a whole new world of reading." Shackleton gave Steinberg lists of books to feed Tupac's insatiable intellectual appetite, a pattern that continued until his death. Steinberg has kept Tupac's books. "It's the only thing I ever travel with [when I move]. . . . If you come to my house, you'll see."[5]

Taking advantage of Steinberg's offer, I visit her cozy Santa Monica bungalow, recessed in a manicured cove on a dimly lit street. I want to lay my eyes on the books, finger through them, and get a sense of the rapper's intellectual habits rising from the ruffle of pages rabidly perused. Steinberg leads me to one of many bookshelves tucked in crevices and along the walls of her house. I drink in the sea of books and wade through the volumes Tupac consumed. There is J. D. Salinger's *Catcher in the Rye,* Robert Pirsig's *Zen and the Art of Motorcycle Maintenance,* Richard Wright's *Native Son,* and Maya Angelou's *I Know Why the Caged Bird Sings.* (In prison Tupac said, "I read a lot of good books; I read a lot of Maya Angelou's books.") There are novels by Hermann Hesse, Gabriel García Márquez, and Henry Miller. Homer's *Odyssey* pops up, as does the well-regarded anthology of Friedrich Nietzsche's work edited by Walter Kaufmann. My eyes run across books by Sigmund Freud—"He read Freud to discredit him. . . . He thought Freud was a frustrated homosexual who never [fully] formulated his opinions," Steinberg tells me—and Carl Jung. The sight of Robin Morgan's *Sisterhood Is Powerful: Anthology of Writings from the Women's Liberation Movement* strikes me. "Did he really read this?" I ask. "He read a lot of feminist writings," Steinberg replies. There's work by Alice Walker, including *In Search of Our Mothers' Gardens,* and George Orwell. (Perhaps he *had* read Orwell's celebrated essay "The Politics of the English Language" before he made his powerful comments on political double-talk during his interview.)

I spot E. D. Hirsch's *Dictionary of Cultural Literacy: What Every American Needs to Know,* an interesting choice to be sure. "When we did our assemblies in the high schools," Steinberg says, "he said that this was a white supremacist perspective on cultural literacy. He wanted to use the second edition to define how whites define what cultural literacy is. Pac paid for this to attack it." As if to counter Hirsch, there is a volume by Jonathan Kozol, *Savage Inequalities: Children in America's Schools.* There are tomes by John Steinbeck, Alex Haley—"He read *Roots* at least two or three times," Steinberg says—and Jamaica Kincaid, including her *At the Bottom of the River.* I notice Eileen Southern's *Music of Black Americans: A History* and Herman Melville's *Moby Dick.* Ira Peck's edited *Life and Words of Martin Luther King, Jr.* is there, and so are Anaïs Nin and Aldous Huxley. ("He was fascinated with Aldous Huxley and the whole sixties psychedelic time period, [which covered] the drugs Afeni did before the crack that almost destroyed her.") Dick Gregory is present, and so is Derrick Bell. "Our friend worked with Derrick Bell and gave us both copies," Steinberg says. I see William Styron's *Confessions of Nat Turner* and Sun Tzu's *Art of War,* as well as George L. Lee's *Interesting People: Black American History Makers,* a collection of the original illustrative biographies syndicated in the National Black Press, 1945 to 1948 and 1970 to 1986. And there is the riveting corpus of Donald Goines, the Detroit writer who specialized in brutal tales of black street life and who died prematurely and violently.

Across the room I spot a familiar book: UCLA professor Susan McClary's *Feminine Endings: Music, Gender and Sexuality,* but Steinberg gently removes it from my hands. "Pac did not read this. But she likes his work." When I see Amiri Baraka's *Blues People,* I reflect on the intriguing similarities that bind the writer and the rapper: huge gifts, fearless outspokenness, and poetically phrased rage. There is Donald Passman's *All You Need to Know About the Music Business* and Fox Butterfield's *All God's Children: The Boskett Family and the American Tradition of Violence.* (When I later talk to Stanley Crouch about Tupac, he mentions Butterfield. "I don't know if you read this book; you probably did. It's called *All God's Children.*" "Oh, Butterfield," I reply. "Yeah, right," Crouch says. "A book, by the way, that Tupac read," I say. "Well, he didn't make much of it that I know of," Crouch retorts. He thinks for a moment and then backs up a bit. "Well, maybe he didn't get a chance to. I'm glad to know he did read it.")

There's poetry by black women. "He loved Maya Angelou, Nikki Giovanni, and Sonia Sanchez," Steinberg says, as I pore over *Black Sister: Poetry by Black American Women, 1746 to 1980,* edited by Earlene Stetson. I also see William H. Harris's *The Harder We Run: Black Workers Since the Civil War,* as well as *Bullwhip Days: The Slaves Remember* and *Souls of Black Folk,* the classic volume by master black intellectual W. E. B. DuBois. *Monster,* Sanyika Shakur's scary gang autobiography, rides the shelf. "They were going to do stuff together," Steinberg says. "They were in touch quite a bit." There is Nathan McCall's *Makes Me Wanna Holler* and Jack Gratus's *Great White Lie: Slavery, Emancipation and Changing Racial Attitudes.* The oversized pictorial *Songs of My People* sticks out, as does *The New Our Bodies, Ourselves* and *The State of the World Atlas,* part 1, by Michael Kidron and Ronald Segal. There is a copy of *The Meaning of Masonry* by W. L. Wilmshurst. "He was very fascinated by masonry . . . by secret societies and the white elite and their control. He definitely was going to dissect [it] and tear [it] down, so he studied." I also notice quite a few volumes on crime and notorious criminals. "He was obsessed with reading about black crimes and white crimes," Steinberg says. "He would read serial-killer books and talk about white crimes related to lots of sick things. And then black crimes as a completely different world of crime [related to] economic struggle." (That insight, however, did not stop Tupac from defending at least one white criminal. In outtakes from an interview that he and Snoop Dogg did for MTV in 1996, Tupac discusses the fact that prosecutors on famous murder trials can write books and make money, but not the criminals. "How can they put a book out and Charles Manson can't put a book out?" he asks. "He did the murders. They didn't do shit. They just talked about what another nigga did. Charles did that shit.")

There is a great deal of spiritual literature, much of which I know, some of it unfamiliar to me. There is Thomas à Kempis's *Imitation of Christ* and several books on Buddhism, including Jack Kornfield's *Teachings of the Buddha.* There are other classics, such as *St. John of the Cross* and *Cloud of Unknowing,* as well as noteworthy contemporary volumes, including Thomas Merton's *No Man Is an Island* and Evelyn Underhill's *Mysticism.* I recognize A. N. Watts's *Wisdom of Insecurity* and Gershem Scholem's edition of the *Kabbalah,* the compendium of Jewish mystical writings. And the *Bhagavad Gita* rests easily against its neighbor, *Tears and Laughter* by Khalil Gibran. *The Tibetan Book of the Dead* sits next to *Secret Splendor* by Charles Essert. The preface to this book, written by David Raffeloc, says, "For many years, Charles Earnest Essert believed that the only reality was experience. And true to his conviction, he sought a varied life." (I think to myself that experience was a huge theme in Tupac's work; maybe this book helped establish its primacy in his thinking.) I pick up *Life Is Corolla* by Joan Grant. "Pac loved her books. . . . She would do stories about other lives, and she would take characters from Egypt." There is also *Serving Humanity* from the writings of Alice A. Bailey. I glance at the table of contents: "The True server"; "The Inertia of the average spiritually minded man"; "The law of service"; "The need for service"; "What is service?" "Forces of enlightenment"; "Preparing for the reappearance of Christ"; "Mystical perception"; "Meditation"; "Discipleship"; "Requirements needed by aspirants."

I turn next to *Messages from Maitreya,* volume 1: *100 Messages,* and then Ruth Montgomery's well-known books, including *Life After Life.* There are literally hundreds of other books—on garlic ("Pac was a great cook, and everything had to have garlic and onions in it, 'cause if you didn't have medical insurance, you ate potato tacos with garlic. That was always our joke"), psychic science, yoga, alternative health, metaphysical science, painting ("He read every book you can imagine on every major . . . visual artist, not just musical or fine arts"), philosophy, psychology, and medita-tion. The range is more than impressive for a poor, black high school dropout and autodidact who never had the benefit of formal higher education.

Tupac's voracious reading continued throughout his ca-reer, a habit that allowed him to fill his raps with acute ob-servations about the world around him. "As an artist, I was initially impressed with his skills and his lyrical ability," says manager Atron Gregory. "And as time went on I got to know him as a human being. He was very inquisitive. He wanted to know as much about everything as he could. I noticed he did a lot of reading." Tupac's profound literacy rebutted the belief that hip-hop is an intellectual wasteland. "There's very little in rap where these kids even encourage people to read books," Stanley Crouch says. Tupac helped to combat the anti-intellectualism in rap, a force, to be sure, that pervades the entire culture. His reading not only gave depth to his lyrics, but it influenced his fellow rappers as well. "I feel what Pac gave to me and gave to a lot of these cats is that you can be street, but you can be smart, too," says rapper Big Syke, who appeared on many of Tupac's last records. Beyond that, Tupac inspired many of his rap mates to read seriously, many for the first time. "He had the words, and he was articulate," Syke says. "That's what made me start reading books. I wasn't reading no books, but the more I started dissecting him, the more I started seeing what all his game was coming from." When Tupac adopted his Makaveli persona and renamed some of his fellow rappers, he spurred their interest in discovering the intellectual roots of the names they bore. "He changed his name to 'Makaveli,'" Syke remembers. "He named me 'Mussolini.' He gave Eddie the name 'Castro,' and [somebody else he named] 'Napoleon.' Gave all of us our names. Now, I had to get a book on Mussolini. And then I got to dissecting Machiavelli. How am I going to find out about him if I don't read?"

Producer Preston Holmes, who worked with Tupac at the beginning of his career (on *Juice*) and at the end (on *Gridlock'd*), believes that Tupac yearned to use his enormous learning and fame to encourage youth to think about big social issues. "He wanted to do a film about Nat Turner and had given it a lot of thought." Holmes told Tupac the idea had two strikes against it: It was black, and it was a period film. But Tupac insisted that the way to make it successful was to include popular young actors who would draw a big audience. "He just thought it was important that he use his celebrity to get young people to think about and learn about some things they might not otherwise [consider]." Holmes points to Tupac's love of literature and art as examples of his open-mindedness and his multifaceted personality. "These kids need to know that this was some-body who loved poetry before he discovered rap. And there is nothing wrong with that. Maybe a little bit of that will rub off on some of these kids running around wanting to be gangsters."

PORTRAITS OF AN ARTIST

CHAPTER 4

"Give Me a Paper and a Pen"

Tupac's Place in Hip-Hop

When I visited with Eastsidaz rapper Big Tray Dee, he surprised me with his frank discussion of his fallen colleague's art. "I'm real critical and skeptical about lyrics or what people say and how they put it from an artistic standpoint," Dee says. "It would be maybe like thirty percent of Tupac's songs that I wouldn't really feel all the time. I would be like, 'That's all right.'" Dee speaks of Tupac's method of creation, highlighting in the process what made him such a big force in hip-hop. "But [his songs] wound up in my head because they would grow on me, and I would see where he was coming from. I had to get that feeling or be in that mood to really relate to what he was saying at that particular time, on that particular song. He showed me how he created music through his heart and through his spirit, showing me that you have to have a certain vibe and continuity. You are not going to appeal to everybody."

Dee's comments underscore a crucial paradox: Tupac's art as a hip-hop emcee was an acquired taste among the genre's cognoscente, even as the masses embraced him through huge record sales and he gained international notoriety as a symbol of rap's fortunes and follies. Tupac was not hip-hop's most gifted emcee by any of the criteria that define the form's artistic apotheosis. He did not, for instance, possess the effortless rhythmic patterns of Snoop Dogg, the formidable timing and breath control of the incomparable K.R.S. ONE, the poetic intensity of Rakim, the deft political rage of Chuck D, the forceful enunciation of M. C. Lyte, or the novelistic descriptions and sly cadences of Notorious B.I.G.—the "mathematician of flow," according to hip-hop luminary Mos Def. Still, Tupac may be the most influential and compelling rapper of them all. It is not that Tupac lacked supreme talent in writing lyrics, composing dramatic stories, and manipulating his voice to haunting effect. But he was more than the sum of his artistic parts. A considerable measure of Tupac's cultural heft was certainly extramusical, especially his well-publicized clashes with the law and his shamanistic thespian efforts. Above all, Tupac was a transcendent force of creative fury who relentlessly articulated a generation's defining moods—its confusion and pain, its nobility and courage, its loves and hates, its hopelessness and self-destruction. He was the zeitgeist in sagging jeans.

"I wasn't a big Pac fan when he was out," Mos Def lets on. "But I'll tell you why people loved him: because you *knew* him." Tupac was easy to know because he was the ghetto's everyman, embodying in his art the horrors and pleasures that came to millions of others who were in many ways just like him—except they lacked his protean genius and a microphone to amplify tragedy and triumph. Despite being pegged a "gangsta rapper," Tupac ranged freely over the lyrical landscape of hip-hop, pursuing themes that bled through a number of rap's subgenres, among them conscious rap, political hip-hop, party music, hedonism rap, thug rap, and ghettocentric rap. Tupac was equally adept at several modes of address within hip-hop, from the dis rap ("Hit 'Em Up") to the hip-hop eulogy ("Life Goes On"), from the maternal missive ("Dear Mama") to the pastoral letter ("Keep Ya Head Up"). There is something fiercely eloquent and haunting about Tupac's accomplished baritone: Its regal, distinct register vibrated directly to the heart and gave him an intimacy and immediacy of communication that are virtually unrivaled in hip-hop. If one were confined to a desert island with the choice of taking only one artist to capture rap's range of expression, Tupac could hardly be surpassed. Tupac's genius can be understood only by tracing the contours of contemporary rap and placing him within its rapidly expanding boundaries.

Hip-hop culture has come a long way since its fledgling start in the late 1970s. Early hip-hoppers were largely anonymous and could barely afford the sound systems on which the genre is built. By contrast, contemporary artists reap lucrative contracts, designer clothing lines, glossy magazine spreads, fashionable awards, global recognition, and often the resentment of their hip-hop elders. If there is a dominant perception about today's rap superstars among hip-hop's purists, it is that they have squandered the franchise by being obsessed with shaking derrieres, platinum jewelry, fine alcohol, premium weed, pimp culture, gangster rituals, and thug life. Although hip-hop has succeeded far beyond the Bronx of its birth, it has, in the minds of some of its most ardent guardians, lost its soul. To paraphrase an ingenious storyteller whose haunting tales elevated and examined the poor—Charles Dickens—these are for hip-hop the best of times and the worst of times. In his embattled soul, Tupac embodied both.[1]

Contemporary rap is filled with stirring reminders of why the marriage of the spoken word to music has revolutionized black culture. Figures like Lauryn Hill, Common, Mos Def, Talib Kweli, and Bahamadia generate black noise to spur the eruption of social conscience. Gifted wordsmiths like Jay-Z, Nas, DMX, and the assorted rappers of the Wu-Tang Clan use their pavement poetry to probe urban existence in gripping detail. But there is still strong criticism of rap's musical vampirism and its dulling repetitiousness. Those who claim the mastery of instruments through the production of original music is the only mark of genuine artistry offer the first criticism. Such purists ignore the severely depleted funding of arts in public schools since the late 1970s, a fateful development that kept many inner-city students from learning to play musical instruments. The critics also overlook the virtuosity implied in the technical manipulation of existing sounds to create new music. Although hip-hop was vulnerable to the claim that it lacked original music at its birth, Tupac was fortunate to have producers who gave melody to his rage. The sounds that bathed his beautiful baritone were often striking. "I loved the kind of tracks that were put together for him to rap over," says contemporary jazz musician George Duke. "They had a lot of the old-school vibe in there. I thought what he did was interesting in terms of the chords. It just felt like something I could play over." Moreover, the fact that so many rappers repeat tired formulas that have been successful for other artists cannot possibly distinguish rap from, say, contemporary rhythm and blues or rock music. And neither can the gutless, uninspiring imitation on which too many raps thrive be said to be unique to hip-hop. After all, contemporary American classical music and smooth jazz—a misnomer worth fighting over, according to jazz purists—do the same.

To be sure, there are more serious criticisms of hip-hop. It is easy to understand the elements of rap that provoke consternation: its violence, its sexual saturation, its recycling of vicious stereotypes, its color-coded preference for light or nonblack women, its failure to engage politics, its selling out to corporate capitalism, and its downright ugly hatred of women. Tupac has come to symbolize the blights on hip-hop's troubled soul. His self-destructive behavior and premature death inspired a great deal of hand-wringing over hip-hop's influence on black youth. Unfortunately, many critics divide the wheat from the chaff in hip-hop by separating rap into its positive and negative expressions. That distinction often ignores the complexity of hip-hop culture and downplays rap's artistic motivations. Instead, rap is read flatly, transmuted into a sociological phenomenon of limited cultural value. Rap is viewed as a barometer of what ails black youth. It is apparent that a great deal of bitterness and anger clutter the disputes between rap's advocates and its critics. It is equally obvious that black youth are under attack from many quarters of our culture. In hip-hop, as with most youth music, that is nothing new. "All art created by young people is despised by adults," says Toni Morrison. "Whether it's Mozart or Louis Armstrong, if it's young, it always has to fight. . . . And what shakes out of that, of course, becomes the best." From its origins, rap music was dismissed or denigrated, even by blacks. The point here is not to berate blacks for missing the boat on what has turned out to be one of the most popular, creative and commercially viable art forms in many decades. I am simply suggesting that there was a love-hate relation between many black folk and hip-hop culture long before Tupac and long before rap's controversial headlines, its tragic deaths, and its worldwide influence.

Early seeds of suspicion have often bloomed into outright rejection of hip-hop as a vital source of art and imagination for black youth. That is why black wags of every stripe have stepped up to denounce the music as misguided, poisonous, and inauthentic, since music that gyrates into the spotlight has little truck with the revolutionary thrust of, say, Gil-Scott Heron or the Last Poets. In other words, hip-hop is not really black music. On such a view, hip-hop is

but the seductive corporate packaging of the vicious stereotypes black folk have tried to defeat since our ancestors
were uprooted and brought to America in chains. Except
now, critics of hip-hop claim, the chains that bind us are
more mental and psychological than physical. And the
great-great-great-grandchildren of slaves who fought to be
free and who hoped that their seed would escape rather
than embrace enslavement create the images that destroy
our standing in society. "Thanks to music videos, the image
people all over the world now have of African Americans is
of violence-prone misogynists, preoccupied with promiscuous sex and conspicuous consumption," says writer
Khephra Burns. "Despite years of striving to distance ourselves from the negative ways in which white folk once por-
trayed us, we have come at last to the point of portraying
ourselves to the world in this way." Stanley Crouch sees an
even more sinister effect of the relentlessly negative and
stereotypical portrayal of blacks. "You can talk to people
who have traveled around the world, and they'll tell you the
contempt that has developed for black people over the last
twenty years is mightily imposing," he says. "You and I
might have a completely different experience, but if we
were in our early twenties, that's another vibration. People
would say, 'Uh-oh, here they come,' and people would be
suspicious and cross the street. That's going on all over the
world."

Burns and Crouch make powerful arguments about the
lethal consequences of flooding the airwaves and video
screen with self-defeating visions of black life. There is little
doubt that the effect is exactly as they describe it, with the

caveat, however, that the global portrayal of black life surely cannot rest on the images or words of barely postadolescent entertainers. This is not to deny that a single video by a rap artist can more successfully shred international boundaries than a hundred books by righteous authors. Neither is it to deny the huge responsibility such artists bear in confirming or combating hateful and ignorant beliefs about black folk that circulate around the globe. But that is just it: These beliefs are part of the ancient legacies of colonialism, racism, and regionalism, legacies that persist despite the efforts of intellectuals, artists, and leaders to destroy them. Is it fair to expect DMX to achieve what W. E. B. DuBois could not, or for Tupac to succeed where Archbishop Tutu failed? The complex relationship between art and social responsibility is evident, but we must be careful not to place unrealistic, or even unjust, demands on the backs of artists. Their extraordinary influence cannot be denied, but the very argument that is often used against them—that they are not politicians, leaders, or policymakers, just entertainers who string together lines of poetic meter—is often conveniently forgotten when it might work to hip-hoppers' advantage.

This recognition does not discount the troubling manifestations of youth culture that merit consideration. One such instance is Tupac's vigorous embrace of "thug life." In the interview taped in 1995 when he was in prison, Tupac explained that "it's not an image; it's just a way of life; it's a mentality." He claims that thug life is "a stage that we all go through. It's just like that for white kids and rich kids. They get to go to the military academy or ROTC, or they take all the risk, energy, and put it into the armed forces. And for a young black male, Puerto Rican, or Hispanic person, you've got to put this in the streets; that's where our energies go." Speaking of his thug life mentality, Tupac says, "The way I was living and my mentality was a part of my progression to be a man." In outtakes from an interview he did with Snoop Dogg for MTV, Tupac clarifies what he means by "thug life." "It's not thugging like I'm robbing people, 'cause that's not what I'm doing," Tupac said. "I mean like I'm not scared to say how I feel. Part of being [a thug] is to stand up for your responsibilities and say this is what I do even though I know people are going to hate me and say, 'It's so politically un-correct,' and 'How could you make black people look like that? Do you know how buffoonish you all look with money and girls and all of that?' That's what I want to do. I want to be real with myself." Tupac's thug life mentor, West Coast rapper Big Syke, eloquently and simply defined for me "thug" and "outlaw," another word Tupac embraced and transformed. "I call thugs the nobodies," Syke says, "because we really don't have nobody to help us but us. And then outlaw is being black and minority. Period."

In a conversation with cultural critic Vijay Prashad, I learned a great deal more about the complex roots of thug. "It's very clear that the word 'thuggee' is a north Indian word," Prashad tells me. "Probably from Murati, from western India, but it's not clear." A British man by the name of General Sleeman made it his mission to eradicate thugs in India. During the early years of the British Empire, there was an increase in the trade of bullion, and brigands roamed the countryside robbing merchants and stealing revenue transactions. Sleeman claimed these thugs were the disciples of the goddess Kali. The thugs used to attach themselves to merchant caravans, claiming to have some talent, like cooking or preparing drinks. They would often drug the merchants and then strangle them with a handkerchief called a *rumal,* leaving a mark on the necks of the victims. Prashad conjectures that there are three possible ways the word entered the United States. "The easiest way is that Sleeman's work was well-known in the U.S.," Prashad says. Sleeman authored a popular nonfiction account of India. But this was mainly to the white mainstream. Prashad thinks the word may have reached black audiences through excerpts in the *Colored American* and other newspapers that were tied in some way to the black church, as the black religious press was deeply interested in India. The third way is through the Caribbean, since there was a large transit of people from eastern India coming into the Caribbean after the 1840s. Given the strong link between black and eastern Indian religions—between Rastafarianism and Shavism, the worship of Shaiva—there were also cultural exchanges, with "thug" passing into the Caribbean lexicon.[2]

In light of the heavy Caribbean influence on the development of rap—its founding light, D. J. Kool Herc, immigrated from the Caribbean to the Bronx, where he transplanted West Indian outdoors parties to the backyards of his American neighborhood—the word "thug" has a specific resonance in black popular culture. "It sounds perfect, in musical terms," Prashad says. "It is better than gangster, which puts you too much in the lineage of the Mafia. This is an alternative kind of thug; it's 'our' kind of thug. It's a unique word; it is known and not known at the same time. It has a flavor to it." When I tell Prashad that Tupac had actually made an acronym of "thug life"—"the hate you gave little infants fucks everyone"—he is in full agreement with the rapper's forcefully subjective interpretation. "It is beautiful, because the word, even though it is an indigenous word to these fellows who were out there to begin with, means the 'hate you gave.' After all, it's the currency transactions that begin because of the empire's influence that will bring the brigands. There is truth there." Prashad ends our conversation by telling me of his experience with some African Caribbean and African American youth. They were sitting on his porch when one of them said, "I'm thugged out." It caught Prashad's attention. "I remember having a chat with them, saying, 'Do you know this word? It's familiar to me.'" The youth were making fun of Prashad's eastern Indian accent, and as a result Prashad and the students began "playing around with words and language." Prashad gave them a brief history of the word they were using, the word that bound at least three cultures together. "They found it fascinating, the story I told them, and we had this interchange, and I said, 'We are inside each other.'"[3]

Toni Morrison, too, has "respect for the genre, because of what it does with language." Morrison is not oblivious to the "bad influence" of "people who are driving [rap] to make it sensational," but she understands the crucial role to youth of an art form that transmits important information. "It is a conversation among and between black youth from one part of the country to another: 'What is it like in

Detroit, as opposed to L.A., as opposed to New York?'"
Morrison's view of hip-hop is admirably international, giving her an appreciation of the genre's inspiring, and subversive, global reach. "Just seeing what happened to it in
Europe is astonishing," Morrison told me. "When I was in
Frankfurt—the center of rap music in Germany—I got
some unbelievable rap discs from a Turkish girl who was
singing in German." Morrison argues that what unifies hip-
hop throughout the world is its emergence from "the 'others' within the empire"—for instance, the Turks in
Germany and the Algerians and North Africans in
France—who ring profound changes in the nation's discourse. "First of all, they're changing the language, although nobody admits it," she says. "But that's where the
energy comes from. . . . It is the necessity for young people
to talk to one another in language that is not the fake language of the press. That sort of conversation curtails
thought altogether. So it is a dialogue." But Morrison does
not neglect the essential *musical* element that frames the use
of language. "The fact that it also is the music you can't sit
down to—you really do *get up*—is what has made it so
fetching." Morrison is, of course, completely aware of the
controversial subject matters broached in hip-hop. "It is always up for grabs about sexuality and violence," she says.
Morrison argues that the establishment accepts such discourse only when "it's separate, like when Shakespeare does
it, or Chaucer, or Boccaccio—those are the most outra-
geously provocative stories and language in *The Decameron*.
They say they want safe language, but that's just the way the
establishment is: It [rap discourse] wouldn't be outlawed or

policed unless it had that quality." As a parting thought, Morrison raises an intriguing question—humorously, to be sure, as she chuckles all the way through it, but, as is evident, it seizes me by the pen. "Are there any other groups of gangsters or robbers or whatever you want to call them who made music? The whole notion of making an art form while you're doing it is . . ." Before she can finish, we're both cracking up at her brilliant thought, her deliriously righteous question, which she caps with a nod to the genius of the folk. "I mean only black people could figure that out. I don't know how far you can go with that! There are sagas about medieval thugs and Robin Hood, but [it's fascinating] to actually invent your own art form while you're in the life, so to speak."[4]

Tupac, Syke, Prashad, and Morrison bring to light the complex fashion—one full of signification and play—in which the thug, the outlaw, the pimp, and the like are evoked in hip-hop. It is true that Tupac tried to make the world believe he really was who he announced on his albums. But at some levels—it is important to stress *some* levels—even that was an act, in the best sense of that word, an ingenious artistic strategy to create a persona. Persona making, after all, is the province of art—and of politics, preaching, and every realm where performance is crucial to self-definition and the transmission of ideas. Too often, however, we deny the artistic milieu in which rappers operate and descend instead into a thudding literalism. The historian Robin Kelley makes this point when discussing Miles Davis and the necessity of a more complex vision of art and persona, even those involving controversial figures like the pimp. "Why is it that we still love Miles despite the fact that he's such an evil figure?" Kelley asks. "It's because the stuff that's so romantic, and evil, can be reconciled in the pimp. And so my thing is, turn the mirror around and look at yourself when you look at the music. And it's deeply romantic, because that's what the pimps are, the great ones." Kelley is not offering an apology for pimping. Instead, he is suggesting that cultural creations have multiple meanings, none of which can be exhausted or suspended by appeals to the responsible behavior of the artist. (Indeed, many of art's meanings exist beyond the intent or desire of its creators.) "I guess I'm tired of this question of what's redeeming or problematic," Kelley says. "We don't have to go to hip-hop to find it. We can actually invent something." Kelley contends that an artistic representation "does both of those things simultaneously" and that a more important question is "Why are we still drawn to it?" As Kelley says, "moralizing [and] saying there's nothing redemptive about this, so therefore we should just critique it, doesn't really tell us anything about how people are thinking."[5]

Taking the time to learn what our youth are thinking and why they create the art they do demands a capacity for deferred justification that most adults lack. They seek to ensure the legitimacy of their moral critique by rendering quick and easy judgments about the art form. Many critics of hip-hop do not have the ethical patience to empathize with the formidable array of choices, conflicts, and dilemmas that many poor black youth confront. Tupac is deeply attractive to millions of young people because he articulates the contradictory poses of maturing black identity with galvanizing exuberance and savage honesty. "Most of my music [tells the truth]," Tupac says in the interview he did in prison. "I'm just trying to speak about things that affect me and about things that affect our community. . . . Sometimes I'm the watcher, and sometimes I'm the participant, and sometimes it's just allegories or fables that have an underlying theme." Tupac's allegories and fables largely estranged his elders, underscoring how the generation gap has grown more menacing.

By almost any measure, the gaps between older and younger blacks are flagrant, even frightening. To be sure, there have always been skirmishes between the generations. Many older blacks have often found the dress, language, and hair of younger blacks offensive. In turn, many younger blacks have often soured on the conservative values and accommodating styles of social existence favored by a majority of their elders. These tiffs have certainly not disappeared. Indeed, every era seems obligated to draw from local circumstance and color in painting a fresh picture of generational malaise. Where the Afro hairstyle raised dander in the 1970s, the 1990s outbreak of hair twists and braids provoked dread in corporate and conservative colored circles alike. And as if the boom in 1970s clothing had not already offended by dredging up bell-bottom pants and platform shoes, the baggy fashions sported by youth—oversized shirts, unlaced shoes, beltless pants sagging to the upper gluteus for maximum exposure—have riled their seniors, especially since such styles are purportedly inspired by prison gear. Although the specific circumstances of black life in the new millennium—unprece-

dented growth of the black middle class, devastating expan-
sion of the ghetto poor, restructuring of industries that em-
ploy large numbers of blacks, sustained drug and criminal
activity, capital flight, increased technologization of the
workforce—shape our understanding of these conflicts,
they appear, in one form or another, in each generation.[6]

What *is* new and particularly troublesome is the sheer
hostility that bruises relations between older and younger
blacks. For perhaps the first time in our history, blacks over
thirty have fear and disdain for black youth. Such a perception turns graver when we consider that *half* of black
America, some 17 million citizens, is below the age of
thirty. That means, too, that half of black America has
come to maturity in an age of bewildering black "posts":
post–civil rights, postmodern, postindustrial, and post–
baby boom. A great deal of the age chasm in black communities can be explained by the chaos that blacks over forty
confronted in seeking racial equity, personal status, and social justice. Blacks who cut their teeth on the sinewy fibers
of violent racial oppression have little tolerance for cries of
injustice from quarters of relative privilege: young black urban professionals who can't hail a cab or coddled college
students who seethe at the racist slights encountered on
elite campuses. Neither do older blacks, whether strong in-
tegrationists or radical nationalists, cotton easily to "the
devil made me do it" theory of criminal behavior and social
disintegration that plagues many black communities. The
purpose of the civil rights and black liberation movements,
after all, was to foster healthy black communities unfettered
by white supremacy. Such struggles were not meant to

justify thugs who hurt other blacks. Neither did those strug-gles intend to ignore the moral deficiency of persons who use racism to deflect attention from their own failings.[7]

For many blacks over the age of forty, Tupac represents the repudiation of ancient black values of hope and positive uplift that tied together black folk across geography and generation. His studied hopelessness—and he affirmed his depressive status by repeatedly declaring "I'm hopeless"—and his downward-looking social glance only aggravated the generational warfare that looms large in black America. As "a brother from another generation, I can't help but hear Tupac, if not totally objectively, at least from a broader per-spective—the bird's-eye view of the forest as opposed to be-ing in the trees, so to speak," says Khephra Burns. "And what I hear generally are words that rip through our commu-nities, our families, and our lives like automatic weapon fire." Burns says that Tupac is full of "discord, death, and re-venge." Bishop T. D. Jakes sees Tupac as an emblem of fin de siècle black social disintegration, a state of affairs markedly different from what previous generations be-queathed to their offspring. Jakes says that the twentieth cen-tury "ended with the sound of gunshots reverberating in the streets of the American black culture." Speaking of Tupac, Jakes laments how the "hearse wheels rolled away the re-mains of a young man who our children watched, admired, and perhaps emulated to some degree." Jakes argues that the "gunshots should have been a wake-up call to us that some-how our cultural pace and our agenda was now being set by young men whose rhythm is at best unsteady." Jakes con-trasts such a scenario with an earlier epoch of black achievement and struggle. He says that our present predicament is "a far cry from the previous decades, when the role models that we were awed by were world shakers like Martin Luther King, Rosa Parks, Medgar Evers, and many others." Unfortunately, these "giants of black faith have in their latter years been replaced by young men whose talent has lifted them to a height whereby they gained the ear of America prematurely, having more talent than statement."

Although youth music has always outraged parents who refused to listen—because it was morally offensive or sexually suggestive, from jazz to rock—the depressing note of hatred and fear of black youth that is being sounded has dire consequences. Sadly, it suggests there is agreement between the regressive forces that target black folk in general—conservative critics who decry our moral laxity, our sexual looseness, our racial obsessions—and black folk who think that hip-hop channels our pathologies into broad daylight. Many older blacks fail to see that the same folk who thought it was just fine to keep black life segregated and economically inferior are now leading the charge to incarcerate their children. And often, with a black authority figure standing literally or symbolically in tow, they point to hip-hop's excesses to justify their actions. Tupac was an irresistible example of how self-destructive and utterly irredeemable our youth had become. Too often the explanations we seek for the disturbing behavior of youth like Tupac are insufficiently sophisticated. As proof we bog down in the understandable but lamentable question: Has hip-hop caused or reflected the violence we should detest?

Even that question buys into the either-or worldview that undermines a sane response to our predicament. Of course hip-hop has become intoxicated with danger, as Tupac's life and career amply testify. Its violent metaphors, profane lyrics, and real-life embodiment of thug fantasies are at some levels chilling. It does no good to reprimand black youth for their addiction to violence. Our nation suffers the addiction in spades, as even a cursory read of pop culture suggests. But it is not just pop culture that is implicated. American society was built on violence, from the wholesale destruction of Native American culture to the enslavement of Africans. "It's violence in America," Tupac says in his interview from prison. "What did the USA just do, flying to Bosnia? We ain't got no business over there." Comparing America's actions to the destructive effects of gang violence, Tupac argued, "America is the biggest gang in the world. Look at how they didn't agree with Cuba, so . . . [they] cut them off." That is surely no justification for hip-hop's artistic elevation of gang-banging or murder, as glimpsed in Tupac's lyrics. "As a rapper, Tupac represented many of the most despicable elements of America's youth on account of the Afro-American extension of what I call anarchic individuality," Stanley Crouch says, "which is: me first." For Crouch, Tupac's anarchic individualism showed most destructively in the glamorization of the gangster in lyrics promoting murder and mayhem, thereby lowering the threshold of resistance for impressionable youth. "You can't pile all of this on Tupac," Crouch says. "But I'm saying that his life and his death and his behavior and the behavior of the people in his circle represent something deeply disturbing."

Crouch's argument underscores the urgent need to address not only rhetorical but literal violence, the causes of which cannot be exclusively or primarily located within hip-hop culture. Although Crouch is tough on Tupac, he avoids blaming him directly for the scourge of violence in the culture or even in black communities. "None of this is to say that there shouldn't be some voicing of the terrible ways in which certain people in this society have to live due to poverty," Crouch says. "That's not something that's supposed to be ignored. That's absolutely irresponsible." Blaming black youth for social violence reeks of the worst kind of scapegoating. Since hip-hop culture is barely a generation old, and black violence is much older, the charge that hip-hop jump-started violence lacks merit. But even if hip-hop didn't invent violence, it can be held accountable for promoting violence. Indulging violence as a reaction to more lethal but less visible forms of violence (for instance, racism and economic inequality), is not excusable, but it is surely a reason to tackle the issues to which black youth are responding.

Neither should we overlook the double standard that prevails in addressing societal violence or its pop culture parallel. It is by now a cliché to state that Bruce Willis, Arnold Schwarzenegger, Tom Cruise, and a host of other big white stars don't come in for nearly the rhetorical drubbing that hip-hop stars regularly endure. "Like with Quentin Tarrantino, when he puts out his pictures, they're all gangster pictures and they're all good and they're all critically acclaimed . . . and they're very creative," Tupac said in the outtakes from his 1996 MTV interview. "But when we do that same thing without the visuals, all wax, just as compelling . . . we get treated like the bad messengers and he gets treated like King Solomon." Tupac also spoke of the video he was directing for the rap song he did with Snoop Dogg, "2 of America's Most Wanted." Tupac said the video's concept drew from the criticism he and Snoop received for portraying gangsters and dirtying the airwaves with their gangsta rap. "We wanted to put the mirror up to show you where we got these gangster ideas," Tupac said. "So we took all these scenes out of classic movies with gangsters in them . . . not gangsters named Doo Dirty and Snoop and Tupac . . . but gangsters named Luck Luciano and Don Corleone and John Caddy, Al Capone and Smitty."

The ready response, of course, is that these white stars don't seek to imitate the roles they play in real life. "James Cagney, Edward G. Robinson, Clint Eastwood, John Wayne, Sylvester Stallone, Arnold Schwarzenegger, Bruce Willis, not one of them has ever had one bullet fly at them in public," Crouch says. When I bring up *The Sopranos,* the hugely successful and much-beloved cable television series, Crouch pounces immediately. "Tony Soprano remains a monster from the first episode to last night's episode," he says. "See, the brilliance of it is he shows you, yes, this man is a human being, but he's a sociopath. He's a predator. He's sadistic. He's a murderer. [Series creator] David Chase doesn't duck any of that, and he doesn't make it seem to you that you're supposed to like it. It's just you see the complexity of what's going on." Crouch contends that Tony

Soprano, the lead character in the series, is full of angst about the life he leads. "He still has all of this guilt, because what he's doing is fundamentally fucked up. But none of that justifies what he does." Crouch presses me. "I mean, you're an expert on this material. There's nobody in rap that I'm aware of in which real questions are asked by the rappers themselves about what the hell they're doing."

Taken in his full lyrical sweep, I maintain that Tupac is such a figure. One of the reasons he stands out in rap is precisely because he offered such a powerful, complex, panoramic view of the young black experience. "If you were going on the path of a social activist, there is something for you in his lyrics," says Everett Dyson-Bey, a Moorish Temple minister and prisoner. "If you were on the path of a straight thug, there is something there for you, too. So to bridge that gap from one end to the next, to run that polarity, from the positive to the negative, spoke to so many people of so many different backgrounds." But Tupac constantly questioned his direction by filling his lyrics with characters who were both the victims and perpetrators of crime, characters who were thugs begging God for guidance through the minefields of self-destruction, characters leaving the ghetto while others stayed, characters who asked why they suffered even as they imposed suffering. In that haze of morbid contradictions, Tupac shone the light of his dark, brooding, pensive spirit, refusing to close his eyes to the misery he saw, risking everything to bear witness to the pain he pondered and perpetuated. In a word, *The Sopranos* offers, in Ernest Becker's term, an "anthropodicy," where we hold each other accountable for the suffering and evil imposed, whereas Tupac wrestles with a theodicy, the effort to square belief in God with the evil that prevails, which is at root an attempt to explain the suffering of those he loved.

Crouch may be right about the motley fellowship of gangster actors who never saw a gun aimed at them off-camera, but it is likely that just as great a percentage of white actors and singers get into trouble with the law as do black rap artists. The list includes Robert Downey Jr., James Caan, George Michael, Hugh Grant, and Axl Rose, among countless others. And in case Tupac and Biggie seem totally anomalous, one must remember James Dean, Sal Mineo, Kurt Cobain, and Bob Kane. And earlier black stars that are now revered had their troubles, including Little Willie John, Frankie Lymon, and Sam Cooke. In their personal foibles and destructive habits, Flavor Flav, Old Dirty Bastard, Bobby Brown, and their cohort have got nothing on legends Marvin Gaye, Wilson Pickett, or for that matter James Brown. None of this explains away the undeniable sadness of the violent captivity of segments of hip-hop culture. It simply gives a broader context to our concerns and cautions against seeing hip-hoppers as uniquely plagued. It is true that the violence that increasingly gets spoken about in hip-hop is self-inflicted and racially perpetuated. Then, too, the violence is so cartoonish and caricatured that fewer and fewer vulnerable minds take it seriously, at least not literally. The biggest knock on hard-core hip-hop may be its tired, cliché-ridden exploration of a subject that demands subtlety, artistic courage, and the wisdom to refrain from using a sledgehammer where a scalpel will do. But the big picture must not be neglected: The real-world violence too many hip-hoppers and black youth confront is so much more troubling than the violence they romanticize, even eroticize, on recording and screen.[8]

Needless to say, the rhetorical violence that is directed at black women is altogether troubling. To be sure, there is a great deal of parody, signifying, and raucous humor that fills a lot of hip-hop's more vulgar lyrical traditions. Those who believe that hip-hop invented these practices have only to listen to blues music from the early twentieth century. Old-school blues bawdiness was every bit as vulgar and sexually explicit as what disturbs contemporary defenders of black morality. Many critics now claim that black youth have lost their way by forsaking earlier visions of ethical caution and racial care. But a review of the concerns of black leaders in the early 1900s confirms that many of them thought their youth were just as morally wayward as the youth of our day. And many of those leaders indicted popular culture for its vicious effects on black youth. The remarkably humbling point to remember is that those youth who were seen as heading to hell in a handbasket became the grandparents and great-grandparents whose behavior is held up as the example we should aim for.

Still, the crude misogyny and sexism that are rampant in hip-hop are deeply disturbing. The sheer repetition of "bitch" as the proper name of females is not only distressing but destructive. It sends the message to young girls and women that their price of admission to hip-hop culture is the acceptance of self-denigration. Unlike the use of the word "nigga" in hip-hop, "bitch" fails to come across as resistant. An argument can be made, as we shall see in the next chapter, that the circulation of variants of "nigger" serves to deprive the term of its negative meanings. "You my nigga" becomes a way of bonding around a term that was historically used by whites to degrade blacks. Thus, it deprives racist whites of the prerogative of naming blacks in harmful ways, since blacks have adapted it to their culture in playful or at least signifying fashion. Of course many black folk disagree and insist that the word can in no sense be redeemed. But the logic of those who contend that the word has use is clear, if unacceptable. The use of "bitch," by contrast, is less compelling. The majority of those using it are the men who continue to dominate hip-hop culture. Thus, its negative meanings are largely held in place. Even when males intend "bitch" to be positive, such as Notorious B.I.G.'s "Me and My Bitch," the term is still loaded with hurtful connotations. It is not clear that women in hip-hop who use the term have sought to use it in ways that question male power or perspectives on women. Their use of bitch usually does little more than second the female-bashing of their male counterparts.

Likewise, the sexual saturation of hip-hop reflects the sexual obsessions that haunt the culture. It seems that nearly every rap video has a stock character: a woman bouncing her bosom, gyrating her gluteus, or otherwise occupied in fulfilling the sexual fantasies of millions of adolescents and adults. Such a specter surely degrades women by reducing them to their lowest erotic denominator. It also suggests to young women that the only viable assets they can exercise are their behinds and not their brains. Hence,

Lil' Kim and Foxy Brown spin lustful, lascivious tales that rival their male counterparts in raunchy abandon. Place that in the company of hustling, drug-selling, death-dealing, sex-crazed Lotharios who increasingly dominate the imagination of hip-hop and, well, the picture is rather grim. For many critics, it simply repackages the stereotypes that black folk have spent centuries resisting: the whorish black woman, the studly black man. The cruel caveat, however, is that now these stereotypes are brashly amplified in the mouths of history-starved misfits whose political illiteracy masquerades as defiant art. Of course there is some truth to this rather harsh, dismissive, and unjust diatribe. Too many black youth have no idea where black folk have been and only dimly know what we've had to do to get where we are. But it isn't primarily their fault. We have reneged on our responsibility as black adults to keep the culture vital by making it relevant to contemporary struggles. That means translating the terms of past struggle into present action. Instead, older blacks often nostalgically rehash romantic memories of the past, failing to acknowledge just how remarkably similar our failures and prospects for triumph are to those of the hip-hop generation.

That shouldn't stop us from admitting that we are much more attracted to the basest, simplest elements of our artistic makeup than to its brightest, most demanding features. This is true for the culture as a whole. That is why *Mission Impossible* outpaces *Boys Don't Cry* and why Britney Spears outsells Bonnie Raitt. The fact that Common, Mos Def, Talib Kweli, Bahamadia, Black Eyed Peas, Jurassic Five, and the Roots don't chart as highly as Jay-Z, Juvenile, Master P, or the latest posthumous effort by Tupac is certainly a problem. But is it hip-hop's problem or ours? Another way of putting the question is to ask whether that trend doesn't reflect a general resistance to art that is explicitly political, sharply critical of the status quo even inside black life, and self-reflective in a way that only mature art will risk. There is no denying that the ethical aspirations of Mos Def, for instance, directly counter the corporate capitalism that commits bigger budgets to market and distribute the latest butt-shaking record. Or another tired, trite, and uninteresting "bling-bling" (the sight produced by light reflecting off diamond-laced or platinum jewelry) video lauding the virtues of material or commercial culture. In that sense, there is a real war going on in hip-hop. On the one side are purists who stake the future of the form on lyrical skill, narrative complexity, clever rhymes, and fresh beats. On the other side are advocates of commercialized hip-hop, marked by the mass production of records that sell because they are crassly accessible. They neither challenge their audience nor move them to reflect on social, racial, or cultural ills. But the issue has never been as simple as politics versus art or positive versus negative.

Mos Def, praised as one of the leaders of "conscious rap," refuses to think in such narrow terms. "They've got their little categories, like 'conscious' and 'gangsta,'" says Mos Def. "It used to be a thing where hip-hop was all together. Fresh Prince [Will Smith's old moniker] would be on tour with NWA [Niggas wit' Attitude, featuring Dr. Dre and Ice Cube]. It wasn't like, 'You have got to like me in order for me to like you.' That's just some more white folks trying to think that all niggas are alike, and now it's expanded. It used to be one type of nigga; now it's two. There is so much more dimension to who we are. A monolith is a monolith, even if there's two monoliths to choose from." Mos Def sees the danger, however, in having only one dimension of the black experience get airplay, which in present terms is usually of the bling-bling or thug variety. "I ain't mad at Snoop. I'm not mad at Master P. I ain't mad at the Hot Boyz. I'm mad when that's all you see. I would be mad if I looked up and all I saw on TV was me or Common or the Roots, because I know that ain't the whole deal. The real joy is when you can kick it with everyone. That's what hip-hop is all about."

Another rapper lauded for his rhetorical brilliance and revolutionary passion, Common, similarly sees the virtue of the range in hip-hop. "I can't put a line between us," Common says about the difference between him and hard-core rap. "Because we are speaking our experiences and we are speaking our voice in hip-hop. Tupac was talking about smoking weed, guns, and so on, and we can't ignore that. I talk about other subjects [than hard-core rappers], but [conscious rappers] still have flaws, and we are not afraid to show those flaws." Mos Def is careful to avoid accepting the praise—and the typecasting—of corporate interests that deny the complexity of black identity and culture. "They keep trying to slip the 'conscious rapper' thing on me," he says. "I come from Roosevelt Projects, man. The ghetto. I drank the same sugar water, ate hard candy. And they try to get me because I'm supposed to be more articulate, I'm supposed to be not like the other Negroes, to get me to say something against my brothers. I'm not going out like that, man." In light of his thug persona, it may be hard to consider Tupac a "brilliant poet as great as any medieval writer," as he is regarded by Arvand Elihu, a talented young graduate student who taught a course on the felled rapper at the University of California–Berkeley.

There is another dimension to the debate as well: Some of the best-intentioned hip-hop, politically speaking, is simply boring or lyrically void of imagination or inspiration. Or it is just musically dead, a real drawback to what folk in the midst of heated argument often forget is first and foremost a musical form. And some of the most apolitical rap is lyrically clever and musically compelling. (Why should it be any different in hip-hop than it is in, for instance, R&B, where Luther Vandross's ethereal love notes rise higher than a musical complaint about racism, though few folk assail that branch of black music for its bourgeois sensibilities that are decidedly apolitical, noninterventionist, and downright misleading in its portrayal of romantic love?) It may well be that we should expand our understanding of what politics is, since hip-hop as an art form has been embroiled in the politics of culture and the culture of politics since its beginnings. In light of Senate hearings about rap's violent effects, it has little choice but to be political, even when its politics have to do with its right to exist at all.

The debate about hip-hop's complexity as well as Tupac's role in rap underscores the need for genre justice. We ought to recognize that there are all sorts of rap music, that not all of rap can do what some of it can do, and that the best rap is the rap that sticks to what it does best. The power of

Tupac's raps is that they encompass a variety of hip-hop genres. One of the liabilities of blanketing rap in general terms is that we fail to recognize its diversity. That means that we also fail to see how many of the debates we try to force on hip-hop culture from outside are occurring with regularity on the inside. Take, for instance, the bravado and posturing that clutter hip-hop and the profanity that is often mistaken for authenticity, for keeping it real. Lauryn Hill, as a member of the Fugees, offered a biting commentary in as brilliant and pithy a fashion as might be imagined when she rhymed: "And even after all my logic and my theory / I add a 'muthafucka' so you ignorant niggers hear me." There are many moods and styles in hip-hop. There is griot rap, including figures like Common, Mos Def, Talib Kweli, Bahamadia, and the Roots. There is radical rap, characterized by the Coup and most recently by Dead Prez. There is materialistic/hedonistic rap, presented by Juvenile, Cash Money Millionaires, and a hundred offshoots. There is ghettocentric hip-hop, including figures as diverse as Jay-Z and the Wu-Tang Clan. There is gangsta rap, including Snoop Dogg and Dr. Dre. There is pop rap, symbolized most powerfully by Will Smith. There is Bohemian hard core, as glimpsed in Outkast and Goodie Mobb. And of course some of these figures and groups bleed into several genres. And many of these genres can be divided not only by theme and style but also by region. So the Dirty South of Atlanta's Outkast and Master P of New Orleans can be contrasted to the West Coast rap of South Central's Ice Cube or Compton's DJ Quick or the Upsouth rhymes of Nelly of St. Louis.

Our expectations of hip-hop's genres should be rooted in an appreciation of their intents. We should not expect pop rap to give us a peek into the inner workings of capitalism or white supremacy. Will Smith will never be Dead Prez. At the same time, Will Smith can beautifully celebrate fatherhood and welcome us to Miami (and to the dance floor) with his delightful pop confections. And that doesn't mean that we cannot be rocked by Dead Prez's brilliant critiques of racial amnesia and cultural genocide in black American life. It's not either-or. And we must not be afraid to enjoy the many intriguing transgressions of Lil' Kim and Foxy Brown, even as we lament their lyrical existence almost exclusively in sexualized zones. Not only are there many genres of hip-hop, but one artist can give us many different looks, feels, sensibilities, styles, and themes. Tupac could both "get around" by sexually exploiting his star status (a fact that hardly makes him unique) and admonish poor young women to "keep ya head up." The edifying and terrifying in this singular artist lived on the same block.

Like Tupac, perhaps its most embattled icon, hip-hop culture lives in conflict and thrives on contradiction. It is both a highly commercialized, corporate-sponsored venture as well as an indigenous art form that reflects (on) the brutal realities of black youth existence. That white corporate types have gotten into the mix doesn't negate the ghetto sensibilities and themes that drive—and sometimes drag down—hip-hop. As Toni Morrison says, "The fact that rap is so attractive to white kids in the suburbs is the risk that all discourses that black people invent have." Hip-hop is a barometer of black youth taste, style, and desires—as they are created and disseminated in local communities and by force of corporate distribution. It is also a sure test of our ability to embrace the best of our youth while engaging in critical conversations about their future. Given its universal popularity and its troubling effects, hip-hop is a vital cultural language that we had all better learn. To ignore its genius, to romanticize its deficits, or to bash it with undiscerning generalities is to risk the opportunity to engage our children about perhaps the most important cultural force in their lives.

Tupac may be the most influential rapper to have lived. His voice rings through our cultural landscape and hovers over our spirits with formidable intensity. Nearly five years after his death, his posthumously released double compact disc, *Until the End of Time,* dwarfed its nearest competition and sold over 400,000 copies in its first week of circulation. It may be that Tupac's bold voice is more necessary now than when he lived. He embraced the history of rap and operated within its limits while always pushing against them, reshaping rap's conventions while blurring the lines between his art and life. His stunning baritone was filled with surprising passion and urgency. He narrated his life as a road map to suffering, wrenching a brutal victory from the ghetto he so loved, and the fame and fortune that both blessed and cursed him. As the supreme symbol of his generation, he embodied its reckless, audacious liberties and its ominous hopelessness. Above all, he was as truthful as we can expect any human being to be about his evolving identity and his expanding artistic vision. "My music is spiritual, if you listen to it," Tupac said in his prison interview. "It's all about emotion; it's all about life. Not to dis anybody, but where other rappers might paint a perfect picture of themselves, I would tell my innermost, darkest secrets. I reveal myself in every one of my records. From 'Dear Mama' to 'Shed So Many Tears,' I tell my own, personal problems, and people can relate to what I believe."

CHAPTER 5

"For All the Real Niggas Out There"

Authenticity Blues

Near the beginning of Spike Lee's film of Richard Price's novel *Clockers*, a group of young black street-corner coke dealers—the "clockers" of the film's title—heatedly debate hip-hop culture. At stake: Who is the "hardest" rapper in the game? Public Enemy rapper Chuck D's name crops up, but he and other "positive" rappers are quickly moved down the list because they "never shot nobody," they aren't "slappin' bitches up," and they haven't "been to jail for murder." One of the drug dealers insists that the "only niggas I hear representin' (hard-core rap) is Tupac, G-Rap, and Wu-Tang."

Long before his tragic death from gunshot wounds, Tupac had become part of the folklore of black popular culture by glorifying guns, gangs, and the ghetto. The scene from *Clockers* captures the bitter contradictions that dogged Tupac's short but hard life. His hard-core image was known widely enough to bleed through the frames of Lee's film. Tupac's acrobatics across the abyss fed many alienated youth's almost erotic appetites for violence. It also suggests truths black youth must learn if they are to stem the tide of urban mayhem. Black youth did not create the violence that plagues them, but some undoubtedly have a hand in its far-flung influence. Unlike the drug dealers in *Clockers* who preach the merits of hard-core hip-hop, real black gangsters do not always scoop up a gaggle of gangsta rap tapes to ease them into the right frame of mind for mutilation or murder. Since they are already living the life, they often seek escape through music with decidedly uplifting themes. Notorious real-life gang-banger "Monster" Sanyika Shakur writes that he favored Al Green. And wiseguys from yester-year loved Frank Sinatra's flying them to the moon and dropping them off in New York, New York. That is a useful rejoinder to those who argue a strict one-to-one correlation between art and social anarchy.[1]

But it is also a useful lesson to black youth about the limits of the real and its relation to the represented. Like the drug dealer in *Clockers* who lauds Tupac for representing the real hard core in his raps, black youth—indeed, so much of black culture—is obsessed with racial and cultural authenticity. Or as the mantra of hip-hop goes, with "keeping it real." If anyone ever exulted in the wildly conflicting meanings of blackness, it was Tupac. He dramatically knifed to the heart of black culture's pursuit of authentic existence. In his own quest for real blackness, Tupac managed to rile large segments of black life, especially his elders. His brazen defiance of authority earned him the admiration of many of his peers. His open embrace of a gangsta lifestyle appealed to some blacks while turning others completely off. The repudiation of the moral innocence and racial correctness of black bourgeois life in many of Tupac's rap songs both endeared him to and alienated him from quarters of black America. The obsession with authentic blackness is driven in large part by the need to respond to stereotypical and racist portrayals of black life. The gestures, nuances, contradictions, complexities, and idiosyncrasies that define black life crowd the artistic visions of black writers, performers—and intellectuals. In fact, in 1996 a reporter from *U.S. News and World Report* said of my own work that I moved "effortlessly from French critical theory to gangsta culture to politics, alternately quoting Foucault and Farrakhan and Ice Cube, Derrida and Tupac and Malcolm, occasionally breaking into an extended and flawless rap groove as he bangs out the background rhythms on the lectern. Seamless, and completely self-assured. But is he a 'real nigga'?" The writer admits that it's a "vulgar formulation from the world of gangsta rap and could easily be dismissed as just another unsavory example of that musical genre's ghetto talk," but says that I didn't "want to dismiss the question, or the culture that insists on it." That is as true for me and my writer peers now as when it was written. Still, the quest for authenticity often restricts the range of what is considered acceptable in black life. The unwritten rule governing many representations in black culture is expressed in the simple slogan, "Always put your best foot forward."[2]

The complexity of black culture is stifled under such a belief, especially when the real is equated with the positive. By contrast, the negative is defined as a force that bears unfavorably on a limited view of authentic blackness. The negative in black life is viewed as the pathology that inevitably accompanies concession to white stereotypes of black behavior. Such a view of blackness is disabling and alienates those whose lives barely darken the outer limits of black respectability. Those blacks who depart from the positive ideal are stigmatized. Some blacks wear that stigma as a badge of honor and relish representations of black life that challenge orthodox blackness. This is particularly true of visions of black culture that are seen as elitist and hence fake. The quest for authentic blackness now comes full circle: It is wrested from the puritanical souls of the black bourgeoisie only to rest in the hands—and in the case of hard-core rappers, in the throats—of ghetto dwellers, redefined in the canon of new black authenticity as real niggas.[3]

Of course the use of the word "nigger" or any of its variants (such as "nigga," the term favored in hip-hop, or as Eddie Murphy says, "nigs") is still highly contentious in black America. Tupac tried early in his career to rescue the term by redefining it, as he did with "thug." For Tupac, *n-i-g-g-a* stood for "never ignorant, getting goals accomplished." For many blacks, such a gesture is at best revisionist self-denigration. Even a word that sounds like "nigger" is wounding to the black psyche. That is why in 1998 David Howard, the ombudsman for Washington, D.C., mayor Anthony Williams, resigned from his job after black colleagues expressed outrage at his use of the word "niggardly" during a debate on the city budget, even though the word means cheap and stingy. (Howard was rehired after the press called this reaction "silly.") The decision by the recent editors of *Webster's Dictionary* to initially define "nigger" as a black person is a sure sign that some whites still underestimate how sensitive blacks are to the word. Not only did *Webster's* definitional chicanery conceal the force of centuries-old racial bigotry, but it also showed how many in our nation try to rewrite history and politics. As if all this were not messy enough, the prospect of white kids—who grew up listening to rappers' liberal use of the word—casually uttering "nigger" in mixed company has upped the stakes of the debate considerably.

Even if white youth understand the word's wretched history and are savvy about its complex use by hip-hop artists or their black friends, the use of the word by even "hip" whites evokes an unspoken history of racial terror. In fact, historically astute and racially sensitive whites have rarely attempted to use the term, even with black friends. When these whites stepped out of bounds, black friends or colleagues readily set them straight. In the wake of the increase in friendly interracial contact, racial utility dictated the development of a durable double standard: Blacks could call each other "nigga," but whites were universally forbidden the privilege. Even though whites occasionally questioned the *fairness* of the practice—"If we're friends, why can't I use the term with you?"—and blacks questioned its *wisdom*—"Why should we voluntarily open ourselves to white supremacist language?"—it was firmly established as a rule of thumb for interactions between the two groups.

The difference now is that hip-hop culture's global influence has authorized the promiscuous use of "nigger" beyond black circles. As a result, the sordid history of the term is obscured, or at least lessened, for many young whites and blacks. "Nigger" began as a term of derision for blacks by slave masters who had stolen them from Africa and forced them into slavery in America. That one word collected the contempt that many whites felt for blacks. It also served as shorthand for the prejudice that was protected under the banner of white supremacy after slavery was legally ended. Even poor whites benefited psychologically from denigrating blacks: No matter how terrible life was for these whites, at least they could take solace in the fact they weren't niggers. Blacks, however, were not passive victims and found ingenious ways to subvert white supremacy in explicit and subtle fashion. One of them was by circulating the term "nigger" in their own circles. They robbed "nigger" of its insulting meaning by deliberately "misusing" it, finding affection where only hatred was intended. But there has always been a big divide in black America about how successful such a move has been. Blacks can be roughly divided into two camps of linguistic usage of "nigga": those who have reservations about its use and those who argue for its revision through aggressive black usage. Black reservationists say that no matter how well intended, the word "nigger," even when uttered by blacks, can never shed its lethal meanings. Black revisionists argue that by rhetorically seizing the venomous term, blacks can deprive it of some of its harmful effects. I am surely a revisionist on this score, though I understand the misgivings of reservationists who contend the term is well beyond rehabilitation.[4]

As historian Robin Kelley points out, black folk have always made multiple and complex uses of the terms, uses that are often overlooked in the overheated rhetoric that surrounds the debate about linguistic propriety. "In some cases you can find even the literature that people think is so important—books like *All God's Dangers*—using 'nigger'" in interesting and provocative ways, Kelley says. "Even slave narratives used 'nigger' not as a mark of self-hatred but sometimes as a way to identify race and class together." Kelley says that terms like "Dixie Negroes" go "back even before the turn of the century" and were meant to negatively contrast to "field niggers" and as a way "to talk about status." Kelley argues that "nigger" was also used "as a term of endearment" and reflects how black folk would "code switch and talk to each other, and that doesn't necessarily mean that it's a kind of internalizing [of white supremacist belief]," which, of course, is one of the major complaints of blacks deploying the term. Kelley says that "older people [who] critique the young people" who use "nigger" in complex ways often "ignore that whole history and assume that because now the word is in circulation in a very public way—because now it's being recorded and sold on CDs for $17, because it's written down on paper, and then being used in a culture that is an increasingly multiracial black culture—that all these white people will talk about 'nigger this' and 'nigger that.'"[5]

Unquestionably most of black America is uncomfortable with whites' use of the term, even those whites who support hip-hop culture. Blacks who favor banning the term blame hip-hop culture for perpetuating racial stereotypes and for giving whites permission to extend white supremacy under the guise of embracing the most current, transgressive meanings of blackness. But such a reading is shortsighted. Whites who possess intimate knowledge of black culture are the very people who know the tortured history of the term and thus refrain from using it, at least publicly. One of the reasons that blacks used "nigger," even in distasteful, unruly fashion, has been to undo white supremacy, especially when it looked like blacks were merely imitating white usage. This is not to deny what to many blacks is a troubling development: that as hip-hop's international influence extends, whites who can barely speak English will often miss the unseemly racial politics behind the term as they refer to their fellow Russians, for instance, as "my niggas." In part, that is the unavoidable consequence of making art in an age of international capitalism, multinational corporations, and global technology. The easiest choice might seem to be to simply stop using a term over which we can exercise little control in America, much less the world. Such a choice, however, denies a crucial dimension of the racial struggles—for self-determination, for self-identification, for self-expression—that all black communities have historically waged, struggles that show up in the music we have produced. Those struggles also attract people to hip-hop and other great black arts from as nearby as Paducah and as far away as Poland.

Despite (or perhaps because of) the rapid proliferation of rap cultures around the world, the word "nigger" remains the ultimate racial taboo. Long before the rise of hip-hop culture, blacks adopted and adapted the term with an eye to making it off-limits to whites by mocking their shameless denigration of black culture. Through the bold and sometimes reckless use of the term, especially in mixed company, blacks seek to remind whites and themselves of the hurtful history of race and how artful blacks have been in overcoming white supremacy's brutal effects. It is also a way of acknowledging that blacks are aware that whites often use the term in private. The public and affectionate use of "nigga" is insurance against the ambush of arbitrary white usage, even as blacks resist being called "niggers" by dictionaries or demagogues—or by the white fans of hip-hop.

Talib Kweli, among the most feted "conscious" rappers, is sensitive to the historic resonance of "nigger" even as he defends Tupac's use of the term. "Tupac was a symbol of his generation," Kweli says. "When he did *Strictly for My Niggaz*, [he helped explain] why he was saying the word 'nigga.'" Kweli argues that black youth influenced by Tupac lack the long view of history to judge the context and propriety of the terms they use. "I think what people ought to realize is that whether we like it or not, whether it's right or wrong, whether it's good or bad, the context of the word has changed." Kweli argues that black youth grew up believing the word was acceptable, even positive, a belief they inherited from generations of blacks: "This has been here when their mothers, their grandmothers, their aunts, their cousins use this word in a positive way." Kweli suggests that the lack of historical perspective has certainly aided the wide circulation of the term. "Kids don't know what happened last week, much less know what happened thirty years ago in the civil rights movement." Instead of conjuring up the acrimonious history of race, "nigger" suggests solidarity for black youth. "All they know is that when they hear the word 'nigga,' they think about their homeboys down the street who got their back no matter what." Jada Pinkett Smith sums up Tupac's beliefs about "nigga": "He always felt he couldn't betray what he would call the 'niggas in the gutter,'" she says, "because they had been there for him. They loved him, and that's who he was here for. I'll never forget what he told me: 'When I'm dead and gone, the *niggas* will understand.'"

If Tupac depended on the "niggas in the gutter" to understand his legacy, he worked diligently in his brief life to understand, and live, their plight. That often meant defining the real nigga as a tragic figure embroiled in violence, a violence that was both conscientiously lamented and vigorously embraced. In the realm of hard-core hip-hop, their own contradictory couplings of authenticity and violence trap the real niggas. Tupac's death is the most recent and perhaps most painful evidence of that truth. I am not suggesting that his still unsolved death resulted from his violent rap lyrics. Rather, Tupac's eager embrace of a dangerous lifestyle that he viewed as the unavoidable destiny of real niggas lead to self-destructive choices. For Tupac and a host

of black youth, thug life and death have come almost exclusively to define the black ghetto. That is a perilous retreat
from a much more complex, compelling vision of black life
that Tupac at his best helped to outline. Tupac rudely—and
refreshingly—opposed explaining all black life through a
narrative of redemptive optimism. He strategically resisted
as well the impulse of positive moral reconstruction in
black life. Instead, he thrust the sharp edges of his lyrics
into the inflated rhetoric of orthodox blackness, challenging narrow artistic visions of black identity. Gangsta rap
and hard-core hip-hop announced a ghetto renaissance: a
flowering of vulgar self-expression rooted beneath polite
discourse. It is not that hard-core rap stories can be usefully
viewed as sociological treatises on black urban suffering.
Rather, such raps are aesthetic creations that also function
to heighten the visibility of degraded youth.

By joining verbal art to rage—about material misery and
racial hostility, about the avalanche of daily suffering that
suffocates black lives—Tupac proved that he possessed a
redemptive vulgarity. At his best Tupac showed that what
was truly vulgar was the way black folk perished from fruit-
less promises of restored neighborhoods and transformed
racial practices. Or how their elders had forsaken young
blacks. Karen Lee, a close family friend and an early Tupac
publicist, recalls Tupac's cursing during a lecture to the
Malcolm X Grass Roots Movement in New York in the
early 1990s. "There was a lady sitting next to him, and I saw
her lean over and say, 'Could you please change your language? It's offensive.'" Lee remembers thinking that Tupac
would make a spectacle of the exchange. Instead, she re-

members, he "made me really proud. He looked at her and said, 'I'm sorry if my language offends you, but it can't offend you any more than the world your generation has left me to deal with.'" Tupac highlighted the vulgar invisibility and silence that cloak poor black life. Every time he seized a microphone to bring poetry to pain, he broke faith with that silence and invisibility. Tupac brilliantly explored this edifying dimension of hard-core hip-hop with a balance that might be campily called "celeterrogation": the deft combination of celebration and interrogation. He rapped about the plight of welfare mothers. He skillfully narrated the thug's life as a cautionary tale of self-destruction, even as he often forgot to observe his own warnings.

Tupac's searing blend of art, conscience, and theater brought him the critical and personal attention he desperately desired. "Pac could walk into a room and he had that kind of energy that would bring the attention to himself," Karen Lee says. "And most of the time he would take that attention and use it negatively because that was the genre of the music, he would say." He was also subject to the harsh spotlight of political attack. John Singleton, the director whose film *Poetic Justice* Tupac starred in with Janet Jackson, says he warned Tupac to "cover your wagons now, because Dan Quayle is talking about how . . . your music influenced some kid in Texas [to kill someone]. He is . . . talking about violence and rap music." Singleton urged Tupac, "who was like a little brother to me," not to "get all wild . . . because they'll be gunning for you." But Tupac refused to shrink from the aggressive swelling of his thug persona. He redefined thug and outlaw in a willfully individual code whose private connotations nevertheless failed to spare him public criticism.

Tupac's manic devotion to tracing the anatomy of the real nigga inevitably invites the question of whether his vision of authenticity is enabling or destructive. Too often that interesting question is sacrificed to harsh judgments driven by racial anxiety. The question asked instead is: Is Tupac's rap positive or negative? But to focus on negative or positive influence is to elevate experience above art and invite a crude comparison between real and false experiences. Instead, we should pursue a far more complex question: Isn't the self—and not just one's public persona, even a thug one—an artistic creation? Can't it draw from the realm of collective experience embodied in cultural myths, racial allegories, and ghetto legends? This line of inquiry puts aside questions of authenticity or its absence to focus on creating, styling, and performing one's self and identity.

Isn't the self best understood in relation to art, and not the other way around, as many of Tupac's critics would have it? As philosopher Michel Foucault questioned, "Couldn't everyone's life become a work of art? Why should the lamp or the house be an art object but not our life?" Foucault also gives a clue to the limited appeal of debates about authenticity—a clue that hip-hoppers could usefully appropriate. In discussing Jean-Paul Sartre's literary criticism, Foucault says that Sartre "refers the work of creation to a certain relation to oneself—the author to himself—which has the form of authenticity or inauthenticity. I would like to say exactly the contrary: we should not have to refer the creative activity of somebody to the kind of relation he has to himself, but should relate the kind of relation one has to oneself to a creative activity." The interesting questions of Tupac's art—whether it furthered the artistic ideals he claimed to represent, whether it musically or lyrically measured up to the best of what the genre had to offer, or whether it suffocated in a miasma of rhetorical posturing—are hardly asked. That's because the morality of the artistic pursuit constantly impinges on its critical judgment. It is not that art should be spared the judgment of its moral meanings. We should simply remember that those meanings will be judged by critics who have their own biases, priorities, and interests to defend. Artists often seek to undermine in their work the ethical prisms through which art is viewed.[6]

The question of authenticity rang especially hard in the case of Tupac's art. "I think Pac is interesting, because he's a cat who most people associate with the real in hip-hop," says intellectual Todd Boyd. "And to me his life is everything other than real. . . . He couldn't distinguish between the real and fictional." Quincy Jones, the entertainment impresario who was initially attacked by Tupac for his interracial marriages but who grew close to the rapper when Tupac dated his daughter Kidada, agrees that many young entertainers find it difficult to "tell the difference between reality and fantasy. . . . It's easy to get vertigo." Still, Tupac managed to strike a chord in his peers, even those, like rapper Mos Def, who are viewed as diametrically opposed to the themes and lifestyle espoused by gangsta rappers. Mos Def sees a profound level of honesty in Tupac's work. "Pac lived everything that he talked about," he says. "He lived the

beauty of it; he lived the horror of it. And that's a lot more than you can say for a lot of people out here."

Did Tupac draw from his own experiences, or did he raid the experiences of others to spin his haunting tales of urban woe and social neglect? If he did, would he be different from any other artist whose primary obligation is to make art out of imagination, fiction, and fantasy? Stories don't have to be real to be true. Wouldn't Tupac have been artistically authentic in borrowing the lives, experiences, and stories of others as the grist for his powerful rap narratives? The motivating force of Tupac's art, as producer Preston Holmes phrases it, was "to keep this connection to the folks he saw as the most depressed," the people "on the streets of Harlem and Baltimore and Marin City." Ultimately, Holmes says, Tupac wanted to take those folk "somewhere else in terms of being able to look at their situation from a standpoint of having some real political insight into why things are the way they are." It may have been that very tension—of trying to remain identified with black street life while trumpeting the urgency of political awareness—that made Tupac's role demanding, if not schizophrenic. "He just really tried to be too many things to too many people," says journalist Allison Samuels, who interviewed the rapper on several occasions. "And you really can lose yourself like that."

Rap is ideally suited as a forum to discuss these ideas since it appeals to its adherents as a unique and authentic culture. As Holmes says, "People talk about 'keeping it real' . . . and that was [Tupac], too." In their most self-important moments, hip-hoppers conceive themselves building a cultural bulwark that facilitates a high level of honesty through narrative self-disclosure. Although "I" may be a dirty word in certain branches of journalism and the academy, it is a moral imperative in hip-hop. The genius of hip-hop is that its adherents convince each other—and judging by the attacks it receives, those outside their ranks—that its devices are meant immediately to disclose the truth of life through reportage. In truth, hip-hoppers construct narrative conventions and develop artistic norms through repeated practice and citation. The artistic métier that Tupac so brilliantly explored was built on just such a combustible premise: "What I say is who I am." The shredding of the artistic and moral lines that separate stories and the truths they embody from "the real" is exactly what worries the critics of hip-hop and black youth.[7]

The aggressive embrace of authenticity is especially characteristic of the struggles to define black masculinity. Indeed, the debate over black authenticity is intimately bound to the clash of visions of masculine identity. The moral equivalency of authenticity and masculinity is an undeniable, if troubling, sign of the degree to which machismo and patriarchy continue to determine the cultural and political priorities of black life. Beyond the plague of gender imbalance in black social concerns, black men of every age confront crises. Older black men face staggering rates of imprisonment, chronic health crises, and persistent forms of racial oppression. If older black men are suffering, younger black males are even more vulnerable—to AIDS, homicide, suicide, poor schooling, and racial profiling. Most troubling, they confront the culture of violence that claims too many lives and seduces young blacks into destructive choices. Tupac's tragically shortened life embodied the troubles of young black men. As rapper Mos Def observes, Tupac captured in the sweep of his brief life the defining experiences of all young black men, the blessed and the unfortunate. "Pac was locked up. Pac had a number-one record. Pac had movies out. He was getting the most out of being a Negro in America," Mos Def notes. "He was living both sides of that [experience]. He was living that thing of having white folks . . . being hostile, and he was put into jail, so that even in the face of his success, he was always cognizant of the fact that to America he was just another nigger." Mos Def wonders, "How does that feel? You know, to go from great privilege to just being locked up, and then watching your own video in the joint?" That sharp and jarring contrast between his personal highs and lows gave Tupac a powerful comprehension of the ups and downs of black male existence.[8]

Tupac is arguably the archetypal troubled black young male, or as the actress Jada Pinkett Smith puts it, "the blueprint for the average African American male." She says that Tupac brought the black male experience "to the light." It was as if Tupac used his life as the object lesson of black male strife. As Smith described it for me, Tupac said, "I'm going to lay my life out; I'm going to lay my soul out for somebody to come and do exactly what you're doing"—referring to my intention of writing a book that explores the heart of Tupac's meaning. "And that's to break it down, so that we understand in a whole what's going on with our black male children and our black men." Smith confesses,

"I have met so many Pacs. We've got an industry full of
them, and they might not be as magnificent and they might
not shine as bright, but I'll be damned if they ain't Tupac in
one way or another."

If Tupac is the representative young black male, his vision of black masculinity emerged, as it happened, just as
black religious and social leaders attempted to address the
crisis of black males. The most prominent, of course, was
Louis Farrakhan. Farrakhan was given a huge boost within
young black America by his ingenious orchestration of the
Million Man March in 1995. The gathering was a dramatic
testament to the magnitude of black male hunger for racial
rescue and moral requirement. Farrakhan tapped into the
generational anxieties of youthful black masculinity, probing the spiritual hunger and communal quests that were the
source of even nefarious activities like gang-banging and
drug addiction. Farrakhan's elevated status after the march
and his continuing appeal to millions of younger blacks,
proves that the march was neither a fluke nor an exaggerated dance of black machismo. Rather, Farrakhan helped
to publicly choreograph black male identity. He helped to
make the Million Man March a ballet of black masculine
self-revelation and reinvention. He understood intuitively
that such a dance of self-declaration had been rehearsed in
millions of miniature but meaningful gestures, both in individual psyches and on the historical stage of collective
racial aspiration. Farrakhan proved to be both brilliantly
perceptive and opportunistic: He seized the day by defining
and packaging in accessible form black men's huge desire—one that is largely invisible to white eyes—to show-

case black identities in all of their splendid, undervalued complexity.[9]

Many black progressives roundly criticized the march as a cathartic gesture that lacked political utility. But Farrakhan understood that a new generation of young blacks hungered for a deepened moral engagement that seems lacking in the political measures and policy recommendations of the civil rights generation. The Million Man March afforded black men the occasion of a symbolic solidarity that had a practical and profound purpose: By combining their resources, black men consolidated a vision of black masculinity that had been largely ignored by the media and other cultural mythmakers. As simple as it sounds, the march took one big swipe at all of the nonsense that masquerades as intelligent opinion about black men. And as disheartening as it might appear—especially in light of the Herculean efforts of black warriors against racial hostility and ignorance—the march rebutted persistent stereotypes about black men. The march showed that black men are concerned about crime in black communities; that they are consumed with the wish to make moral mayhem a thing of the past in black neighborhoods; that they are more diverse than cultural beliefs suggest; that they are sensitive and sharing; that they are brothers who can embrace one another across the chasm of class and economic circumstance.[10]

While Farrakhan focused on rehabilitating black men's images, members of the younger black generation appeared to reject the moral compass supplied in traditional religious and civic life. Tupac's life and death certainly captured the anger of young black men. But boxer Mike Tyson's sad decline embodied another dimension of the wide moral gulf that separates older and younger blacks. Before Tupac and fellow slain rapper Notorious B.I.G. ascended to this throne, Mike Tyson—whose fight with Bruce Sheldon Tupac attended the night he was fatally wounded—was the king of "troubled black youth." Tyson's hulking image loomed large over youthful black masculinity's identity crises, particularly as he embodied the authentic street brother whose athletic glory never undermined his identification with the ghetto from which he sprang.

As a youth Tyson spent time in a detention center, had street brawls while a professional fighter, and as champ was accused of being a "serial buttocks fondler." Most recently, with two bites to Evander Holyfield's ears in their 1997 heavyweight boxing championship fights, Tyson renewed his kinship with the dragons of self-destruction and reclaimed his kingship. Tyson's act was made more ugly by the sense of inescapable tragedy that envelops his life. Although Tyson has skillfully punched his way from concrete to canvass, he has often appeared to be a street brawler trapped in the body of a world-class athlete. He mastered the mechanics of ruthless ringmanship, but his womanizing and sidewalk set-tos left him reeling from hostile reactions to his will to disintegrate. Since he became, at age twenty, the youngest heavyweight champion ever, Tyson has seemed spectacularly uncomfortable with the twin imperatives of black athletic success: to nobly represent black culture while striving to undo its unfairly bestialized image in the public's mind.[11]

At the same time, Tyson crystallized the contradictions of a sport built on blood and brutality. His success inside the ring depended on his ability to harness an outsized fury that outside the ring could lead to great mayhem. Tyson's occasional blurring of the boundaries between his two worlds—symbolized in allegations that he pounded his first wife, actress Robin Givens—bruised a major premise of the "sweet science" of boxing: that it is civilized violence. More sharply, Tyson tapped the unconscious vein of white fear and fascination with sexualized black masculine identities, just as other despised black youth figures have done—including Tupac, Notorious B.I.G., Lil' Kim, and Snoop Doggy Dogg. Tyson became for many whites a sad brute. He was a beast in boxer shorts whose primitivism was made a spectacle to be bought on pay-per-view. When Tyson joined forces with fight promoter Don King, they seemed to supply each other's missing parts. They were a seamless conjunction of the savvy and the sensational, two brilliantly bothered black men whose showy success made some white folks mad. In King, Tyson seemed to find the father figure who could turn whites' demonization of him into more than dollars, while offering him a psychic shield from whites' attacks. For King, Tyson's raw youth represented his most enduring and biggest paycheck. Equally important, Tyson became King's field general in the ghetto rebellion against the more sedate, sophisticated style adopted by the black bourgeoisie. Tyson gave flesh and blood to King's belief that the real forces that underpin capitalism are shrewd intelligence and relentless intimidation. In King's business dealings, Tyson glimpsed the logic that had motivated his own fisticuffs: If you can beat 'em, they'll join you.

But his partnership with King did not squarely address Tyson's desperate need for moral mentorship. If Tyson suffered from white demonization, with King he endured, to a degree, black exploitation. As a result, Tyson lacked a force to protect himself from his own worst tendencies, especially his seemingly uncontrollable urge to grope or fondle women against their will, which eventually led to his conviction for rape. Even here, the support Tyson received hurt him. Desiree Washington, the woman whom Tyson was convicted of raping, was pilloried in many black communities, while Tyson was the subject of prayer meetings. When he went off to prison to serve his sentence, Washington became the "ho"; Tyson became holy. Even Tyson's conversion to Islam had a perverse underside: In the minds of many, it was a justification of the hurdles he had to overcome to attain perfect faith. Washington became a pit stop to his spiritual evolution. When Tyson emerged from prison a changed man having converted to Islam, many black women were angry with just this sort of logic, whose immediate outcome was a Harlem parade to honor Tyson. These black women acknowledged that Tyson had served his time, but they wondered if he, or for that matter most men, had learned their lessons. Tyson was, in essence, being forgiven without having confessed his sin.

It is ironic, though too predictable, that the pain Tyson caused black women wouldn't be recognized or make sense until Tyson left his teeth marks on the body of a black man. There is still a lamentable hierarchy of hurt in black

America. If men are harmed, there's solidarity in crisis. If women or children suffer, sometimes at the hands of black men, their grief is enshrouded in silence or invisibility. This is where Tyson's embodiment of generational decadence loses its raison d'être: The denial of the importance of women's lives crosses every era in black American history. There's no question that Tyson has faced enormous racism in his quest for pugilistic supremacy and personal dignity. Tyson's second bout with Holyfield had an ugly religious undertone. Holyfield was the righteous warrior fighting for all that evangelical Christianity, contrary to its roots, has come to symbolize: rigid domestic rules, ahistorical piety, and a claustrophobic view of faith in the public square. Tyson the Islam-reformed thug met his end in Holyfield's halo. Tyson was rebestialized, but this time more subtly. He was now Mecca's monster. But none of this—not even Holyfield's smoothly managed, unsportsmanlike conduct of head butting and low blows in their two fights—can account for Tyson's terrible act. The best counterargument against Holyfield would have been a fist in his face, not an etching of Tyson's bicuspids and incisors in his ears. The supreme irony may be that the only white man in the ring, referee Mills Lane, had to stop a hero of despised young black masculinity from tearing the flesh of another black man. For many, Tyson's apology for his ring actions rung hollow, a futile gesture in a grotesque choreography of self-pity. Just as Tupac did, Tyson still faces his greatest challenge: taming the demons inside.[12]

Tyson is not the only young black male who has had to confront his demons in public. Hip-hop mogul Sean

"Puffy" Combs, viewed by Tupac as his sworn enemy, along with Combs's protégé, Biggie Smalls, also traded on a thug persona to create a multimillion-dollar empire and stake a claim in hypermasculinized black authenticity. Combs has also had a series of highly publicized encounters that have shaped perceptions of him as a smooth figure outside the law who is capable of both retaining street credibility and corporate cachet. All of that was recently threatened by a very public run-in with the law. Early in 2001, after a seven-week trial, a Manhattan jury acquitted Combs of four counts of illegal possession of a gun and a single count of bribery. Combs faced up to fifteen years in jail if found guilty of charges stemming from a 1999 shooting in a Manhattan nightclub that left three people injured. Combs's ordeal has forced him to rethink his image and perhaps help other black youth question the indissoluble links among masculinity, authenticity, and violence. Combs built his reputation as a hip-hop impresario on the controversial embrace of black culture's outlaw features. Naming his company "Bad Boy Records" perfectly captured Combs's symbolic indulgence in girls, glamour, guns, and gangsterism. For the most part, none of this was to be taken literally, especially when Combs the rapper took to the microphone. His posturing on records and the video screen was seen by fans and critics alike as an attempt to hype his image as a "real nigga," a necessity that he perhaps gleefully exploited, given the ascendancy of hard-core and gangsta rap.

Of course there have been moments in Combs's career when the lines between art and life have fatally blurred. The most tragic occurred on a March night in 1997 when

Combs's biggest star and rap's king of rhyme, Notorious
B.I.G., was gunned down in Los Angeles. It happened again
when Combs was alleged to have summoned associates to
beat up record executive Steve Stoute. Combs was angered
by Stoute's refusal to cancel a Combs guest appearance on a
crucifix in a video he shot with rapper Nas, claiming the image was sacrilegious. His missteps aside, Combs has built a
$300-million empire, including (besides his record label) a
fashion line, two restaurants, a film development company,
and a technology company. His extraordinary success is due
in no small measure to his ability to bridge two apparently
irreconcilable worlds: white suburban wealth and black
ghetto grit. He is as at home in Martha Stewart's tony digs
as he is in Sylvia's famed soul restaurant. Puffy is at a critical
juncture in the public reconstruction of his persona. That
so much of the nation bought his thug act has brought him
millions of dollars and worldwide fame, and in 2001 it
nearly brought him prison. Ironically enough, Combs may
have contributed to the narrow perceptions of black youth
even as his real achievements as an entrepreneur broke barriers and crushed stereotypes. His rebirth as "P Diddy," a
symbolic renunciation of his previous thug persona, not
only may signal a crucial turn in his private conception of
authentic black masculinity but may provide a crucial cultural moment of the public rethinking of the "real nigga."

The question whether Tupac was real, much less a real
nigga, when he rapped makes sense only when artists, and
their audiences and critics, presume to know true black
identity when they see it. Tupac certainly laid out the predicate of a real nigga: someone willing to die for his homies,

love black women *and* keep bitches in their place, tell the truth about black suffering and uphold the ghetto even as some of its fiercest advocates joined the Negro-riche. His critics were equally adamant in their opposing morphology of correct blackness: Real blacks, positive blacks, don't call women "bitches," don't call each other "nigger," don't promote predatory behavior, and don't celebrate hopelessness and cynicism, especially to sell records. In fact, we must entertain the notion that rappers like Tupac "may ultimately be agents of our autogenocide," says writer Khephra Burns. "Rappers talk about keeping it real," he says. "But it ain't real; it's theater." Burns argues that gangsta rap lyrics don't portray "the reality of most black people's lives, nor even the reality of most rappers' lives." Calling gangsta rap a "posture—a stance and style adopted once recordings of outlaw rappers proved successful," Burns claims it was embraced by the music industry, with "every wanna-be rapper craving attention, the adoration of millions of fans, and all the toys conspicuous consumption could provide them."

As much as Tupac railed against the "respectable Negro," he pioneered a dangerous trend in hard-core hip-hop that, ironically, draws from the moral energy of the orthodox black culture from which he sought thuggish refuge: He yearned to live the life he rapped about in his songs. That golden ideal was the motive behind the gospel desire to close the gap between preaching and practice, between what one said and what one did. Applied to gangsta rap and Tupac's career, it brought disastrous results. "In the beginning it wasn't about all that thuggishness . . . and the street stuff," Singleton says. "He wanted to be a poet; he wanted to be an actor." Singleton reveals that Tupac "used to wear crystals" and tried to be "this artsy cat." But "for the sake of the whole rap game, I think, in my mind, he crafted the image [of the gangsta] for himself. He started to live that image out, and that's what led to a lot of his troubles." Producer and rapper Dr. Dre, who worked with Tupac on his groundbreaking double compact disc *All Eyez on Me,* was harsher. "Tupac . . . liked to stir up stuff and then watch it explode in others' faces," Dre says. "That's a hard way to live and a quicker way to die." I am not suggesting that Tupac had no firsthand experience with many of the themes he explored in the studio, from poverty to probation, from homelessness to getting high. But his emulation of real gangsters and thugs implied surrender to the stifling literalism that trumped many of his critics. Many critics are unable to acknowledge the ingenuity of artistically exploring the attractions and limits of black moral and social subcultures. They endorse a "positive" perspective that is as artificial and uncomprehending of the full sweep of black culture as is the exclusive celebration of pimps, playas, hos, macks, and thugs.

In the arc of his secular, gangsta ambitions, Tupac's embrace of the gospel's guide to black behavior proved painful. In 1993 Tupac was charged in the shooting of two off-duty Atlanta police officers. He had various convictions in Michigan and New York on assault and battery charges. Tupac served eleven months in jail after being convicted in a 1994 sexual assault of a woman in a New York hotel room. During his trial he was shot five times in what appeared to be an armed-robbery attempt in New York's

Quad Recording Studios. In April 1996 he got into trouble for violating his probation. In May of the same year, he pleaded guilty to a felony weapons charge in Los Angeles. And that June Tupac settled a lawsuit with a limousine driver who alleged that Tupac and other members of his entourage beat him severely in the parking lot of Fox TV after Tupac taped a segment of *In Living Color*. It would be simplistic to suggest that Tupac's death came solely from his own destructive desire to forsake the represented for the real. After all, he was in part playing out the cards dealt to him, extending and experimenting with the script he was handed at birth. Some of his most brilliant raps are about those cards and that script—hunger, ghetto life, the narrow choices of black men, and the criminality that some seek as a refuge from a racist society. In falling prey to the temptation to *be* a gangster, Tupac lost his hold on the frustrating but powerful moral ambiguity that makes the rhetoric and representations of gangsta rappers effective. In fleeing from art to the actual, from appearance to reality, from the studio to the streets, Tupac lost his life. He also lost the most devastating weapon he possessed to fight the problems he saw: his brilliant representations of the reality he confronted, and the powerful reality that his representations, like those of all great artists, helped to bring about. His art changed people's lives. His stirring raps made many people see suffering they had never before acknowledged. It helped many desperately unhappy young people reclaim a sense of hope and humanity. That's why a young man approached me after a lecture at a midwestern university to tell me, "Tupac saved my life. If I had been listening to so-called positive rappers, I would have been dead. When he said, 'I'm hopeless,' I could identify with that, and I didn't kill myself like I had planned to do because I believed he understood how I felt."

It is perhaps the saddest feature of a life cut short in troubled youth that Tupac didn't live long enough to trust his own genius, to believe in its saving power for himself. Unlike fellow gangsta rappers Ice T, Dr. Dre, and Ice Cube, video director Eric Meza says Tupac "didn't live long enough to make enough name, to make enough fortune [so] that he could get out of" the gangsta rap game with its attendant pitfalls. Mos Def sees Tupac's importance as taking "something that was negative and associat[ing] it with us [young blacks] and trying to flip it. . . . I think it was really just a noble ambition of Pac's mind that he never really got to even fully expand on. . . . He died so young." No matter where you stand on the argument about authentic blackness, that tragedy is real.

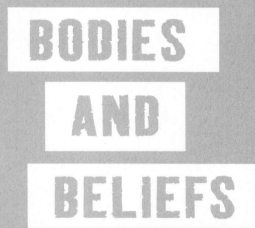

BODIES AND BELIEFS

CHAPTER 6

"Do We Hate Our Women?"

Female Per Versions

In retrospect, the gnarled sympathy Tupac fostered for women is already evident in the interview taped when he was seventeen. The teenager conjures an image from his recent past, lamenting the mistreatment of young women by his male counterparts.

"I've seen guys speak to women with this much respect," he says, "and I deplore that." Tupac professes an "ultra-respect" for women that he occasionally defends by fist. The chivalry he gained at his mother's knees brings him the admiration of his peers. It also entails a drawback that the youthful Tupac had not anticipated: wounded pride when his gentle outreach to the opposite sex was rebuffed.

"I was liking this girl in [Tamalpais High], and I'm extra nice," he says. "Extra gentleman. I'm extra just, like, 'Oh, you're beautiful, and you deserve the best.' And she told me I was too nice. I couldn't believe it. It wouldn't work because I was too nice. That was the ultimate stab in the back." His stabbed back led to a broken face that Tupac seeks to restore.

"I went through a week of just going, 'Forget it. I'm just going to be like [the bad boys] because they seem to get the girls, and they call girls the *b* word, and they smack and beat [them], and they're getting girls. And I'm going 'Peace,' and, 'I think you're beautiful,' and they're going, 'Well, I like him because he's masculine.'" But Tupac's sparkling intelligence and gung-ho innocence forbid permanent cynicism. In an elaborate bit of gender strategy, Tupac casts himself as the sacrificial lamb to woo black men into respectful behavior.

"My plan is that I keep telling girls not to let them call you these names, and if I keep saying it, it's going to catch on," Tupac insists. "Because the girls won't allow them to be their boyfriend if they're going to speak to them like that. And they're going to want me. So in order to not get them to go with me, they're going to have to change. So that's how they change. So I'll be a scapegoat. No problem, as long as it changes." The fragments of Tupac's conflicting thoughts about gender coalesce in his revealing story: performing chivalrous deeds, identifying with female suffering, chastising men for harmful actions, chafing at irrational female preferences, envying the erotic fortunes of the "bad boy," and insulting women with the epithets he formerly loathed. Although Tupac remained steadfast in his love of women, a troubling sexism seized his microphone and throbbed in hateful lyrics. And although few observers believe that Tupac was guilty of the sexual abuse conviction that landed him in prison, his conflicted vision of women reflects hip-hop's convulsive gender beliefs.

Hip-hop has been distinguished by an assault on women that is as remarkable for its virulence as for its crushing lack of creativity. There is a small but deadly clot of epithets that circulate in the stream of rap rhetoric, none more derogatory than "bitch." The mother of all female insults is especially damaging because it is rooted in unjust social conditions. Patriarchy has undermined the equal footing of men and women in our society, despite the gains of the feminist movement. Perhaps the most visible signs of that inequality are the sexual assault and domestic abuse to which women are subject. The clash between male supremacy and feminist resistance has necessarily strained gender relations, as men grapple to preserve their uncontested social authority. Since the rule of law has reflected a slow but positive shift toward gender justice, the political and cultural realms become even more highly charged battlegrounds to resolve conflicts of identity and power. Among the skirmishes that flare in the sex wars, few are as important as a woman's right to reproductive choice or her ability to gain public assistance in support of a family in hardship. Moreover, the question of how women should be treated by men in power—at the workplace, in a bar, or even in a dorm room—has forced our culture to ratchet up the conversation about appropriate boundaries, spaces, and limits. And the cultural symbols of sexism—including the use of explicitly antifemale language, the endorsement of rigidly defined gender roles, the stereotypical portrayal of women in the media, and the revival of family values as a cover for male dominance—have come under duress. As a result, two opposing trends developed: the codes of male privilege were challenged even as the culture of misogyny doubled in force. In the hazy afterglow of simultaneous triumphs and setbacks, feminist struggles over identity sometimes settled for, and in, crucial debates about nomenclature. As the debate over the word "nigga" makes clear, what we are called and what we answer to is a deeply political matter. In such a view, gender epithets are seen as linguistic bombs exploding on the identities of assaulted women. Or to switch metaphors, "bitch" is a one-word thesaurus for male supremacy.[1]

To be sure, there are attempts by women to rehabilitate "bitch" for their purposes, similar to the efforts of some blacks to do the same with "nigger." Instead of acceding to its derisive nuances, women pour on flattery where formerly insult prevailed: "We are *proud* to be called 'bitch,'" they seem to say, "if that means we are aggressive, assertive, independent, self-determining, and wholly unashamed of the power we wield, especially when it terrifies sexist men." Of course racial and generational differences intervene. Independent and aggressive white women are certainly viewed as "bitches," but that is because of their threat to male power. By contrast, independent and aggressive black women are often viewed as "bitches" because of their threat to the social order, a major part of which undeniably rests on the pillar of patriarchy. Black women threaten not only male privilege but white society, culture, and values as well. The difference is that white women share in the meanings of whiteness even as they separate themselves from masculine dominance. White women are still "us" to white men, despite their attempts to topple male supremacy. Black women, however, are "them" on two counts—race and gender—and thus are doubly degraded as "bitch." But there is more: Because of the intragender and interracial competition for jobs and education, black women carry yet another burden of "bitch" placed on them by white women who are their ostensible sisters. And when one adds the hostilities often directed at black women by black men— because they challenge the sexual economy of the black household, because they appear less threatening and therefore more acceptable to white men than black men, or because they seem more harsh and intolerant of black male behavior than white women—the meaning of "bitch" for black women is unquestionably complex. Thus, the choice of white women to claim the "bitch" mantle is an entirely different affair for black women. If one's existence, and not one's function, is reason enough to be called "bitch," the choice to call oneself "bitch" is fraught with peril. Another way of stating this is that *a certain group* of white women are thought of as bitches—the "obstreperous" ones with attitude, say, or those who demand control—whereas black women *as a group* endure the stigma. It must be remembered that much of this is not consciously reasoned but draws from myths and stereotypes about black female identity that are deeply rooted in our culture.[2]

The burden of being thought of, even unconsciously, as

a bitch in the wider culture makes it excruciatingly painful for many black women to bear that term when it is thrust on them by their own children and, sometimes, by other women. Many older black women feel betrayed when they hear "bitch" trip from the lips of children who were not alive when they marched, protested, or otherwise supported the movement for black freedom, which included the liberty to speak our black minds. For this generation of black male youth to use that liberty to crush black females in derision is simply intolerable. If many black women have found it difficult to exult in their bitch status, a younger generation has little compunction in laying hold to the title. Many younger black women, and some older ones, too, are proud to be bitches. They wear the label as a badge of honor and roll the word's resonant sound in their mouths with high delight. (Afeni Shakur told me: "I know I'm a bitch. You can call me that. And if you're a bitch, you know you're a bitch. And if you're not, you know that, too.") Many black women think of this practice as little more than willful self-hatred, the same way blacks that call themselves "nigga" are self-hating. When they hear female rappers like Lil' Kim or Foxy Brown calling themselves "bad bitches," black women fail to see subversion or the entitlement to redefinition reflected in the rappers' rhetoric. All these black women see is that these girls are consenting to their own degradation by a vicious word whose meanings travel further back and deeper down into history and culture than they care or know to look (although these same women appear to be more forgiving of older black women who call each other "bitch" in private as a form of playful solidarity or gentle chastisement).

The same is true for black boys, but their relations to black women have been complicated by the exigencies of the poor urban household where fathers leave mothers to fend off hunger and want with ever more meager resources. Welfare reform extended the already harsh circumstances that force black mothers to choose between work and family. More than one generation of black boys has matured under the regime of piecemeal benefits tendered by the state and eaten away by the addition of more siblings. The choices made by many of these mothers—live-in boyfriends; the loosening of hierarchical child-parent bonds in deference to lateral and multiple male affections; the often unwitting sexual sacrifice of boys and girls to abusive partners; and the resort to drugs and alcohol to drown the pain of poverty—turn out to be the cruel but faithful calculus of black female resentment by young black boys. Of course it is patently unfair to blame poor black mothers with severely limited resources for the social hardships their children endure. And yet poor black urban culture seems to nurture *femiphobia*—the fear and disdain of the female, expressed in the verbal abuse and protracted resentment of women. I am not suggesting that femiphobia erupts exclusively or primarily in the ghetto. I am arguing that an especially visible and troubling form is rooted there.

Hip-hop culture has been particularly virulent in its femiphobic sentiments. Many of the genre's angriest and most articulate artists have grown up under conditions that make them vulnerable to its harshest expressions. But then the collective unconscious of hip-hop has been shaped in the crucible of female disdain; femiphobia has become the rhetorical reflex of rap. Femiphobia no longer depends exclusively on the individual experiences of rappers to articulate its vision. Rather, femiphobia has become a crucial aspect of the culture of signification in rap that influences the lyrics of hip-hop artists, measures authentic rap—and hence, male—identity, specifies a pervasive machismo, and forges masculine bonds within the culture. Tupac unquestionably reveled in the femiphobic passions of hip-hop, even as he sought to balance his beliefs with kind behavior toward women. Although it borders on cliché to say so, Tupac's troubled, complex relationship with his mother decisively shaped his vision of women. The fragments of his relationship with Afeni were distributed in his interactions with women, both literally and through his art. How can we account for Tupac's contradictory views?[3]

On first blush, Afeni's struggles with poverty and homelessness gave Tupac a model of valiant mothering against huge odds. Despite her revolutionary commitments, her crack addiction undoubtedly had a negative impact on Tupac's vision of female association. Tupac claims that in Baltimore Afeni's boyfriend physically abused her, a state of affairs that was precipitated, perhaps, by her drug and alcohol addiction. This surely had a devastating effect on a developing boy's psyche. Maxine Waters gained crucial insight into these issues in her work with young black men in the projects and in gangs. "I learned that many of them had seen too much with the advent of crack and the impact of crack on their mothers and the neighborhood," Waters says. "They saw their mothers and older women who were supposed to be their protectors get caught up in and addicted to crack. Crack caused women to do unspeakable things." Waters claims that the emergence of "the 'strawberry' who performed [sexual] acts and exposed even their children to unspeakable things" also ruptured the sense of social stability that should ground all children. As a result, there were frightening consequences. "I saw young men who had seen too much of that, and I thought they were the most dangerous young people that I'd ever met. I think that once young people are exposed to certain kinds of things at a very early age, particularly as it relates to women and their 'mamas,' they are capable of killing." Waters argues that these young people kill as a way of exacting retribution for "what they have seen and what they have experienced."

If Tupac's femiphobia was not rooted in murderous rage—"he didn't have a hatred in his heart for black women" according to publicist Karen Lee—it might have been stoked by his experiences on the road, which mirrored those of his rap peers. "I think that was part of his experience with women," Lee says. "I think there *were* bitches and whores. Being out here with these young brothers on the road, there's plenty of them." In many ways it appears too easy, and just downright sexist, to blame women for the hateful sentiments that pass for gender commentary in hip-hop. Most rappers inherit their beliefs about women long before they find fame and fortune in hip-hop. Still, it is undeniable that they encounter young women whose chief goal is to bring pleasure to rap stars and to procure, in

Snoop Dogg's term, "superstar dick." Groupies are a staple not just of hip-hop but all forms of masculine endeavor, from the dugout to the pulpit, from the blues hall to the boardroom. It is one thing to cast aspersions on women deemed to be loose and destructive in their sexual demeanor. It is another to judge all women as bitches or whores or to defend oneself, as rappers often do, by claiming, "I'm not talking about *all* women, just the ones I meet who act like bitches and hos." The problem is, they never seem to meet or describe any other women besides "bitches" or "hos." (But the hypocrisy of the double standard must not be missed. Groupie sexual culture attempts, however desperately and self-destructively, to right the imbalance in the circulation of sexual pleasures that allows men to be promiscuous as a condition of their maturing masculinity, whereas women bear the stigma of "ho" for their equally aggressive erotic experimentation.)

Neither does such a judgment take into account the political economy of the "ho." If social empathy for young black males is largely absent in public opinion and public policies, the lack of understanding and compassion for the difficulties faced by poor young black females is even more deplorable. There exists within quarters of black life a range of justifications for black male behavior. Even if they are not wholly accepted by other blacks or by the larger culture, such justifications have a history and possess social resonance. Young black males hustle because they are poor. They become pimps and playas because the only role models they had are pimps and playas. Black males rob because they are hungry. They have babies because they seek to prove their masculinity in desultory paternity. They rap about violence because they came to maturity in enclaves of civic horror where violence is the norm. Black males do poorly in school because they are deprived of opportunity and ambition. Yet there are few comparable justifications for the black female's beleaguered status. The lack of accepted social justifications for black women's plight would lead one to assume that black women do not confront incest, father deprivation, economic misery, social dislocation, domestic abuse, maternal abandonment, and a host of other ills. If they do, these factors apparently have nothing to do with their crippling lack of self-esteem that leads to ugly, self-defeating actions. Neither do these factors have anything to do with the sexually compensatory behavior in which these young girls might participate. Obviously, these young women were not seduced into becoming seducers by the messages of a culture addicted to sexual stimulation. And perhaps there's no excuse for poor young black women believing that their bodies are their tickets to pleasure—besides, that is all the cues they get from pimps, playas, teachers, preachers, daddies, hustlers, and mentors. Apparently, there are no cultural influences—no magazines or television shows—that lead them to believe that their sexuality might suspend their misery, if even for a few gilded moments at the end of the night in the backseat of a car on the edge of town—and perhaps their sanity. The factors that might contribute to a young woman's behaving promiscuously, or recklessly or even daringly are rarely considered in hip-hop, since the political economy of the "ho" is severely undervalued. (Of course it must be conceded that the definition of "ho" for many men is infamously slippery. If women give sex easily, they're "hos." If they don't, they're "bitches.")[4]

In its punishing hypocrisy, hip-hop at once deplores and craves the exuded, paraded sexuality of the "ho." As it is with most masculine cultures, many of the males in hip-hop seek promiscuous sex while resenting the women with whom they share it. This variety of femiphobia turns on the stylish dishonesty that is transmuted into masculine wisdom: Never love or partner with the women you sleep with. Such logic imbues the male psyche with a toleration of split affinities that keep it from being fatally (as opposed to usefully) divided—the male can enjoy the very thing he despises, as long as it assumes its "proper" place. In order for "it"—promiscuous sex—to assume its proper place in male lives, women must assume their proper places. They must occupy their assigned roles with an eye to fulfilling their function as determined by men. If they are "hos," they are to give unlimited, uncontested sex. If they are girlfriends or wives, they are to provide a stable domestic environment where sex is dutiful and proper. The entire arrangement is meant to maximize male sexual autonomy while limiting female sexuality, even if by dividing it into acceptable and unacceptable categories. The thought that a girlfriend or wife might be an ex-ho is a painful thought in such circles. The hip-hop credo can be summed up in this way: I want to chase women, but I want *my* woman to be chaste.

Hip-hop culture has helped to reduce the female form to its bare essence. Black women appear in rap videos in increasing stages of undress as a way for black men to bond in masculine solidarity. Even the ostensible perks of the rap video—it features black women's bodies, which are usually degraded by the larger culture, especially the black derriere, and it provides a launching pad for a career in "the industry"—fail to make men into the advocates of female opportunity that some claim to be. Praising the rump, while certainly praiseworthy on some scores, is not a feminist or particularly liberating gesture in itself, though it might be if it figured in a larger scheme to tell the complete story of black female identity. Instead, the degraded black female body is revictimized when it is eyed primarily to satisfy the male sexual appetite. Hip-hop reflects the intent of the entire culture: to reduce black female sexuality to its crudest, most stereotypical common denominator. As Sonia Sanchez says, the country tries to "asphyxiate our daughters in a state of undress, and convince them that they're hos. Even in college they [try to make them] hos. Any place [young women] walk, the country says, 'I'm going to take you back to hoedom.'" I am not arguing that there are not interesting ways that explicit sexuality is engaged in hip-hop that appeal to signifying traditions in black culture. I am addressing some brutal sexual beliefs within hip-hop that reflect the sadistic sexism of the larger culture. If hip-hop has any virtue in this regard, it is that it uncovers what the larger culture attempts to mask. The bitch-ho nexus in hip-hop is but the visible extension of mainstream society's complicated, and often troubling, gender beliefs.

Tupac was certainly caught in the bitch-ho nexus in hiphop. On "Keep Ya Head Up," he gives a "shout to my sisters on welfare," praising them for rearing children alone as he damns the cowardly fathers who flee their roosts. On "I Get Around," he and his mates brag about their sexual dalliances and celebrate their promiscuity. Many critics have suggested that this made Tupac a hypocrite. Such a reading, however, is misguided. Human sexuality is a complex amalgam of competing interests that claim space in our evolving erotic identities. If human beings are to test the integrity and strength of their sexual identity, they must experiment with a variety of partners and circumstances to define their erotic temperament. At different points in life, different identities emerge, different priorities surface. (In explaining the changes he had undergone, Tupac said, "After you get past your mad, angry 'F the world' stage, you really get into your freaky 'I want to F the world' stage, and that's where I'm at now. It's just straight-up freaky, freaky. I'm ready to put it down.") If Tupac's position—and by extension, hip-hop's views—can be said to be hypocritical, it is because it reserved that prerogative exclusively for the male gender. When women exercise that prerogative, they are scathingly attacked. When men do so, they are seen as normal and healthy. What may be even more hypocritical—since many rappers claim to stand against white dominance—is hip-hop's broad endorsement of conservative beliefs about black female sexuality. When rappers express femiphobic stances, they often recycle stereotypes of poor black women promoted by right-wing hacks: All they want is welfare, more babies, no work, and the freedom to party as they destroy the family and drive the men away.[5]

Another feature of femiphobic culture is the simplistic division of women into angels and demons, both of which are problematic. If women are viewed as angels, the moment they depart from prescribed behavior they're made into whores or bitches. If they are viewed as demons, it denies the complex sexual personae that all human beings express, parts of which I described above. Tupac's femiphobia was certainly of this Manichean variety. "He definitely believed there were two kinds of women," Jada Pinkett Smith says. "Which was a danger for Pac, because he had a way of putting you on a pedestal, and if there was one thing you did wrong, he would swear you were the devil." Smith says Tupac's views of women reflected the extremities of his entire existence. "Everything about him was extreme. That's what made him so complicated to love. There was no mercy."

If Tupac's mercilessness grew from his stringent demands on women, as unfair and complicated as they were, it also gestured toward the expectation that they carried redemptive power. The danger of such an expectation is that it exempts the expectant party from trying equally hard to bring about the desired redemption. Further, it foists onto women a charge to redeem that assumes they are awaiting the fulfillment of the masculine vision or that they are spiritual tabulae rasae with no dissenting views of how such transformation might take place. Underneath, however, is a hopeful projection of the possibility of real communion. This communion would not necessarily have to be permanent, just useful, spurring two people's emotional growth for as long as they are connected. In a discussion of film ideas that was recorded less than a month before he died, Tupac reflected on what may be termed the emotional util-

ity of intimate relationships. "This is what I do believe
about some relationships," he says. "Even though they end
bitter, it's like, this person was supposed to just come, be
with you, do this, and leave. Don't be mad. . . . People always want to latch onto the person that do the most for
them." Tupac explains an encounter with a young woman
that he initially believed was strictly physical, "nothing but a
fuck." But then he understood the deeper meaning of their
rendezvous, since it gave the young lady, who had never
been out of her home state, contact with Tupac, who
brought a wider view of the world to her doorstep. "Now I
understand what I'm supposed to be doing," he says. "She's
never been out of California. I'm supposed to be there to
just give her some experience." If this sounds condescend-
ing, unidimensional, and even oddly paternalistic, it is surely
a measure of the relentless pursuit of Tupac by women of
every color and culture. (He met her as a fan in a mall.) His
anecdote also gives a sense that he was evolving in his understanding of the purpose of relationships beyond the
cramped vision provided in much of hip-hop.

Despite the harshest dimensions of his femiphobic
views, Tupac was capable of warm relations with women.
"He was—charming is the word, especially toward older
women," actress Peggy Lipton says. "He could charm anybody. He was moody and interesting." Allison Samuels confirms Lipton's estimate of Tupac's appeal. "All the women
that knew him, that I know, loved him," she says. "They
thought he was adorable." Tupac's almost universal appeal
among women who knew him makes it difficult for any of

them to believe that he was guilty of the sexual abuse conviction that got him locked up for eleven months.

In 1993 Tupac was in New York filming *Above the Rim,* in which he played a gangster named Birdie. While there, he formed a relationship with a Haitian-born music promoter, Jacques Agnant, after whom the rapper-turned-actor chose to model his character, according to some of Tupac's friends. In the flush of success—his second album, *Strictly 4 My N.I.G.G.A.Z.,* had debuted at number one, and his second film, *Poetic Justice,* was faring well at the box office—Tupac and Agnant ventured on a November night to Nell's, an upscale downtown New York club. Tupac greeted other stars that night, including the New Jersey Nets basketball star Derrick Coleman and New York Jets football legend Ronnie Lott, both of whom feted his accomplishments. Their kudos thrilled the rapper and in a way betokened the sturdy black male mentorship that Tupac lacked but sorely needed, especially in light of the trauma he was about to confront.[6]

A friend of Agnant's introduced twenty-two-year-old Tupac to nineteen-year-old Ayanna Jackson. The couple danced and worked their way into a dark corner, where Jackson allegedly proceeded to give Tupac oral sex. They retired to Tupac's Parker Meridien suite, where they smoked marijuana and had intercourse. The next day Jackson left several messages on Tupac's voice mail, one of which praised him for his prowess. Four days later Man Man (Charles Fuller), Tupac's friend and road manager, arranged for Jackson to visit Tupac at his hotel again after he finished a New Jersey concert. When she arrived, Jackson found Tupac, Man Man, Agnant, and a friend of Agnant's in the room. After they all watched television, Jackson and Tupac went into the bedroom, where the other three men joined them later. There is great dispute about what happened next. According to Jackson, she was forced to give Tupac oral sex as Agnant partially undressed her and held her from behind. Then, she says, Tupac held her while she was coerced to perform oral sex on Agnant's friend. Man Man, she says, did nothing. Tupac says he departed the suite when he saw where things were heading but lacked the interest to participate, exhausted from his grueling schedule. Therefore he saw nothing. John Singleton says Tupac was consistent in the story he related to the director. Singleton remembers that Tupac said, "This girl comes to see Tupac [who is] in the room sleeping. He doesn't really want to see her, but she starts giving him a massage." She wants to have sex with Tupac, who is not in the mood. "The guys in the room are like, 'Well, I want to fuck' . . . and [Jackson] comes and begins to partially have sex with everyone in the room, except for [Tupac], and . . . he doesn't want to have anything to do with it." That is when things turn bad. "There's one guy in the room that crosses the road: He tries to stick his dick in her ass, and she goes crazy, screaming, 'What the fuck are you doing?'" She runs out of the room, and Tupac unsuccessfully attempts to track her down to console her. In the meantime Agnant's friend departs.

After she left the suite in tears, Jackson reported the incident to the hotel security; they in turn phoned the police. Tupac, Man Man, and Agnant were arrested. "This was two weeks from the incident in Atlanta, with the shooting of the two undercover police officers," publicist Cassandra Butcher says, referring to Tupac's earlier confrontation with plainclothes cops in Georgia. "So while we are in One Center Street [police central booking], I hear two police officers say, 'That's that motherfucker who shot those cops in Atlanta.'" The three were indicted for sexual abuse, sodomy, and weapons charges, since two guns were found in the hotel suite. Agnant's lawyer successfully got his client's case severed from that of his two codefendants, because only Tupac and Man Man were charged with the possession of weapons. This prompted Tupac to suspect that Agnant was a government informer who had set him up, a claim he later made on record, for which Agnant sued Tupac's estate and his record company, publisher, producer, and the engineer of the song. Tupac was eventually sentenced to one and a half to four and a half years in prison for two counts of sexual abuse for forcibly touching Jackson's buttocks (although Tupac always maintained that he was innocent of the abuse charge)—a compromise verdict of sorts, since he was acquitted of the sodomy and weapons charges.

It was reported that Tupac broke down and cried when he was sentenced by the judge, but Karen Lee says that is not so. "When we got to court, and before they gave him the sentence and [the judge] asked him if there was anything he wanted to say, he got up and he spoke to the judge first," says Lee, preparing to paraphrase Tupac. "He told him, 'You have not looked at me one time during this whole case. You doodled, you have written on pieces of paper, so

how can I ever expect justice?'" She says that it was only when he spoke to his friend Man Man that he cried. "He spoke to the girl [Jackson] and apologized to her, not because he did anything, but he apologized for the situation," Lee says. "And then he looked at Charles [Man Man], and that's when he broke down. He said, 'I came and told you that I was going to take you out of the gutter and bring you with me, and we were going to the top. And little did I know that being with me would take you further down than you had ever been.'" Bail jumped "from $50,000 to $3 million," Lee says. The fee was beyond reason, reflecting that Tupac had struck a nerve in the justice system. Before his appearance in court to be sentenced, Tupac had been shot five times in an apparent robbery attempt in a Times Square recording studio where he went to guest on the recording of a rapper who allegedly had ties to Agnant. After Tupac's sentencing, Agnant's indictment was dismissed, as he pleaded guilty to two lesser charges.[7]

Tupac maintained his innocence to the end, though he took responsibility for failing to monitor the situation in his own suite. Allison Samuels interviewed Tupac about the incident and says he "didn't waver" about "what happened to the girl," but he was "pretty responsible" in his insistence that he shouldn't have allowed "the other guys to do it." Lee says, "There wasn't venom in his heart like that to sexually abuse a woman. That's always about power. His power was in his words. He wasn't looking to overpower somebody." Chastising Jackson, Lee asks, "Who gives a brother a blow job on a dance floor? Respect is not the first thing that comes out." Jada Pinkett Smith says that she chided Tupac for being in the room under such dire circumstances, especially since he always made sure she was safe. "If that . . . had happened to me," Smith says, "he would have killed somebody." She says she told the rapper that regardless of what happened, he should have protected Ayanna Jackson at all costs. He agreed. "He understood that, and that was part of what ate at his soul."

Although Tupac admitted that he should not have ignored the problems at hand in his hotel suite, Lee says he chafed at the thought that a black woman would charge him with sexual abuse. "He was devastated by that," says Lee. "It took a while for him to understand. He said, 'I spent all this time praising these black women, and this girl does this to me.'" No doubt Tupac was referring to songs like "Brenda's Got a Baby" and "Keep Ya Head Up," although he might have forgotten "Lunatic," where he boasted, "This is the life, new bitch every night." Or his boasts on "I Get Around." Writer Khephra Burns calls such sentiments self-serving. "There's no love there," Burns says. "It's totally selfish sex in which the women are simply props to massage his dick and ego." Burns also spots a flaw in the metaphors that sexist rappers deploy. "[Tupac] ain't got time for commitment because he's a playa. In fact, the game is the primary metaphor. But games are the province of children. Like N'aim Akbar said of the players, 'Children play.' Grown folk are about something more serious—sacrificing and building community, starting with a commitment to family and the raising of children." Burns's point about Tupac's selfish sex is powerful and convincing. And his insistence that community, family, and children are central to a mature social vision is eloquent. As for the metaphor of life as game, the thought is not original with black ghetto lover-men. Philosopher Ludwig Wittgenstein spoke insightfully about language games in a way that shed light on human existence. According to Wittgenstein, games are indeed the province of human beings engaged in the critical process of self-reflection. As for distinguishing children and adults by play, it is helpful to remember that play is also a grown-up endeavor that is studied by both sociologists and philosophers. It is also good to realize that the play of professional athletes—basketball, football, tennis, and baseball *players*—is a decidedly adult affair that involves serious talent and a great deal of money. It is the deadly seriousness of hip-hop's linguistic inventions and rhetorical play that makes rappers feared social commentators and reviled cultural influences. Although the verbal venom that circulates in rap is especially troubling, it would be disingenuous to deny the traditions of rhetorical play in earlier black oral cultures, which Burns acknowledges. These cultures feature sexual explicitness, commentary on gender relations, and mutual put-downs between males and females.[8]

Still, Burns and Akbar are brilliant social critics who compellingly challenge the lethal sexism of hip-hop. C. Delores Tucker, who joined forces with conservative former secretary of education William Bennett to oppose rap's misogyny, was a target of Tupac's acid tongue. (Although it was reported that Tucker filed a suit against the dead rapper for interfering with her husband's conjugal duties, she tells me that is not true and that she filed suit against the newspapers that reported it, charging slander. Afeni Shakur says the judge threw out the suit against her son because Tucker "had never listened to one single, solitary sentence that he had said—not one word, not one song"). On his song "How Do You Want It," Tupac castigates Tucker by name: "Delores Tucker, you're a motherfucker, Instead of trying to help a nigga, you destroy a brother." And on his "Wonda Why They Call U," Tupac's justification for calling women bitches, he offers Tucker a closing salvo: "Dear Ms. Tucker, . . . I figured you wanted to know, why we call them hos bitches." But Tucker offers a surprising defense of her youthful accuser. "I don't believe that he meant a word of it," Tucker says. "I really don't." Tucker thinks that Tupac felt pressured to verbally assault her. Despite her understanding, his words stung. "Still, it's a message that reached down to the children, and I'd walk around, everywhere I walked, 'That's C. Delores Tucker, the motherfucker.' And he's the one who uttered the words.'" Even in prison Tupac maintained his opposition to Tucker's rabid campaign against rap's rhetorical excesses. "Delores Tucker just want to get a name, which she won't find," he says in the interview in prison. "I don't see how she could say she's helping the black community to strike back at us. We are the black community; we are part of the black community."

Besides his revolutionary heritage and rap career, Tupac's insistence on his identification with the black community had a lot to do with the love he felt from its female members. The director Reginald Hudlin argues that Tupac "was handsome in a way that women [would say]: 'Well, I hate gangsta rap, but that Tupac is cute.' He was a guy who was the exception to the rule." But Hudlin says that Tupac's exceptional appeal was driven by a female culture that prizes the naughty rebel. "Women always have this kind of 'bad-boy' thing, where they want the aggressor, the tough guy who has the heart of gold. And Tupac was that. So women naturally wanted to mother him, protect him, be loved by him because he was that classic archetype." Yet that is the very archetype that caused Tupac pain at seventeen. Stanley Crouch sees that archetype as particularly harmful. "Once that kind of guy was created—the Afro-American version of what Marlon Brando and those guys on motorcycles represented for white America in the late fifties—it began a certain kind of behavior," Crouch says. He suggests that black communities have suffered primarily because females bought into the bad-boy archetype. "My theory is the day that the black females decide they're tired of that, that's the end of that," Crouch argues. "They can talk all that stuff about this is the true black culture, this is the real brother, and all of that. If the real brother can't get no date, the real brother is going to become another kind of real brother." Crouch sees a particular danger in the bad boy's becoming a sex object: He will be knighted by popular culture and encourage younger boys to emulate him. "The guy who might have, when he was twelve, questioned whether or not he should knock your wife in the head, by fifteen or sixteen, he might not even question that," Crouch says. "Because guys who act like that are millionaires." Tupac was a prime example. "One guy said that he was working on a set when they did *Above the Rim* here in New York. He said he had never before seen that many women, black and white, show up for anybody as came to New York looking for Tupac on the set when he was playing."

Tupac was torn his entire short life about what he wanted and expected from women. If his heart was bruised at seventeen because the bad-boy archetype trumped his nice-guy image, he vigorously compensated for its defeat in the few years he had remaining. And if the psychic wounds and soul scars he suffered as an adolescent provoked femiphobia, he was equally capable of genuine affection with the women he loved. Though confusing for him as a youth to know what to do to get the kind of woman he wanted, it was equally difficult for him in his twenties to get the kind of woman who wanted *all* of him. "He said it was really hard for him to find a woman," lawyer Shawn Chapman says. "Because women who were attracted to his sensitive side couldn't understand his thug side. And the women attracted to the thug side couldn't understand the sensitive side." That is a dilemma Tupac took to his grave.

CHAPTER 7

"But Do the Lord Care?"

God, Suffering, Compassion, and Death in the Ghetto

When Tupac was murdered, Baptist pastor Reverend Willie Wilson received calls from a couple of local radio station personalities. "Reverend, can you do something?" they asked. "We're getting a flood of calls from young people who are in such grief and pain." Wilson agreed to hold a memorial service for the slain rapper in his Washington, D.C., church. It drew youth from across the city who were, in Wilson's words, "befuddled, bewildered, lost [and] disillusioned." In Wilson's mind, the service would give "these young people a place to channel their feelings." Wilson's eulogy may have startled some in the religious community and beyond. "Hip-hop artists in many instances are the preachers of their generation, preaching a message which, too often, those who have been given the charge to preach prophetic words to the people have not given," Wilson said at the service. "The Tupacs of the world have responded and in many instances have reflected . . . that Scripture that comes to mind: 'If you don't speak out, then the rocks will cry out.' I think in a very real sense these pop artists are the rocks that are crying out with prophetic words." About Tupac's role in what might be termed a postindustrial urban prophecy, Wilson was clear: "He was their preacher, if you will, who brought a message that [young people] can identify with, related to what was real, that spoke to the reality of the circumstances, situations [and] environments they have to deal with every day."

If Wilson's words appear outlandish to some, perhaps even sacrilegious to others, it might help to remember that Tupac was obsessed with God. His lyrics drip with a sense of the divine. In "So Many Tears," he asks God to intervene in his suffering, "God can you feel me? / Take me away from all the pressure and all the pain." In "Only God Can Judge Me," Tupac seeks an answer for his existence and his friends' deaths, and in "I Wonder if Heaven Got a Ghetto" Tupac declares his sympathy for thug life while pondering his destiny. In "Staring at the Word Through My Rearview," Tupac questions the divine presence when he says, "Go on baby scream to God, he can't hear you." In "Are You Still Down?" Tupac pleads for salvation: "Please

God come and save me / Had to work with what you gave me." On "Picture Me Rolling," Tupac wonders if God's forgiveness is forthcoming as he asks, "Will God forgive me for all the dirt a nigga did to feed his kids?" "White Man's World" combines Tupac's request for divine favor and retribution in a fashion reminiscent of the Psalms: "God bless me please / . . . Making all my enemies bleed." In "Hail Mary" Tupac evokes prayer tradition. "Bomb First" exhibits an ecumenical religious sensibility as he observes, "Spirits spurting spiritual lyrics / Like the Holy Koran." And in "Life Goes On," Tupac, as Martin Luther King Jr. said the slaves did in earlier generations, turns into a declaration what had been his constant question of the afterlife's accessibility to thugs: "There's a Heaven for a 'G.'" Finally, Tupac's song "I Ain't Mad at Cha" was famously made into a premonitory video that brimmed with religious imagery. In the video he codirected shortly before his death, Tupac is shot five times by an unidentified assailant as he walks the street with a friend, who helplessly watches as Tupac dies. A character playing Redd Foxx greets Tupac at the Pearly Gates, and the two are quickly joined by figures playing other black legends who have died, including Nat King Cole, Billie Holiday, Dorothy Dandridge, Sarah Vaughn, Jimi Hendrix, Miles Davis, Louis Armstrong, Sammy Davis Jr., Josephine Baker, and Marvin Gaye. Tupac eventually returns to earth as an angel, dressed in white and smoking a cigarette, keeping watch over the friends he left behind. When the video first appeared, his mother is alleged to have said that it was her son's way of making peace with God.[1]

To be sure, Tupac's religious ideas were complex and unorthodox, perhaps even contradictory, though that would not make him unique among believers. From his youth, Tupac was interested in spiritual matters. "He studied every spiritual teacher you could imagine," his early mentor Leila Steinberg says. "His songs were calculated to take you back to the Bible. Take the song 'Blasphemy,' for example, where he talks about ten rules to the game. What were the ten rules? What did the Ten Commandments say? That there are ten rules to the game. He really wanted you to examine hypocrisy and the truth." Although he was deeply spiritual, Steinberg says that Tupac sought to question organized religion. "He always talked about the holy triangle, the most volatile area in the planet," she says. "The corners [are] Christianity, Islam, and Judaism, the three strongest, vocal organized religions." According to Steinberg, Tupac was especially interested in making people think about conceptions of sin: "He really wanted you to question [sin] so that you'd understand that there is a spiritual element to life. That if you don't get the sense of God in your breath and your being on this planet, you've lost it, [and that] you have to really come to the truth there is a spiritual force in this universe . . . to help correct what the Bible should teach." It is apparent that Tupac aimed to enhance awareness of the divine, of spiritual reality, by means of challenging orthodox beliefs and traditional religious practices. Steinberg says that Tupac aimed to use his spiritual beliefs to tear down ethnic and national barriers. The world's "others" would be instrumental in such a project. "Pac really thought that [these] 'others' would usher in a new consciousness where to be . . . black or 'other' would be okay. And that was his dream, to embrace diversity." Steinberg says that Tupac yearned as a youth to create a society where spiritual enlightenment could be fostered and respected, "whatever the teachings were, whether they were Hindu or Muslim or Jewish. . . . He really wanted to be a vehicle for that dialogue."

Tupac's hopefulness and ambition befit a seventeen-year-old. Still, it is notable that a poor black youth who was bounced from home to home with little means of support should harbor such grand aspirations. On the surface, his desires may be read as compensation for the stability and trust absent in his own life. But that would ignore the sped-up maturity in other spheres that resulted from his poverty and his mother's addiction. It would also overlook Tupac's attempt to wrestle with the great ideas that came his way through his arts education, but especially his own reading. Perhaps his harsh circumstances fueled in him the desire to destroy all barriers to human community, including religious and racial hindrances to brotherhood. Instead of a liability, his youth may have been an advantage, in the way that a naive belief in the possibility of solidarity often trumps hoary antagonisms to such a belief. To paraphrase Thomas Edison, it may be the youth ignorant of the limitations on true religious and racial harmony who achieves that end over the protests of the learned elder. "We're not talking about me having discussions with somebody in their late twenties at Hunter College," Steinberg says. "We're talking about Pac . . . [discussing] what could be done on this planet. It was tangible to him." Tupac truly felt that he and others could help transform the world. "It wasn't like some people [who say], 'I can't make a difference.' Pac thought every single one of us could . . . really make a difference and [that] it was at the tip of his fingers," that it was "not an unachievable goal." If his ideals for spiritual communion were optimistic, his views of spiritual transformation were decidedly realistic, even surprisingly mature and critical. "We would sit at the Bohdi Tree Bookstore and get books on . . . the spiritual movement," Steinberg recalls. "He thought that spirituality, as many people explore it, is racially biased. It's a privilege to be able to ponder the great spiritual truths. Because if you are a poor person in the ghetto with no money, how can you expound on life? So [Tupac said] it's very racist to have the luxury of exploring your humanness, because when you're in the hood, you don't get to ponder because you're trying to eat. And Pac wanted to open the doors for all of us to be able to have spiritual conversations and to ponder the meaning of life." A lesson, to be sure, crassly overlooked by many a would-be guru who tutors remedies for spiritual malaise that discount the circumstances and experiences of the oppressed.

It is also worth noting that unlike many advocates of revolution, the younger Tupac entertained a holistic view of social change that did not downplay the crucial role of spirituality in a transformed world. According to Steinberg, this sharply contrasted with the worldview that she and Tupac inherited from revolutionary mothers. "We sat one day talking about our mothers, how both of us felt like our mothers were our children," Steinberg says. "Well, both of our mothers were products of the idea of revolution . . . [but it] has to be multidimensional, and neither one of us felt like our mothers quite got it. . . . They were younger than us. We came in older, and so we had to take their hands and teach them." Steinberg says Tupac believed that revolution "had to be emotional . . . had to be spiritual" to be effective. "You can't have a spiritual revolution that is not all-inclusive," that does not embrace the "physical, sexual, and political."

Tupac's passion for spiritual matters never left him, although its form and function in his later life may have become almost unrecognizable by earlier standards. Besides, the young person who argued for holistic spiritual revolution had not yet been tested by fast fame and instant wealth. By his own admission, Tupac was "bitter" about the poverty he was reared in, but only later, through his lyrics, did the world discover just how much he had really suffered. That suffering led him to deepen his understanding of spirituality and of God. "He had his own special relationship with God," Jada Pinkett Smith says. "I think there was a part of Pac that knew that God had his hands on him." Smith believes, however, that Tupac's heavy reliance on weed and alcohol made it difficult to discern his faith. "It's hard to make sense out of it, like in our terms of what makes sense. You can't rationalize what is really going on in the mind of a man who is not clear, and who is as brilliant as he is . . . but I just know that he did have a very strong relationship with God." If the anatomy of his belief was hard to trace, its effects were nonetheless discernible in the love he had for his people. Rapper Big Tray Dee, who performed a song with Tupac on the *Gridlock'd* soundtrack, said that Tupac "had a lot of things on his mind that he addressed through his songs. And I knew he was a real spiritual person, maybe not as far as proclaiming it, but you can hear it in his songs, in his art. He is looking for an answer, trying to find it with his people, through his music."

The answers Tupac found in his music and the people he found them with often offended traditional believers. According to Bishop T. D. Jakes, Tupac's messages were certainly prophetic, but in a way that revealed his pain and suffering, not in a manner that helped society clarify its direction. Tupac's message was "so prophetic that in many ways" it warned of the "inevitable outcome" of his own despair. Tupac "cried a blood-curdling scream that we called music, which in many ways may have been a cry for help." For Jakes, Tupac represents a generation that "had trodden underfoot the principles of God, leaving their ideas over God instead of God's ideas reigning over theirs." Jakes says that "Tupac and others like him epitomize for us the perils of our times," full of entertainers who are not real leaders. "My fear is that in the absence of strong unity in our community, these entertaining voices have been mistaken for the messiahs of a generation who has lost their way and desperately needs a compass that directs them beyond a lyric that excites them." Such a view, however, overlooks the urgent spiritual crises passed on to the hip-hop generation by older black generations. It also slights the initiative and ingenuity of poor black youth who filled a leadership vacuum with artistic expression. Jakes is right to say we must not confuse the venting of despair with prophetic ardor. Yet countless sacred narratives are hardly distinguishable from contemporary rap by this standard. The prophet Jeremiah belched despair from the belly of his relentless pessimism. And the Psalms are full of midnight and bad cheer. This is not to argue that the contrasting moral frameworks of rap and religion do not color our interpretation of their often-opposing creeds. But we must not forget that unpopular and unacceptable views are sometimes later regarded as prophetic. It is a central moral contention of Christianity that God may be disguised in the clothing—and maybe even the rap—of society's most despised members.[2]

"I remember when [Tupac] died, someone at Columbia University said, 'Why would you write a poem about Tupac?'" poet Sonia Sanchez recalls. "'He was a thug.'" After telling her questioner that all black men and women in America at one time or another may be similarly viewed, she pointed to some icons that were also scorned. "Martin [Luther King Jr.] was considered that way when he was arrested. And certainly Jesus was, too." Sanchez argues that "this theological space in hip-hop" is not unfamiliar to radical believers who recognize that Jesus was judged harshly by religious folk. "And he might be viewed as a criminal by good, holy Christian people going into these churches," she argues. "I always say to [them] when they really get kind of nasty, 'If Jesus would come in your church, he'd be crucified again.' Because Jesus was a bad dude. He was challenging what I call the orthodox criminals." Sanchez contends that Tupac did the same, challenging those figures that oppress black communities and distort black identity. "Pac was searching for his black Jesus," Sanchez says. "He was searching for something that could replace this thing that he had seen," referring to harmful religious ideas that stunted the quest for black liberation. "He is really at some point looking and trying to figure out: exactly how do you get back to yourself, to your black self?"[3]

If the point of hip-hop spirituality is to support the quest for authentic black selfhood, the question of the kind of selves produced in hip-hop is paramount. The debate in hip-hop over authentic black identity is contentious enough to warrant a disclaimer: Different visions of the culture yield different identities. Those hip-hoppers concerned with the elevation of the race through edifying stories of black achievement view themselves as custodians of their generation's moral memory. A high premium is placed on recognizing and exploiting the historic continuities between black generations. There is also a strong emphasis on combating self-destructive habits—glamorizing violence, promoting gang culture, encouraging misogyny, and codifying self-hatred—that find expression in quarters of hip-hop. Hip-hoppers who address thug life, gang culture, and ghetto existence view themselves as urban poets whose job it is to tell the truth about poor black life on the streets. Great stock is placed in tales of urban woe that depict in chilling detail the consequences of living outside the law, beneath the middle class, and without social legitimacy. There is in this arena of hip-hop a shameless glorification of figures otherwise stigmatized in society, including the player, the pimp, the mack, and the hustler. Needless to say, explicit sexuality, illegal behavior, sexism, and violence are encouraged. These conflicting views, of course, produce competing views of black selfhood and the moral visions they support. If such visions of black selfhood imply a spiritual foundation, then a conception of God is not far away. It is easy enough to detect the divine in hip-hop communities that value traditional expressions of religious sentiment. But what of thug culture, or, to quote Tupac, "Is there a Heaven for a 'G'?"

The gangsta's God—or the thug's theology—is intimately linked to his beliefs about how society operates and who is in control. For many thugs, God is the great accomplice to a violent lifestyle. Big Syke, Tupac's mentor in thug heuristics, states a belief that may shock outsiders. "God is a killer, too," he says. "Don't get it twisted. God kills a lot of people. He wipes them out in masses. God is real." This may ring true for the vengeful deity depicted in the Old Testament, where the principle of a life for a life prevailed. But the last couple of millennia have witnessed a transformation of God's image. To an extent, thug theology is willfully anachronistic or at least staunchly traditional. To those who claim that thugs are brutal and vicious and incapable of decency, it may be well to remember the beliefs they appeal to in justifying their behavior. "You make a pact with God, and ask him to forgive you and move on, because sometimes you get put in the path to kill. . . . I feel I'm in cool standings with God." Syke argues that God is aware of how the social order reflects a retributive philosophy. "God knows I'm not running around here trying to do anything wrong to anybody. But if somebody is trying to do something wrong to me, then I know I did wrong to people before, so now I have to realize that it could be just the repercussions from what I did. Now I've got to accept it like a man and go to God if I get killed. But it might be that I got to kill this cat, because he was in here doing something he ain't supposed to do. That's just how life goes."

Syke says he did not have "deep conversations with Pac" about God. "We were just always talking, 'God, please forgive me,' because it's serious out here. It's the only thing we got." In justifying the thug lifestyle, Syke appeals to the Bible to make his point. "I'm not a Bible person, but from what I'm told, Moses was a killer," Syke says. "[There are] killers in the Bible that God used for him, after they were cleaned up. 'Okay, you did what you did, but I need you over here. You are going to be one of my soldiers.'" Still, the rules of the universe reflect God's will. Think of thugs as natural law theologians after a fashion. "We can go with some spiritual-type thing that gives answers to everything that you are looking for, if you look for it. Like, 'What goes around comes around.' That's true. You . . . keep doing shit, and this is going to come back around to you. To this day, I wonder, 'Do I still have to answer for some things that I did in my past?' But if I do, I'm cool with God, because God knows I changed, so it's all right. I'm ready to leave any day."

The readiness to die is characteristic of thug theology, as much because of the intensity of the suffering they observe and endure—and quite often cause—as the belief that they have squared themselves with God. Suffering—as misery and unhappiness, as pain and evil observed—was a constant theme in Tupac's work. "Pac was one of the most valuable Americans of his generation," rapper Mos Def says. "But he was also one of the most flawed and conflicted and really unhappy persons as well. Pac was unhappy

here. I think we all sensed that. We didn't listen to him [when he said,] 'I'm not happy.' He wasn't happy here; he was given a rough time." Tupac's suffering affects Mos Def to this day. "I cry a lot thinking about him, because I felt like we couldn't help him. He was begging for it." If there is a wide perception that Mos Def is right (and many who knew Tupac agree), what was the cause of Tupac's unhappiness? Leila Steinberg traces it to his brutalizing prison experience. Ironically, Tupac as a young man often told Leila that a prison stay, a staple of black male existence, would give him invaluable experience to draw on in writing his raps. But he had a different story after being locked up for eleven months. "I asked him, 'Did it give you insight? Did it give you any more respect?'" Leila says. "Jail killed my spirit," Tupac replied. "It wore me out. I'm tired now. I don't know if I'm making any difference." It was a disconcerting retreat from Tupac's earlier optimism about each person's ability to change the world. "I saw a change when he came home," Steinberg says. "I mean, there was new fire, because he was twenty-four–seven, working like crazy. But he wasn't happy anymore. That light and the wit, the way that he would shine, it was completely changed, dimmed after that experience. It was so sad to see the change in his spirit because of what happened. It was heartbreaking."

Jada Pinkett Smith agrees. Before he went to jail, Tupac had pledged to Smith to renounce his dangerous lifestyle. "I'm going to stop thugging," he told Smith. "I am getting rid of the guns; I'm getting rid of all these niggas around me. I'm changing, Jada. I don't want to do this rap thing anymore. I'm just going to act." Despite his wish to transform himself, Tupac was trapped by his past. "And then he went to jail and turned into a totally different person," Smith says. "I think a part of Pac just died right there, and then he just sold his soul. I mean, the one thing about Pac is that he thought he could work around God . . . and work around the devil. . . . He really thought he had some tricks up his sleeves." Instead, Tupac was defeated by the very experience he once deemed crucial to the black male existence. "That was the [downward] spiral of his life," John Singleton says. "That was where the Tupac that I knew ended." Singleton thinks the key to Tupac's unhappiness in prison rests with the extreme humiliation he endured, a humiliation that may have been sexual. "Nobody wants to talk about that," Singleton says. "Not one muthafucka that you're going to talk to is going to talk about what they think did or did not happen to Tupac in jail. . . . Nobody wants to speculate. People are saying he was raped in jail, but nobody wants to talk about it." Whatever happened, it is clear that Tupac's energy for life drastically changed. "The light that was in his eyes [before prison] wasn't there. When he got out of jail, I think he was a perfect nihilistic vision of what people kind of believe a black man in America as a hip-hop artist should be, because he really did not give a fuck, and he just put it all in his music."

Although prison certainly exacerbated Tupac's unhappiness, it did not create his misery. Long before he went to jail, Tupac anguished over racism and poverty. He decried a dysfunctional society that profited from these ills while forcing poor blacks to become thugs and outlaws. Tupac rejected the argument that other choices loomed for poor blacks in attacking social suffering—choices that were, in fact, made by most poor blacks, such as going to school to become upwardly mobile, attending church or temple to boost one's faith, or protesting injustice through marches. Tupac thought those were futile strategies for folk whose aspirations to excel were aborted at birth.

Many critics think that his remedy—an elevation of thug rhetoric and a glorification of gang behavior—only increases the suffering. Khephra Burns argues that Tupac's rationalization of thug behavior as the only recourse open to folk who have "no legitimate options for survival" is wrongheaded. "Black folk coming through Howard and Morehouse and Spelman and [other black colleges] throughout the South by the thousands give the lie to that line of bullshit," Burns says. "And these are black folk coming from Compton and Cabrini Green and Harlem and black communities all over the country." Burns points out that "despite circumstances similar to those the thugs came up in, [they] simply opted to pay attention and do their homework instead of hanging out." Stanley Crouch agrees, insisting that the thug mentality threatens the survival and moral health of poor black communities. "The question that a guy like Tupac Shakur raises is whether or not the chaos with which certain people in impoverished situations will find themselves surrounded by should be answered by chaotic behavior," says Crouch. "When you answer the chaos with more chaos, then that creates a double burden for everybody else." Crouch argues that thuggish behavior only hurts "a community that's got a bad relationship with the police department, [where] people are unemployed, you've got teenage pregnancy, [and] people don't necessarily know how to take the best care of themselves in terms of their health. . . . I think that that's adding to the problem." It is clear that Tupac wavered between conceding thug life's brutality even as he embraced its lethal inevitability. That tension made him an ideal spokesman for the moral ambiguities at the heart of hard-core hip-hop.

In embracing thug life, he was at once plague and prophet. Tupac believed he spoke for the desperately demobilized and degraded lumpen who were, as he said on one of his songs, "young [and] strapped," those who "don't give a fuck." Perhaps the key sentence is the one that concludes this litany of woes: "I'm hopeless." Tupac's personal battles with hopelessness had to do with "that convoluted thing of wanting to have hope but not wanting the hope to be dashed," Singleton says. Still, Tupac managed to transmute his hopelessness into anger at hypocrisy in American politics. Speaking about Bob Dole, C. Delores Tucker, and Pat Buchanan, Tupac said, in outtakes from an MTV interview, "Those are the people destroying the values . . . that keep us together." Tupac also targeted "those people that beat those Mexicans up that was trying to come in our country," referring to the infamous police beating of fleeing illegal Mexican immigrants in California that was broadcast on television news programs around the country. "That's what they should be trying to ban, you know what I mean? You should see how many times they play that [video of the beating] 'cause they love seeing people suffer. So why shouldn't we rap about it? Why shouldn't we talk about it? If all we see is suffering and all we see is profit from suffering?"

Tupac answered suffering in part by acts of care and compassion. Tupac's compassion grew from his belief that, as Mos Def says, "we are responsible for one another." In taking that responsibility seriously, Tupac sought to care not only for his family but also for those beyond his circle of kin. He displayed a remarkable sensitivity to the suffering he saw around him. Publicist Karen Lee says that on Tupac's first promotional tour in Washington, D.C., he made media appearances and visited schools "because little kids were just totally mesmerized by him." As the limousine whisked them to the airport to travel to the next stop, Tupac watched a television report about a young black girl who had been attacked by two pit bulls and rushed to the hospital. "He has the limo driver turn around," Lee says, "and we go to the hospital. He doesn't know these people." When Tupac arrived at the hospital, the girl was in surgery. "I just wanted to come and let you know that I'm praying for you," Tupac told her parents, who were overwhelmed by the gesture. The girl survived. "The mother and child moved to Atlanta and became very, very close with [Tupac's] family. But nobody talked about that." By most accounts, Tupac liked it that way.

Cassandra Butcher tells a similar story of Tupac's reading about a gravely ill child while he was on a plane trip and demanding to be taken to the hospital before fulfilling any press obligations. "But he didn't want any press. He felt very strongly about that." John Singleton witnessed Tupac's generosity to his kin, which became burdensome in its own way. Singleton says Tupac's success "complicated his life" by encouraging his family to depend on him. "Everybody wants money from you, and everybody wants you to take care of them," he says. "Everybody wants you to buy them cars and weed and everything like this. And Tupac was very much a man of the people, so he never ran from that. He always felt that he had a responsibility to take care of the people around him who felt that they needed him. . . . He had a big heart like that."

Tupac's big heart was apparent when he went on location in Harlem to film *Above the Rim*. "Tupac loved his people more than anything," Butcher says. "To see him in Harlem, in those communities, it was really remarkable." According to Butcher, most actors give little more than perfunctory greetings to residents in the neighborhoods in which they film, retreating for the most part to their trailers. "Tupac wasn't like that. He couldn't just eat in the catering area with all of the crew and see that these people were hungry or see that these people wanted to talk to him. He really connected, and these were his brothers and sisters, and he meant it from his heart, like nothing I've seen before." Although Al Sharpton says that Tupac "didn't want to be a role model and a leader," he was still sensitive to his impact on the youth with whom he interacted. Los Angeles radio personality Big Boy, a former hip-hop bodyguard, illustrates the point with a humorous story. After doing a show in Seattle, the van that Tupac and several other groups were traveling in was stopped by the police. When the police were distracted by a mob of fans, Tupac sought to "make the best of our time," Big Boy remembers. "So Pac pulls out a joint, and he was about to put it to his mouth, and there was this little girl [who saw him]." After spotting her,

Tupac pulled the little girl close to him. "Listen," Tupac said, "you just caught me doing something real bad, something that I shouldn't be doing. But this is a secret between me and you. . . . Don't tell anybody. This is how you got me and I got you." Big Boy laughs as he recalls the little girl's "just sitting there and just looking at him, and just nodding, 'Okay, okay.'"

Tupac's sensitivity to children drew from a vulnerability that flashed in critical moments, despite his hard reputation. "Pac was emotional," says Leila Steinberg. "He cried around me a lot. He was man enough to cry; he would always tell you that." Before he had to protect his thug image, Tupac was more willing to expose his heart. "You've got to know that he was a very different young man at seventeen," she says. "Pac was very gentle" and had "a feminine quality that most men don't balance" with their masculinity. Even as a famed entertainer, Tupac flashed a soft side. "There was something vulnerable about Tupac that was extremely captivating," says Congresswoman Maxine Waters. "I think it was felt by anybody who paid attention to him. . . . It's a kind of quality that I saw in Richard Pryor [whose voice Tupac sampled on his "Heartz of Men"], very vulnerable, very bright." It was that same vulnerability that made Tupac aware of the vulnerability of the people he loved. When a videographer asked Tupac during the filming of *Above the Rim* what it felt like to be on his "old stomping grounds" in Harlem, he directed the filmmaker to the several hundred fans grouped around him. "He did not want the cameras on him to take attention away from what was going on in the hood," says Cassandra Butcher. "And he says to the camera,

'Man, I'm not the story. Talk to some of these niggas on the streets. That's the story. That's where you can make movies all day. Talk to them.'" Butcher also experienced the rougher edge of Tupac's compassion. Once, after crying when it appeared the rapper would stand up a major network media show, Butcher was duly reprimanded. "Don't fucking cry in here," Tupac barked. "Don't cry. Don't be like my mother. Don't cry." Butcher says that Tupac was "so mean and angry at the time," but that she later realized his motive: "He just could not stand to see the pain of someone else."

If Tupac was incapable of witnessing others' pain, he was equally incapable of enduring their rejection. "One of Pac's problems was he loved a lot, and he loved hard, and he was very passionate about what he loved," rapper Talib Kweli says. "And he loved freedom, and he loved black people to the point where it pained him, and you could hear it in his records. When he felt like that love wasn't reciprocated, it hurt him." It not only hurt Tupac to be denied the love he believed he deserved; it angered him. "A lot of the people he lashed out against were people he was genuinely hurt by, whether they felt like they hurt him or not." Near the end of his life, Tupac lashed out at a number of rappers, most notably rapper Notorious B.I.G. ("Biggie") and his producer and label head, Sean "Puffy" Combs. Tupac proclaimed publicly that Biggie and Combs set him up when he was shot during the attempted robbery of a New York recording studio. Although there was never any proof for Tupac's claim—and in fact, a person close to him told me that Tupac "knew in his heart that Biggie and Puffy had nothing to do with his getting shot in New York" and that the "shot that went through near his groin area, the bullets came out of *his* gun" tucked in his pants—the rapper escalated their personal conflict into what eventually became an infamous and violent beef between East and West Coast rappers. Tupac released an especially effective and hateful single, "Hit 'Em Up," that spilled his vitriol into a recording. It also signaled a recklessness that was potentially fatal. "It looked to me that he was spiraling out of control," says Talib Kweli. "And I used to say to myself, 'Something bad is going to happen to him if he continues.'"

The sense that Tupac was spinning out of control was widespread, even if most onlookers felt helpless to stop him. His self-destructive impulses were at full blast in the last year of his life. He claimed to have slept with Biggie's wife, singer Faith Evans. Hostilities flared and a gun was pulled when members of Death Row, Tupac's label, and Puffy's Bad Boy label clashed at the Soul Train Music Awards. "We were inside the show," says publicist Karen Lee, "and I knew something was going on because all of a sudden all these cops went outside." Someone told Lee that Tupac and his comrades were in the parking lot in a scuffle with some of Puffy's employees. Lee says Tupac missed his first award, and "by the time he comes in to accept his second award, I can see he's pumped up and way out of control." When the show was over, she approached Tupac, who hugged and kissed her. "I said, 'Come here.' I pulled him from the bodyguards. I said, 'What are you doing? This is all we have. There is no other show looking to book you, darling.'" But Tupac seemed bent on exploiting the coastal tensions in hip-hop to dangerous, polarizing effect. Two days before he was fatally shot, he attended the MTV Music Video Awards and got into a scuffle. He even turned on Dr. Dre, the superstar producer with whom Tupac worked when he joined Death Row. Tupac took credit for forcing Dre from Death Row, the label Dre ran with Marion "Suge" Knight. Although he acknowledges Tupac's "incredible work ethic," Dre has harsh words for Tupac's destructive behavior. "He was a person who liked to be in the middle of things that didn't concern him," Dre says. "And that was a problem." Tupac was determined to push other people to their limits, to dance with danger and ultimately, death.

Always obsessed with death, Tupac seemed to forecast—and by his actions, nearly guarantee—his demise with frightening intensity. Maxine Waters says that Tupac was "wild and unpredictable, and even troubled. I thought that he didn't know the word 'caution.' . . . He thought he was invincible. But I do think that he stared danger in the eye and didn't flinch one bit." Waters regrets that she "and others could not find a way to protect him, his talent, and his genius." C. Delores Tucker, whom Tupac considered a nemesis, says the rapper "was truly gifted," but that "a demon inside of him" didn't want him to use his talents for the good. Others, however, believe that Tupac felt haunted by destiny. "I think he absolutely knew that [his death] was coming soon," says Leila Steinberg, the first to see Tupac's poem "In the Event of My Demise," written when he was twenty-one years old. "He knew he was never going to hit thirty," says director Vondie Curtis Hall. Such a belief is dangerously liberating. "It allows you to live with a certain level of abandonment. It allows you to accept destiny without fear."[4]

The fearlessness, even recklessness, with which Tupac confronted death had a great deal to do with the death he witnessed and made records of, the mourning he did in its wake, and the God with whom he struggled to make sense of it all. There is a culture of death in pockets of hip-hop and in poor black communities that is alarming for its pervasiveness and tragic in the way it victimizes the young. The obsession with death has to do with the relentless murder and mayhem to which youth are exposed. Gang violence, drug wars, domestic abuse, social dislocation, and displaced rage at poverty erupt in ghetto death. The plague of what is usually called "black-on-black homicide" overruns black communities. The term is a misnomer, to be sure, since its cause is often the barbarisms of economic misery and its consequence, the death of another black person, is encouraged by the persistence of white supremacist myths and practices that promote black self- and other hatred. In all of its forms, death is a destructive landmark in urban black geography.

Death is also a staple of the psychic landscape of poor black youth. The dead black body—whether strangled by a relative, shot by a robber, stabbed by a jealous lover, or suffocated by a babysitter—is so common as to become metaphor itself: Suffering black flesh is the window onto the spiritual trauma that afflicts an entire generation. The yearning for death, for its relief of suffering, is marked in death envy, the soul-crushing desire to become *identical to* the dead black body. (We must remember that even the desire to be *identified with* a dead body—say, wanting to be seen as the second coming of a dead sports star, rap artist, or leader—is still life-affirming, since the recognition reaped by such an identification underscores the efforts of the living person.) The sports scholar Keith Harrison illustrates this insight with a chilling anecdote. "I went to a funeral a few years back of one of my uncles," he recalls, "and one of the things that moved me at . . . the church was the number of black men that were eighteen and nineteen getting up [and] saying how they wished they were going where my uncle Len was."

The sheer repetition of death has caused black youth to execute funeral plans. In its response to death, black youth have reversed perhaps the emblematic expression of self-aware black mortality, Martin Luther King Jr.'s cry that "every now and then I think about my own death." They think about it constantly and creatively. With astonishing clinical detachment, black youth enliven King's claim that he didn't contemplate his death "in a morbid sense." They accept the bleak inevitability of death's imminent swoop—which, in truth, is a rejection of the arbitrariness we all face, since death to these youth is viewed as the condition, not the culmination, of their existence. Black youth summon funeral directors to portray their dead bodies with a style that may defeat their being forgotten and that distinguish them from the next corpse. If these youth are cynically viewed as the canary in the coal mine—since we all die, and death really is the mark of life, their actions embody the route we all eventually take to prepare for our demise—the sacrifice of their bodies for spiritual wisdom is a symbol of our inhumanity. Even if our reasons for allowing their suffering are not nearly as callous as that, the culture of death that suffocates black youth is nonetheless damning.[5]

It makes sense that autopsy is a central mode of rap rhetoric. In hip-hop examining the dead black body—its beauties, its contributions, its distinct marks, its arrested aspirations, its foreclosed opportunities, its lost life, its representative expressions, its causes of death—is both science and magic. By detailing the horrors that enclosed the lives of their fallen friends, rap music helps to chronicle the social pathologies that grow inside the body politic and that claim black and brown lives with unacceptable regularity. But the gesture of examination is also one of self-protection: It secures the place of recent ancestors in the urban cosmology by giving them their just due. In so doing, survivors extend their lives, blessed by the memory of late comrades who intercede with the powers that be on their behalf. That is why postmortem poetry in the form of eulogy and mourning song is so powerful: It captures the collective grief of a hurting generation and bears witness to persistent terrors for survivors.[6]

Tupac was especially adept at this branch of postmortem poetry. By now the frequency of death and its remembrance has generated conventions for the rap elegy: recalling the moment and conditions under which a dead friend expired; speaking of pouring out liquor as a sign of reminiscence in the hip-hop version of African libations; calling the dead person's name on record in rap's ancestor evocation; conjuring shared activities and memories between the rapper and the departed; and the invocation of peace on the loved one's soul. Some of Tupac's most forceful and poignant work is in this vein. In "So Many Tears," Tupac remembers his friend Kato with the lyrics, "Call on the sirens, I seen him murdered in the streets / Now rest in peace." In "To Live and Die in L.A.," Tupac remarks on how he and his comrades "Shed tears as we bury niggas close to heart / What was a friend now a ghost in the dark." And in the haunting "Life Goes On," his eulogistic masterpiece, Tupac pays homage to his slain brothers: "Rest in peace young nigga / There's a Heaven for a 'G.'"

As brilliantly as he mourned death, Tupac was equally capable in his raps of wishing his enemies dead. His lyrics teem with vengeance and malevolence, as Tupac flaunts "my murderous lyrics," promises "we gonna kill all you muthafuckas," and suggests "these tricks should die." Then, too, Tupac, was scarcely able to curb what he rapped as his "urge to die," as song after song records his brutal struggle. It is precisely this combination—of mourning death, seeking to kill, and desiring to die—that makes Tupac perhaps the most powerful symbol of the multiphrenia that divides the young black urban mind. By rhetorically embodying the person murdered, the person wanting to murder, and the person mourning a murder, Tupac captured a huge range of desperate black response to death's dominion.

It was this divided soul and the people he loved and loathed that Tupac brought to the God he never gave up on. His relationship to God during his rap career took the form of an ongoing argument about the suffering he saw and the evil he endured and expressed. The compassion he summoned as well as the raps he wrote were meant to expose and relieve the pain he witnessed. In traditional theological circles, the branch of thought that seeks to answer the unmerited suffering of believers is termed theodicy. It has an analogue in social science as well, where theodicy is concerned with discerning meaning in the suffering of the masses. As an inveterate thug and a tireless, if unorthodox, believer, Tupac operated with a thug's theodicy. He may be considered what I've called a hip-hop Jeremiah, an urban prophet crying out loud about the hurt that he constantly saw and sowed.

In Tupac's raps all parties to death, evil, and suffering get a hearing—and lashing—including the crack addict, the welfare mother, the hustler, the thug, the pimp, the playa, the bitch, the ho, the politician, the rapper, the white supremacist, the innocent child, the defenseless female, the crooked cop, and the black sellout. If his love for his people and his God were intertwined with the cruel and self-defeating impulses of the lost, one must remember Tupac's proclamation on "Black Jesus": "In times of war we need somebody raw, rally the troops like a Saint that we can trust." At the end of the song, one of his comrades prays for a Black Jesus who is "like a Saint that we pray to in the ghetto." By both rejecting and embracing suffering, Tupac offers a complex prayer that does not merely glorify violence but interrogates its meaning and howls at the pain it wrecks.

"i Got Your Name Tatted on My Arm"

Reading the Black Body

"One day he had his shirt on," Johnnie Cochran remembers of an early encounter with his then new client Tupac Shakur. "He took his shirt off, and across his stomach he had 'Thug Life' on it. There's all this writing. It [was] all over the place. I would kid him about not coming to court with a lot of jewelry and stuff on. He was a very handsome boy, very handsome. He had earrings, too, you know; that is the style. But he had all this writing on his body. I asked, 'Why do you put all that stuff on your body? Is that necessary?'"

For Tupac, writing on his body was a necessary gesture of self-expression. The tattoos that dotted his physique were road signs along Tupac's unfolding, meandering identity. The ink on his body gave the world an inkling of the passions that raged in his breast. Besides "Thug Life" across his abdomen, "2 Pac" appeared on his right breast and "Nefertiti" on the left. "Outlaw" was tattooed—"tatted" in hip-hop parlance—on his right forearm, and a serpent with open jaws decorated his right shoulder. Christ in flames and a crown of thorns flashed on his right biceps. "Playaz" was inscribed on the nape of his neck. "Fuck the World" ran across his trapezoids; the same phrase, this time in script, ran across his shoulder blades. On the lower sides of his back were "Laugh Now" with a mask of comedy and "Cry Later" with a mask of tragedy. A German cross with "Exodus 18:11" stretched over his back. And "50 Niggaz" covered his sternum. As his body of work expanded, the work on his body increased.[1]

The writing on Tupac's sinewy surfaces, however, is but one feature of his riveting, spectacular presence. It may be a truism that the body is crucial to the performing artist, but in Tupac's case it is especially so. The self he projected depended heavily on the body he uneasily lived in—his expressive almond-shaped eyes, his thick lips and eyebrows, his long lashes, his radiant smile, his well-formed nose, his lithe and muscled frame, his silky mustache, his diminutive stature, and his bald head. Beyond his natural gifts, Tupac fashioned his persona—particularly as homeboy and thug—through symbolic accessories: nose studs, earrings, head rags, low-sagging jeans, designer sweatshirts, Rolex watches, diamond-encrusted Jesus piece, designer suits, skullcaps, stylish bracelets, bullet-proof vests, baseball caps, and modish rings. As a relentlessly signifying artist, Tupac embodied the idioms of black male anger: middle fingers thrust defiantly in the air as he hangs out the window of a fleeing automobile, spitting hostilely into the camera of a journalist, walking like a duck to mock injustice in the courtroom, and punching and kicking an enemy the night he was fatally wounded. Finally, Tupac's bullet-riddled body is an unavoidable symbol of the rage and murder that destroy precious black bodies.[2]

As a famously controversial black icon, Tupac's body was never completely his own. It bled into the hungry ink of a media bent on deifying, destroying, or dissecting his reputation, sometimes in the same breath. His limbs stretched across the cineplex as he attacked his craft with imploding intensity. His sturdy black back provided carriage for a slew of relatives and fictive kin who rode his notoriety to banquet tables and casino halls. The state even pinched a piece of his hide, parceling him among jails and prisons on either coast. And thousands, perhaps millions, of young black males believed his body was their body. That belief depended on a prior and remarkable identification Tupac made with masses of suffering and hopeless black males who heard their pain in his. Tupac had stopped being a star and had become a grammar: His moves, gestures, and performances were a startlingly faithful articulation of their conflicted, confused inner lives. Much of his art insisted that their bodies were his. It was if he were saying, "I will be your sacrificial lamb. I will suffer for your sake, in your place. I will tell the story of your entombment in poverty and stunted social ambition. I will narrate your lives through my chaotic, desperate, self-destructive public life. And when I die, it will be to immortalize the similar deaths of anonymous black males whose names will never scar the tissue of public attention." If all of this appears maudlin and melodramatic, perhaps even hyperbolic—and at points, it surely is—it does not negate the impact of Tupac's embodied response to the crisis of young black America.

If Tupac was in the position to sacrifice his body, especially for young black men, it was in large part because of the love he got from women. In crassly immediate terms, that meant that Tupac had his pick of the ladies, a prerogative he ardently indulged. In broader terms, it meant that the charisma and sexiness he exuded on stage and on screen created a huge market for his talents. Tupac was almost universally adored for his vibrant sensuality and his striking good looks. Actress Vivica A. Fox, who appeared in Tupac's "Dear Mama" video, says that Tupac "wasn't hard on the eyes at all. He had nice lashes, great lips; he was just working it." Actress Kim Fields says that Tupac's great charm, and his great emotion as well, was in his eyes. "There is an expressiveness about his eyes," Fields says. "It is just that there was an interesting combination in his eyes, the sadness, the determination, anger, passion, you know." Fields says that as an actor, Tupac's eyes kept "pulling me in," making her want "to know what he knew about life." She confesses that Tupac appealed to "the pure female side, too." "The way he held that lollipop in *Poetic Justice* and certain pictures that I've seen. He makes a sister want to be a lollipop the same way we wanted to be a trumpet from *Mo Better Blues*," she says laughing, referring to the Spike Lee film that starred Denzel Washington and Wesley Snipe as musicians. But even in nonsexual terms, Tupac's eyes proved to be a window onto a larger landscape of social compassion. "Some people think that young people just love him because he was hip or he looked like he was into everything," says Sonia Sanchez. "But when you looked into that young brother's eyes, at the core of his eyes was love."

Even off stage and away from the microphone, Tupac's physical presence generated intense interest. Shawn Chapman, one of Tupac's legions of lawyers, spent a good deal of time with him and observed his effect on everyday people. Chapman recalls the many times that Tupac "would have to make an appearance in the Criminal Courts Building," waiting in the hall with elderly white jurors. "They had no idea who he was," Chapman says. "But within minutes he'd have everybody just eating out of his hands, just being so funny and polite. These old white jurors were loving him. . . . He really had that effect." Chapman also felt Tupac's charms a little closer to home. Seeking to get Tupac to sign some legal documents, Chapman asked him to come by her office. Instead, he suggested they meet at the Los Angeles eatery Monty's. When she arrived, Tupac had already ordered "a bottle of Cristal, some orange juice, and some strawberries." After ordering dinner, which Tupac didn't eat because he was talking nonstop, he made his move. Again. "He's always trying to tell me why I should go out with him," Chapman says. "And I'm telling him, 'I can't go out with you; I'm your lawyer. I'm older than you.'" But the clincher is the way his body is written in ink. "I said, 'Look, you have 'outlaw' tattooed on your arm." Without missing a beat, Tupac wittily protests, "That's a work in progress. It's going to say, 'Without law, society is in chaos.'"

His romantic efforts aside—where he clearly interpreted the writing on his body for sexual advantage—Tupac's body of work, his work on his body, his work *in* his body, were clearly works in progress. In part, the imperatives of thug life and his bad-boy image led to the draping of his frame with signs and war robes, each the symbolic shroud of an intentionally esoteric gangsta code he was desperate to decipher in pubescent terms. His willingness to distill swagger and verve to their masculine essence increased his erotic register. Music videos and films alike were accoutrements of his visceral sensuality, stamping his manly presence into the eye and the collective unconscious the way his compelling baritone vibrated his aural appeal.

With Tupac the body was risk, was *at* risk, perennially exposing itself to delight and danger in fell swoops: smoking weed, fighting, brandishing weapons, getting shot, receiving oral sex in public, and chugging Alizé and Cristal. His openness to placing his body in harm's way—his willful disregard of safety through provocative machismo and irritating bluster in gang circles where symbolic gestures were lost on males who had no sense of metaphor in their pledge to keep it real—was occasionally matched by his relaxation of the body's defensive postures. "There were so many parts to Tupac," publicist Cassandra Butcher states. "I remember doing a photo shoot with him when they were doing *Poetic Justice.* . . . [Photo editor] Charlie Holland thought, 'What is

he going to do when he comes to the photo shoot?'" Tupac's bad-boy reputation made Holland believe that she was in for a tough time. "He's probably going to smoke some weed," Butcher told Holland, who suggested they dress Tupac in a pinstriped suit. "She was very British," Butcher says of Holland. "I said, 'Well, he's not going to wear that, I will tell you that. Tupac likes fatigues, and he likes regular clothing, jeans—they need to be sagging. That's what he's going to wear.'" Holland protested, saying she'd like to see Tupac "in something really different this time." When Tupac arrived at the photo shoot, he was asked what music he'd like to hear. His answer gave Butcher her first surprise. "At the time he walks in, they're listening to Mozart, and he says, 'Leave that on.'" And as expected, Tupac promptly enjoyed a few drags of his cherished joint. Holland asked Tupac to try on the black-and-white pin-striped suit. Tupac wordlessly obliged, and in a mellow mood he graced through the photo shoot with surprising poise. It was a moment Butcher never forgot. "It was just amazing and beautiful to see him moving to Mozart and Beethoven. . . . I see people do it now, and it's fun; it's all a game. But this guy could appreciate it. And that's when I re-alized this guy has a gift, and he's got a heart, and he's got a soul, and he can appreciate all forms of art. And as long as you could come to him with some form of creativity, he could appreciate that. It didn't have to be in a bottle."

The bottle, however, and the joint, too, were never to be slighted in Tupac's taxonomy of addictive escapes. From the time his mother abused alcohol and crack to the time he attempted to become a low-level drug dealer—only to be

saved not by his revolutionary forebears but by street people in Marin City—up until the moment he drank his last
drink and smoked his last joint, undoubtedly the night he
was shot in Vegas, Tupac understood the seductions and
magic (as well as the destructive, demonic consequences) of
mind-altering, body-changing substances. The creed of
weed is romanticized in hard-core hip-hop and in the hood.
The usual cry that it got the creative juices going is not the
most important claim in these circles. Weed is viewed as the
necessary adjunct to ghetto fabulousness, a bit more accessible to the hood's rank and file than Cristal and Alizé, the
drinks of choice in the Negro-riche cliques of thugged-out
movie stars and rappers (though these are increasingly one
and the same, like Snoop Dogg in Singleton's flick *Baby Boy,*
DMX in *Exit Wounds,* or Ice Cube in his duo of *Friday*
films). Befitting the outlaw character of the hard-core rapper, ingesting huge amounts of legal and illegal substances
amounts to a ghetto pass and union card. Getting high is at
once pleasurable and political: It heightens the joys to be
found in thug life while blowing smoke rings around the
constraints of the state. "Getting your buzz on," whether
from alcohol or marijuana, is also about taking off the inhi-
bitions and prohibitions that regulate the distribution of
ghetto goods, services, and pleasures. That is why there is a
close parallel, if not outright identification, between weed
and freedom. Besides the countless odes to the pleasures of
dope, hard-core hip-hop is rife with metaphors drawn from
marijuana usage.

But there is another dimension to the weed creed, one so
resolutely practical as to almost slip the notice of its heavi-

est indulgers: addiction. This may be classic self-denial, the belief that addiction happens elsewhere, with other drugs, to other bodies. But droves of youth are entranced by the joint as a gateway drug into other, more dangerous, substances, like ecstasy, heroin, and cocaine. Even as hip-hop's potheads deny the addictive character of weed, they display the addictive habits that trump the quasi science behind their denials. Glamorized 40 ouncers round out the picture of proletariat pleasures in rap. But the hard truth is that thousands of poor black youth are trapped in a haze of smoke, whether from ganja or the gun. Their smooth confluence in hip-hop's hard-core symbols only heightens the almost erotic glow they bring. Young black men and women often smoke blunts to blunt the consciousness of the social pain they endure, including violence of every kind. But the violence they engage—sometimes extending it, often seeking to avoid it—shares with the means of its escape a highly addictive quality. When they dovetail in a figure like Tupac, the combination is dangerous, even explosive, and often irresistibly sexy.[3]

Tupac's dear friend Jada Pinkett Smith was one of the few to peer through the haze. "People don't like to talk about [the fact that] Pac was an addict," she says. "He wasn't clear about too much of anything. He was really in his own world. You know, he was an alcoholic, and he was high. He was high all the time, drunk, whatever. His mind was never clear." Tupac's early publicist, Karen Lee, agrees. "The boy could smoke some weed," she declares. But Lee says that when Tupac went to prison, his head cleared up. "One of the things that just breaks my heart [is that] he was just coming into being a man when he died," Lee says. "I saw him pretty regularly when he was [in prison], and he was clearer there than he had ever been. He wasn't getting high, and . . . for the first time he set goals. Pac never set goals, and when you start talking about writing scripts, whether or not you realize it, it's a goal." But Smith disagrees. "He was even getting high [in prison]. Whatever you need is there. I remember somebody was in there making some alcohol, and he would get his little buzz on in there one way or another." Smith believes it was Tupac's altered state of mind that led him to propose marriage. "I'll never forget one of his little desperate moves, calling my mother to ask for my hand in marriage, thinking he's doing something honorable," Smith recalls. "And he's doing it the old-school way: 'I'm going to call her mother before I even talk to her . . . and ask for her hand in marriage.'" Smith says that her mother was gentle but firm. "And my mother, [who's] known Pac for a long time [says], 'Pac, I love you. You guys have a very special relationship. But you can't expect me to be happy about you asking for my daughter's hand in marriage.'" Then Smith's mother lowered the boom. "'And you're an addict. When are you going to get clean?'" Smith says that Tupac pledged to clean up his act, but she knew the odds were against him. "His whole thing was, like, 'I know I need to clean up.' But I think he also knew he had too much to take on to [be able] to cope without the alcohol and drugs."

Of the myriad forces Tupac had to confront, few were as urgent as his own demons, especially the chronic absence of self-worth that spurred a lot of his self-defeating behavior.

Despite his "kind face," as scholar Vijay Prashad phrases it, Tupac never bragged about his good looks, never seemed to believe that he was all that special and therefore deserved someone special. "I know too many girls that had been with Tupac," says friend and journalist Danyel Smith of the rapper before he found fame. "And you didn't have to do nothing to be with him. You just had to show up, and show up with nothing." Smith believed Tupac's choices of girlfriends reflected his painful lack of self-worth. "Tupac is the kind of brother, he's so attractive," says Smith. "Just walking down the street, the brother looks good. But the women I would see him with . . ." Smith's voice trails off in disbelief. "I'm not acting like if you're cute, you just have to go on ahead and be with somebody just as cute as you. I'm not that superficial," Smith protests. "But you don't have to be with somebody that's just raggedy and looks like she has no self-esteem and nothing going for her, and maybe combs her hair and maybe didn't." Smith says that when Tupac chose someone who was less than promising, his own lack of self-worth prevented him from helping her do better. "If you pick somebody like that, [self-worth leads you to say], 'Let's try to work it out so we can both look a little better . . . [so that we are] just moving forward positively. It wasn't about that [with Tupac]. It really wasn't." If Tupac lacked self-esteem, he also lacked the vanity that made him believe that his handsomeness was the predicate of his erotic exploits. That does not mean that he didn't use his looks, his masculine charm, and manly appeal to get girls. But the raison d'être of female pursuit drew from the imperatives of the masculine culture that embraced him and that he clung to for dear life, for thug life. A real thug had many women, was true to none of them, pursued sex with athletic intensity, and subordinated "bitches" to "niggas."

And a true thug marked his body in loving solidarity with his homeboys. "I remember when he went and got his tattoo," says Cassandra Butcher, referring to Tupac's "50 Niggaz" emblem. "I said, 'What does that mean?' He said, 'This means when you come up against me, it's like coming up against fifty niggas, because I've got the souls of all my brothers in me.' And he believed it. . . . It was what he felt in his heart." Tupac's thug life mentor, Big Syke, argues that only when he found a reason for marking his body—the true love of his homeboys—did he inscribe his flesh with the memory of fallen friends. "We spray paint and we tack up," Syke says. "L.A. cats got gangs [and] tattoos all over their stomachs and up on their arms. It was normal. I didn't do it back then, because it was a fad. But now that I found something that I know I'm dying with, regardless [I get tatted] . . . I tell cats, 'If you don't have nothing to live for, find something to die for.' . . . I'm going to die for my thug life and my outlaw, and I'm going to live for my thug life and my outlaw." Syke, who has "2 Pac" tattooed on his left forearm, reveres his late comrade because he made thugs acceptable by making them fashionable. "The only reason they start to accept us now—and this is why I loved Pac so much—is because he made it cool. It's cool to run around with a rag on your head with gang-bangers. If you would have done this in '92 or '93, you would get pulled over on every corner. [The cops would say], 'You got a rag on your head. Are you crazy?' Now it's a fad, so it's cool."

If the marked, designed body is part of Tupac's thug legacy, so is the body marred by gunshots, intruded upon by medical paraphernalia, and incinerated to ashes. Tupac legend has it that he told his comrades to smoke his ashes when he died. His beautiful body was riddled with bullets, mangled and twisted by hot lead piercing his flesh, unprotected by guards or forewarning. But he wore his premonition as a cloak, which, in truth, had the opposite effect of the bullet-proof vest meant to shield him from harm: It invited the fury of his demons and that of his enemies to conspire against him, to rebuke his body and to crush it with terrifying finality. He had often wished when he was shot the first time that they hadn't "missed," that his body had disappeared, returning to the cruel earth from which he sprang. The thought of Tupac's body lurching backward in suffering as he sought to dodge his murderer's assault is the thought of black males left vulnerable to arbitrary destruction. Whether it is of their own making or the doing of sinister forces outside their communities, though important to know, cannot finally deter the love that must embrace and save them.[4]

Because he was young and vital, Tupac's body has become metaphoric in the way that John Brown's body has, or even John Henry's. But his breathing and walking body, his living and loving body, his rapping and acting body, his angry and defiant body, is the body that matters most, because without it, we would have no record of his spirit in our lives, no trace of his transcendent meaning etched into our hearts and minds. It is that body that it is hard to believe is no longer here. "I couldn't believe it when he took those five bullets," Danyel Smith says. "And I just really feel sometimes—I never doubt that he's dead, but it's amazing and unbelievable, even though I know it's true." Smith conjures as well the memory of a college student she had a crush on as a high school student when she worked at a local swimming pool. The young man had a motorcycle accident and eventually died from his injuries. Smith was devastated, not least because it killed the body that signified to her his valiant youth. "It was just unimaginable to me that somebody so young, someone who is in my same age group [could die]. And just because he had such a beautiful body, too, [it was hard] to imagine it mangled."[5]

By extension, it was hard for Smith to picture Tupac's bullet-barraged body. A former boyfriend who had been shot just one time in the leg told her of the enormous pain of a gunshot wound. "Your mind is never right after that," he told her. "Because you imagine that that kind of pain can just come from nowhere and fast . . . and the fact that there's almost nothing you can do to erase a bullet wound off of you. . . . It's just the invasion, the hot metal going through your body." That makes it hard for Smith to "imagine Tupac in his last moments. Did he feel at that moment that he was going out in a blaze of glory?" as he had often said he wanted to do. "Or was he peeing on himself? Was he scared to death? This is what hurts me, and this is why maybe we let him down. It's just no way for anybody, white, black, young, or old, to go, by a gun and with nobody there for you. And it makes me think: None of us knew how to grab that nigga by his collar?" Smith, who has grown intensely emotional, composes herself, pauses, and then raises her final, telling question. "But then I say, 'Well, what would we have said?'" Smith probably realizes that so many words—of warning and love, of criticism and concern—had already been spoken to Tupac. But he kept throwing his body—his beautiful, tattooed, wounded, conflicted, drugged, lurching, representative, fighting, cursing, defiant, loving, needy, sacrificial body—in the way.

"How Long Will They Mourn Me?"

Posthumous Presences of a Ghetto Saint

In the last weeks of his life, Tupac Shakur was charged with drug possession in a felony criminal case in Los Angeles. Already on probation for two other misdemeanors, Tupac faced an unmerciful district attorney seeking to put the rapper back in prison. Tupac's lawyer, Shawn Chapman, decided instead to have him plead guilty "open to the judge," which granted the judge sentencing discretion based on a report the defendant was to submit. Chapman hired Dr.

Sheila Balkan to prepare the sentencing report. The expert in these reports is required to spend a great deal of time with the defendant and the defendant's family and friends in preparing a document that recommends a sentence to the judge, who may agree or impose his or her own verdict. After fulfilling her duties, Balkan recommended that instead of going to prison, Tupac give a free concert. Even Chapman deemed the idea "absolutely ridiculous" and believed the judge, a white man, would agree. The judge summoned both sides to his chambers.

"You know, I have read this report, and this young man seems to me to be absolutely remarkable," the judge said. "I'm going to sentence him to give this concert." Chapman and her client were ecstatic. Shortly afterward, Tupac was murdered.

A hearing date had been set before Tupac's death. Chapman huddled with the DA, and both concluded there was no need to follow through, since it was widely known that Tupac had died on September 13. Moreover, the judge had moved from criminal to civil court, making it highly unlikely that he would want to hold the hearing. But when they called the judge's clerk, they were informed that he wanted to keep the date. Baffled, the two headed to the hearing.

"We get there, and the judge had nothing to say to us," Chapman recalls. "It was clear to us both immediately—and the court verified this later—that he just sort of needed to be in the presence of people who knew Tupac. It's that Tupac had made an impression on him in the short time that he had appeared before him, and he needed to be with the people who had introduced him to Tupac."

The grieving jurist was not alone. In the wake of Tupac's death, his fans around the globe mourned his passing in the presence of others who had come to revere the artist in the short time he appeared on the world stage to make his case for the voiceless black poor and to be judged by enemies and forgiven by friends. Tupac Amaru Shakur, the bright, burning flame, had been extinguished by murderous violence. Or had he?

No sooner had Tupac's bullet-riddled body been cremated than rumors of his faked death began to circulate. Tupac was not really dead, one rumor had it, but in Cuba with his "aunt" Assata Shakur, or on another Caribbean island, seeking relief from the intense drama of his fettered life. Tupac lives, another rumor maintained, because he assumed, on his first posthumous album, the persona Makaveli—a hint that he imitated the strategy of ultimate political survival by faking one's death as advocated in Machiavelli's *The Prince,* from whom the rapper borrowed his musical alter ego. But others immediately believed the rapper was dead, especially in light of the death wish he seemed to carry. "I never doubted it for five minutes when they said he was dead," says Danyel Smith. "I never had a moment of, 'The nigga is in Cuba or Jamaica or some neverland where Elvis and Bob Marley are.' When they said he was shot, I knew he was going to die. And I feel like I knew he was going to die a year before. It's ugly that it was whoever it was [who killed him], but I just feel it was going to be somebody." And the director Reginald Hudlin was acute in his observation of the effect of Tupac's real, not faked, death on his legacy. "There's no doubt that leaving a corpse is a great setup to becoming a legend." Mixed with the mystery cult that quickly attached to Tupac's memory were more ordinary responses to grief—primal disbelief ("I cannot believe he is dead"), psychic separation ("I cannot imagine him dead"), conditional denial ("He is too young and beautiful to have died"), suspended acceptance ("I cannot accept that he is dead"), traumatic indifference ("The hurt is so great I cannot afford the emotional investment of grieving"), and irrational tempest ("I am mad at you for dying").

In truth—and this is not atypical, although in his case it is even more so—Tupac's death says as much about us as it does about him. His death is beyond our control, and his, too. But an intriguing feature of the human psyche flares in the face of death: Although we forgive the dead a great deal, we also demand that they be responsible. It would seem that dying relieves a person of ethical obligations, especially since the notion of personhood is fundamentally changed once the body is no longer here and the person can no longer receive claims or make them. (Of course we can do so in the person's name, but that is not the same thing.) The shift in tenses that death brings—he *was* a rap superstar—suggests that Tupac, for instance, *was* a person, *is* now a memory, a spirit, and therefore is exempt from the claims we the living regularly make on each other. (The first sign that this is not always true is the way Tupac is still blamed for the violence in rap or the lapse in moral judgment among black youth. But it works in reverse, too. Martin Luther King Jr. is still praised for changes in present racial culture more than thirty years after his death.) As with taxes and debt, death sometimes only shifts obligations, to one's estate or—in the absence of its sufficiency to answer financial or legal claims—to the living, the survivors. The living are not disentangled from their loved one's death. They manage the affairs of the dead, or they manage the memory of their loved one through memorials and the like. But survivors often hold the dead responsible, especially for how they lived, which may have had something to do with how they died, say, by smoking or drinking or overeating. Or by making self-destructive choices in a rap career. Thus the line between responsibility and resentment is blurred, and the hunger of memory may not be as innocent as our consciences might lead us to believe. Death creates as much as it destroys.

In Tupac's case the crush of rumors that circulated in the aftermath of his demise suggests a huge investment in the denial of death. Many youth simply could not abide the destruction of a beloved icon. Rumor is the attempt to shape the *consequence* of death since its circumstances are well beyond control. This is not to deny the greed of rumor: Its aim is to foreclose a feared possibility by diverting attention from its confirmation. But rumor interrupts the normal state of affairs by throwing a wrench into the gut of perception: Things are not as they appear to be. But if it shapes, even distorts, perception, rumor is also a means to question knowledge: whose knowledge is superior, what is its source. Remember, rumor seems to say, that the official circuits on which information is carried are often defective.

None of this can be coordinated; in fact, it works best when it takes on a life of its own. The rumors that engulfed

Tupac's dead body revived it, kept it from perishing in the ground of neglect or blowing as cremated ash in the winds of amnesia. The point of the rumors about Tupac's staged death was to deny the power of death by denying it had even occurred. This was crucial above all to young, poor black people who had endured the ravages of arbitrary destruction. Tupac's death symbolized the ultimate arbitrariness of death, since it struck down an icon favored by destiny to rise from the conditions in which they were still mired. But that very recognition only reinforced their investment in his alive, though disappeared, body. His death revealed their vulnerability: Since their identification with him had been so strong, his death symbolized the possibility of their deaths. Hence, investment in Tupac is also self-investment. But there is another level at which the investment in rumor operates. Since Tupac is the symbolic representative of a generation, his death symbolizes its death to some degree. The results of such a belief are phrased clearly: If he is dead, then we are, or could be, dead. Keeping him from dying, insisting on his bodily persistence in a secret location, forestalls that realization. The manipulation of the rumor through secrecy is a crucial component of its success. The mystery that shrouds Tupacian mythology—where he is, how he faked his death, how long in advance he knew of his demise—is as important to the preservation of his memory as is the fact of his staged exit.

Aided by rumor and the cult of mystery, Tupac has become an urban legend. Of course urban legends have helped modern citizens negotiate the landscape of postindustrial culture. The rise of the big city, with its attendant opportunities and ills, spurred the development of myths by which dwellers could articulate their moral values, express their fears and aspirations, and facilitate the transition from one living space to another. That process has been profoundly influenced by racial conflict and class antagonisms. As black and brown people began to occupy the fringes, and then the centers, of urban terrain through immigration and relocation, they clashed with white neighbors. These conflicts eventually resulted in patterns of racial exit—or in truth, white exodus—from the urban front with retreat into suburbia. In the meantime racial hostilities were articulated through urban mythologies of black and brown identity, solidifying the free-floating anxieties of whites into stories or legends. So stereotypes about brown and black people—involving culture, for instance, and sexuality—proliferated, permitting whites a level of intellectual control over social and racial forces and people that were foreign to them and caused them fear. The urban legend translates the unknown into the easily accessible language of myth.[1]

Black and brown people also use urban legends but often in a different fashion. Black and brown urban legends allow these minority populations to address the specific conditions of their existence while combating the pervasive influence of white supremacy. As do their white counterparts, black and brown people often generate stories about the threatening presence of youth, especially in gangs. The supposed rituals and esoteric practices of these unwieldy social groups have become the subject of much fascination and

fear and mythologizing among urban citizens. That is because a non–gang member could be caught in a gang ritual
that had deadly consequences for the uninitiated. (Hence,
one urban legend held that one should never flash one's
headlights when meeting an oncoming car, since gang
members were said to use that as a signal of what person to
harm that night.) But urban legends have further utility:
They express the collective determination of black and
brown people not to be tricked by the deceptive and racist
strategies of white society. Thus, an urban legend developed that suggested Church's Chicken intended secretly to
sterilize black people in its recipes at stores that dotted the
ghetto landscape. Another urban legend held that fashion
designer Tommy Hilfiger was contemptuous of black people, despite their heavy patronage of his enterprise. (This
urban legend almost failed one of the tests of its makeup:
easy verification, since it was said, but never proved—and
in fact was even *disproved*—that he went on *Oprah* and
spilled his venom for blacks. But when such a legend takes
hold, empirical proof is almost irrelevant because a greater
good is being served: social critique.) Urban legends in the
ghetto are often grassroots attempts to fight against anonymous social power by giving it a face and motivation. The
urban legend—and the conspiracy theory—allows black
and brown folk to grasp hold of the machinery of oppression and tweak it through their subversive rhetoric.

To suggest that Tupac is an urban legend underscores
the racial and generational utility of his memory. Tupac has
become a signifying, trickstering figure in the collective
black urban imagination. His legend hangs on paradox: He

has showed up more fully by disappearing. By having ascribed to him the intent of faking his own death, he becomes the apotheosis of the urban legend's on-the-ground morality: to defeat the lethal limits imposed on black life by whiter and older people. The elements surrounding his death have an even more heightened role in the mythologies that reveal his subversive intent. That he died in Las Vegas, the American capital of gambling, hustling, magic, and illusion, is an irresistible goad to his growing legend. That on the night he was murdered he attended a fight by Mike Tyson, the ultimate champion for the thug life that Tupac prized and promoted, is further proof of his solidarity with demonized urban exiles, those who have the most to gain by his artful defiance of death, since they can cheer on one of their own. That he hung around for seven days—from Saturday, September 7, to Friday, September 13—was his unification of opposites: seven, the number of religious perfection, and thirteen, the number of secular bad luck. Friday the thirteenth is even more the emblem of an ominous tide turning inward on Tupac, but he mastered his fate by escaping through the portals of ghetto cunning. In life he had warred mightily against the essential separation of the cursed and blessed, a point he now signified in his strategically timed demise. The numerological esoterica that ring his metaphoric body join the ghetto occult to its hustling ambitions: When it comes down to it, it's all about playing the numbers.

Robin Kelley sees the significance of linking Tupac to historic black figures like Simon Kimangu and Charlie Parker. "Kimangu is like Tupac in that he was an outlaw character, a luminary in the movement, except he was really religious," Kelley says. Kimangu was a leader in the Belgian Congo in the 1920s and 1930s, although his movement spread throughout Central Africa; "he was a great martyr, and there was a whole movement called Kimanguism." When he was jailed, people claimed to see him in other spots. And when he died, people claimed that he lived. To this day there are people in the Congo who claim to see him. Kelley finds similar parallels between Tupac and Parker: "After Charlie Parker died, the first thing people did was run all around New York and write, 'Bird Lives,'" Kelley says. "And then people would claim to have seen him." A big difference between Tupac and Kimangu and Parker is the means of their projection into posterity and the larger culture. Since all icons are a product of their times, even as they are scripted for enduring timelessness, Tupac's rise in the age of technology is especially auspicious. "Tupac is the product of a technology that allows us to see him in movies and videos after he's dead," Kelley says. "Some of those things were not seen until after his death. That's kind of powerful. It reinforces the myth of Tupac's death and makes it even more unbelievable that he could be gone."

Tupac's posthumous appearances have certainly expanded his myth. In fact, the seemingly ceaseless outpouring of albums and movies exemplifies a postmodern conception of authorship, just as the proliferation of Web sites and chatrooms dedicated to Tupac allows fans to keep his persona alive. It would seem that an almost disembodied force of production wills itself into expression. Tupac's constantly mediated existence is a metaphor for the way black life is constantly mediated—through investigative journalism, scholarly monographs, television news, film, and video. Tupac's mediated status fused with his own larger-than-life persona, where he had defeated death before. "He survived so many things that should have killed him," Kelley says. "It's the idea of having nine lives." That same expectation greeted Charlie Parker when he lived. "Parker was so much like Tupac in that he lived by absorbing everything he could, taking everything he could from anybody, whether it was women or drugs, and was still extremely brilliant. He spoke in terms of identity as political and introduced musical ideas that people just didn't know where they came from. He lived a very short life, and you could almost predict his death."[2]

But if Tupac's legend has serviced the psychic and cultural needs of poor black youth, it has also lifted him to the lofty heights of mainstream mythmaking. Tupac is perhaps the first black figure to survive death in the way that only a few white icons have managed. Although supermarket tabloid reporters have not yet spotted him toasting his hidden life at a remote location, Tupac burrows deep into the popular cultural imagination. He has been viewed as the equivalent of James Dean, Elvis, even Marilyn Monroe. Rapper Big Syke calls his friend the "ghetto Elvis." Tupac's lawyer and Harvard professor Charles Ogletree agrees: "People think you exaggerate when you talked about how he would be the next Elvis Presley or James Dean," Ogletree says. "But he is that and more, because of the power that he had. When people think of an Elvis or a

James Dean, they would see Tupac as an icon of art who was not counterculture but just changing culture. He was sending culture in a whole different direction." Elaborating the James Dean connection, John Singleton hoped that Tupac would avoid what looked like unavoidable fate. "There was a time in which I was hoping that he wasn't going to be our James Dean," Singleton says. "I remember telling somebody, 'It looks like he's still alive; he ain't going to be James Dean.' And then it happened."[3]

Of course the quest for equivalence—finding a comparable figure to match him with—is doubly meaningful with Tupac. On the one hand, it involves the standard procedure in cases of icon identification: drawing comparisons between unique historic personages—for instance, Marilyn Monroe is like James Dean, the argument might run, but not like Montgomery Clift. But it also means looking for the white analogue to Tupac's entrance into the pop pantheon. In both cases, of course, comparisons help but do not exhaust the possibilities of interpretation. All figures that attain mythological status answer a unique need that has gone begging in the culture. The baseline requirement is simple yet brutal: Early death and unfulfilled potential mean the possibility of achieving after life what could not be achieved in life. But the route to cultural mastery turns on a risky democracy: The figure must find favor among peers and progeny. Their creation as icons in the first place is only the down payment on their legacy. Such figures have permanent futures because they have useful pasts, pasts that point the way to some key insight or crucial moment that helps define the culture. The needs they fulfill may change,

and their lights may lessen or grow brighter. This sort of icon worship, after all, depends on who's in charge of the cultural liturgy. (This is why Tupac is an important test case: Can a largely white and increasingly multicultural society continue to embrace this black rebel over the next few decades, as tastes change and tolerance of blackness waxes and wanes?)

Black equivalency is even more difficult to finesse. It sends us ranging into fields beyond the person's scope of endeavor, especially when the major feature of comparison is race and not, say, profession. It is not that vocation is an unimportant line of demarcation, which is why, for instance, we compare Martin Luther King Jr. to Mahatma Gandhi or even John F. Kennedy, and not to Marilyn Monroe or James Dean. But race is important in searching for equivalencies among black figures simply because race has become an independent variable in shaping our perception of human beings and what they mean to us. A huge part of King's meaning is tied to race, especially to blackness, as is true for Tupac. Despite the obvious dissimilarities between them—as Danyel Smith says, one moved people by design, one by the accident of art—it still might make sense to derive insight through their comparison. (Of course it is also helpful to compare Tupac to John Coltrane and Jimi Hendrix, both because they were artists and because a similar devotion to their memories developed after their deaths. Tupac is distinguished from them by his candidacy for cultural canonization that privileges the surviving body, not simply the surviving body of work.)[4]

In my book on Martin Luther King Jr., I compared King to Tupac, but only as a way to provoke a conversation about the contrasting meanings of two icons who enjoyed more similarities than many observers were comfortable to admit. By no means did I suggest that King and Tupac were moral equivalents—that their vision of struggle was joined at the ethical seams. Rather, I sought to show how the perception of two defining figures allowed one to be exempt from a variety of moral criticism to which the other was routinely and, I believe, unfairly subject. Race becomes a substance that demands to be accounted for even as we figure its role in larger issues like death. That Tupac was a black man, as King was a black man, has everything to do with how we have understood his message and responded to his challenge. Race is an equivalency, even if a rather restricted and formal one, but a significant one nonetheless. One may not gain anything by comparing two figures *simply* because they are black, but one can gain a great deal by comparing even two strikingly different figures and seeing how race has perhaps unified them in ways that have everything to do with race. The point, of course, is to underscore how determinative race has been and how it impinges even on death.

That is why the prospect of black survival is revealing and the absence of such survival equally noteworthy. That Tupac has become the first black figure with a serious chance at the persistent cultural memory accorded Elvis, Marilyn Monroe, and James Dean suggests the integration of immortality, or at the least the desegregation of survival.

But it also suggests that black survival, of necessity, has taken different forms than those of mainstream icons. As proved by Kimangu and Parker, black icons occasionally are believed to survive their physical demise—that is, not to have died at all—especially when they have served huge social or cultural purposes. But black icons have not primarily flourished in such modes of survival. Rather, black survival has taken the form of spiritual rejuvenation, moral renaissance, and social struggle as embodied in the spirit of the departed figure. Black survival, then, has usually been by analogy: The spirit of King is alive because we behave as he behaved, we believe what he believed, and thus we grasp hold of and extend his legacy. But no one believes that King is alive except in the rich social traditions he inspired. By contrast, the sort of survival suggested by the rhetoric around Tupac is survival by reference, in this case, to a literal presence, a physically alive, embodied person who enjoys existence in a hidden plane. The irony, of course, is that survival by reference is itself a metaphor for the hidden existence of anonymous, ordinary people, the people who invest in the legends by which their private lives—their most intimate experiences—are publicly narrated. Anonymous, ordinary individuals project their lives onto the legendary figure, merging with it where they can, fostering an even more intense identification with that figure. By contributing to the creation of a legend—what we might term the posthumous persona—ordinary people are in fact creating themselves.

If the posthumous persona is a means to self-creation, then legends have not only personal meaning but social and political utility as well. In some instances the posthumous persona is a political judgment of the society that creates the need for its existence. To be sure, all societies have and perhaps always will have the need for myths and legends. But a society rife with inequalities—of race, gender, class, social status, sexuality, geography, and age—will produce legends that funnel social critique even as they organize collective memory, articulate social vision, and project communal values. Tupac's posthumous persona serves many needs: It transmutes grief to glory; it transforms mourning to celebration; it projects onto his body the hopes and aspirations of other, less famous, anonymous bodies; and it situates black urban identity in the pantheon of national survival. But it is also a fairly unsubtle critique of a society that produces the need for the thug persona Tupac grew into during his twenty-five years. Tupac spoke constantly of being forced into the choices he made: He blamed the violent persona he adopted on a society that created a vacuum of somebody-ness and filled it with the nobodies of American life—poor, black, desperate, hopeless, urban citizens, the thugs. Of course many critics, some of them black, disagreed, as we witnessed in earlier chapters. But hordes of youth identified with Tupac's tragic sense of ghetto life, an existence that was often maligned by the powerful and ignored by the wealthy. Choosing to remember Tupac, to keep him alive, to insist that he is not dead, to proclaim his posthumous persona, is at once an acknowledgment of his unique role and a sharp criticism of the forces in society that made Tupac necessary.[5]

In this sense, Tupac's cultural meaning more closely resembles King's in yet another way: He has become for some fans and followers a martyr. "He was a martyr before it even happened," says Robin Kelley. "So much of his music was about the inevitability of his demise, and at the same time he also had this almost Jesus-like voice, where he would preach and, in his own body and experience, would articulate all this pain and hope." The immediate, cynical response might be that the downsizing of martyrdom cheapens its use and that if a figure like Tupac—who glorified violence, glamorized thuggery, and proclaimed a misogynist gospel—can be a martyr, the word has lost its redemptive meaning. Some, or even most, of that criticism can be conceded without doing damage to Tupac's martyrdom in the eyes of those disappointed by more traditional martyrs. The very notion that Tupac was a martyr—for the cause of thug life or black male hardship or economic inequality or hopeless urban existence—means that competing martyrdoms failed to adequately represent just what those who love Tupac and proclaim his martyrdom lost: a figure who, in the spirit of his song "Black Jesus," loved like they loved, smoked like they smoked, hurt like they hurt, died like they may die.

At least four notions are crucial to the conception of martyrdom: embodiment, identification, substitution, and elevation. The martyr's death embodies, and in some cases anticipates, the death of those who follow. It may be that his death signifies the manner in which his followers, adherents, or comrades could die. The martyr is identified by and with the community that follows him. He is identified as the leader of a group of believers or followers who identify with him as a member of their own tribe or community. The martyr's death often substitutes for the death of his followers; he dies in their place, at least symbolically. For instance, when King died, his death changed the black political future in this nation. He died in the place of millions of blacks, since it could easily have been one of them who perished from racial violence. Finally, the martyr is elevated to a high status, even as he elevates the condition of his followers through his death, drawing attention to their hidden or overlooked suffering.

Tupac's martyrdom was clear to many youth and followers. He embodied the harsh, callous death of thousands of anonymous black males victimized by arbitrary violence and, often, the violence they provoked. But the line tends to be blurred, as it was in Tupac's life, since it is not clear who killed him, though it is clear that the path he trod certainly invited death. That ambiguity, the lack of ethical clarity, is precisely the condition of thousands of young black males caught in ever increasing cycles of violence and retribution. Tupac was identified clearly, irrevocably, as a young black male. He wore it as a badge of honor. As a second-generation Panther, he took pride in his defiant manhood in the service of black revolutionary truth, though what that meant was vastly different from a generation before. His strong identification as a black male marked him in ways that marked millions of others. Although these youth lacked his platform and privilege, Tupac used them to broadcast their pain, which made them identify with him even more. Tupac identified with the legions of hurting, beleaguered black youth whose only option appeared to be to "ride or die," to blast or be blasted into oblivion. His identification may have been self-destructive, wrongheaded, and morbid—but it was thorough and heartfelt. As a result, millions of youth have identified with him, with his swaggering courage, with his sexy defiance and splenetic rebellion, with his pain and vulnerability, with his hunger for the end even as he clung, like they cling, fiercely to life.

Tupac's death has functioned as a symbolic substitution for the youth he loved and for the urban castaways for whom he spoke. He has been elevated to a cultural demiurge, his death drawing attention to and elevating black youth whose own lives of violence and misery were folded into the recesses of public consciousness. His remarkable reappearance as a spiritual force—through unreleased music, through films and videos, through a posthumous persona—means that his martyrdom might cast a big light on the people he loved and cherished. It might also underscore the perilous circumstances that claimed his life, even if to decry the destructive path he took, the self-annihilating impulse he followed, and how contemporary youth recklessly take up his mantle.

It is a testament to Tupac's already vast and complex legend that it unites a posthumous persona and martyrdom in one body—whether disappeared or sacrificed. There is a fail-safe method to Tupac's cultural canonization that seems to split the difference between the two branches of belief that embrace him. It is as if they got together to decide how to cover the bases in keeping Tupac alive. Those who proclaim his martyrdom believe that he is physically dead, but not really dead, because his memory and spirit live on. The advocates of his posthumous persona say that he isn't physically dead and that his arranged absence only underscores how much more vital and present he has become. What is constant is the zealous cultural response that settles around his myth, his legend, and his body. If his body has gone to the ground or if it has been grounded on some paradise far away from the *Sturm und Drang* to which he was fatally addicted, he has in any case managed to be present while absent. What he may most resemble, then, is a religious figure with special power—a ghetto saint.

Tupac's ghetto sainthood features all of the elements that render historic figures as embodied presences of divine inspiration. It is surely difficult to trace the anatomy of his spiritual power, though the acclaim he continues to receive from youth across the world is adequate testimony to his enduring significance. But Tupac evoked black gods—of pain, truth, and poetry—with a beauty and power that are reserved for those who transcend greatness and leap straight into a mythic, spiritual, and saintly stratum. His strong black body bore the sins of his generation with restless fury. His eyes recorded the pain and agony that millions of others saw but could never as eloquently express. His hands wrote words of unsparing honesty about the self-destruction that dogged him once he made a name for himself. His voice spoke poetry of such haunting sincerity that all who heard it were moved—not necessarily in a positive fashion, but he could not be ignored. He is the mantra millions of youth invoke to calm their fears. They play his words to soothe the demons that thump their breasts. They chant his lyrics to make war on the absurdity of racial oppression and poverty. They finger the metaphoric rosary of images he projected as a gift of intercessory prayer. And they view his risen, disappeared body as the absent evidence of his eternal ascension. Tupac has joined those black saints who tarry with the ancestors to watch over our blighted black babies. His spirit may be restless, but his heart is a haven for many who feel lost without his words. His future and legacy depend on their constant, unfolding adoration. As a ghetto saint, he beckons us to watch his transformation. And even if we do not subscribe to his bitterly, relentlessly truthful theology that ripped from his divided soul, we can at least gauge the tenor of our black youths' soulful journeys by referring to his life-changing artistry.

NOTES

Chapter One

1. This quote and following quotes from the "prison interview" are taken from a videotape made of Tupac when he was in Clinton Correctional Facility in 1995, which Tracy Robinson, Yanko Damboulev, and Mike Pope graciously shared with me. Frank Cooley conducted the interview.

2. Kelley, *Yo' Mama's Disfunktional.*

3. Stavig, *The World of Tupac Amaru.*

4. Seale, *Seize the Time.*

5. Pearson, *The Shadow of the Panther.*

6. Lasch, *The Culture of Narcissism;* Kelley, *Yo' Mama's Disfunktional;* Wilson, *The Truly Disadvantaged* and *When Work Disappears;* Massey and Denton, *American Apartheid;* Davis, *City of Quartz.*

7. Webb, "Dark Alliance," *San Jose Mercury News.*

8. Anson, "To Die Like a Gangsta," *Vanity Fair;* Bruck, "The Takedown of Tupac," *The New Yorker.*

9. This quote and following quotes from the "school interview" are taken from a videotape made of Tupac when he was in Tamalpais High School in 1988, which Leila Steinberg graciously shared with me.

10. Olsen, *Last Man Standing.*

Chapter Two

1. Jones, *The Black Panther Party Reconsidered.*

2. Keeling, "'A Homegrown Revolutionary'? Tupac Shakur and the Legacy of the Black Panther Party," *Black Scholar;* DuBois, *The Souls of Black Folk.*

3. Shakur, *Assata: An Autobiography.*

4. Churchill and Vander Wall, *Agents of Repression.*

5. DuBois, *W.E.B. DuBois, a Reader: 1868–1963;* Lewis, *W.E.B. DuBois: Biography of a Race, 1868–1919;* Dewey, *John Dewey on Education;* Freire, *Pedagogy of the Oppressed.*

6. Puzo, *The Godfather;* Fanon, *The Wretched of the Earth.*

7. Davis, *Angela Davis: An Autobiography;* Jones, *The Black Panther Party Reconsidered.*

Chapter Three

1. Bruck, "The Takedown of Tupac," *The New Yorker.*

2. Anson, "To Die Like a Gangsta," *Vanity Fair;* Bruck, "The Takedown of Tupac," *The New Yorker.*

3. George, *Buppies, B-Boys, Baps and Bohos: Notes on Post-Soul Culture.* I borrow the term "boho" from George's book.

4. Twain, *The Prince and the Pauper.*

5. Teilhard de Chardin, *The Phenomenon of Man.*

Chapter Four

1. Rose, *Black Noise;* Neal, *What the Music Said;* Boyd, *Am I Black Enough for You?* George, *Hip-Hop America.*

2. Sleeman, *Rambles and Recollection of an Indian Official,* and *Journey Through the Kingdom of Oude, 1849–1850;* Barrett, *The Rastafarians;* Dyczkowski, *The Doctrine of Vibration.*

3. Hobsbawm, *Primitive Rebels,* and *Bandits;* Seal, *The Outlaw Legend;* Duncan, *Romantic Outlaws, Beloved Prisons.*

4. Boccaccio, *Decameron.*

5. Davis and Troupe, *Miles: The Autobiography;* Carr, *Miles Davis: The Definitive Biography.*

6. Patillo-McCoy, *Black Picket Fences;* Massey and Denton, *American Apartheid;* Wilson, *The Truly Disadvantaged,* and *When Work Disappears;* Kelley, *Yo' Mama's Disfunktional.*

7. Kasher, *The Civil Rights Movement;* Morris, *The Origins of the Civil Rights Movement;* Dittmer, *Local People;* Fairclough, *Race and Democracy;* Hine, *Hine Sight;* Giddings, *When and Where I Enter;* Garrow, *Bearing the Cross;* Carson, *In Struggle;* White, *Too Heavy a Load;* Norrell, *Reaping the Whirlwind;* Branch, *Parting the Waters,* and *Pillar of Fire.*

8. Guralnick, *Sweet Soul Music;* Wolff, *You Send Me.*

Chapter Five

1. Price, *Clockers;* Shakur, *Monster.*

2. Herbert, "The Making of a Hip-Hop Intellectual," *U.S. News and World Report.*

3. Boyd, *Am I Black Enough for You?* Kelley, *Race Rebels.*

4. White, *Ar'n't I a Woman?* Berlin, *Many Thousands Gone.*

5. Rosengarten, *All God's Dangers.*

6. Foucault, *Ethics: Subjectivity and Truth.*

7. Rose, *Black Noise;* Neal, *What the Music Said;* Kelley, *Race Rebels,* and *Yo' Mama's Disfunktional;* George, *Hip-Hop America.*

8. Golden, *Black Male.*

9. Alexander, *The Farrakhan Factor.*

10. Ibid.

11. Berger, *Blood Season;* Hoffer, *A Savage Business.*

12. Giddings, *When and Where I Enter;* Hine, *Hine Sight;* White, *Too Heavy a Load.*

Chapter Six

1. Rose, *Black Noise;* Roberts, *Killing the Black Body;* Cloward and Piven, *Regulating the Poor.*

2. Giddings, *When and Where I Enter;* Hine, *Hine Sight;* White, *Too Heavy a Load.*

3. Rose, *Black Noise.*

4. MacLeod, *Ain't No Making It;* Butterfield, *All God's Children;* Boyd, *Am I Black Enough for You?*

5. Murray, *Losing Ground.*

6. Bruck, "The Takedown of Tupac," *The New Yorker.*

7. Anson, "To Die Like a Gangsta," *Vanity Fair;* Bruck, "The Takedown of Tupac," *The New Yorker.*

8. Wittgenstein, *Philosophical Investigations;* Gintis, *Game Theory Evolving;* Sutton-Smith, *The Ambiguity of Play;* Terr, *Beyond Love and Work;* Ackerman, *Deep Play;* Harris, *Language, Saussure, and Wittgenstein;* Rose, *Black Noise;* Boyd, *Am I Black Enough for You?* Neal, *What the Music Said;* Levine, *Black Culture and Consciousness;* Kelley, *Yo' Mama's Disfunktional.*

Chapter Seven

1. *Jet Magazine,* October tk, 1996, pp. 60–62.

2. Cone, *God of the Oppressed;* Gutierrez, *A Theology of Liberation.*

3. Thurman, *Jesus and the Disinherited;* Horsley, *Jesus and the Spiral of Violence.*

4. Shakur, *The Rose That Grew from Concrete.*

5. Carson and Holloran, *A Knock at Midnight;* King, *A Testament of Hope.*

6. Barrett, "Dead Men Printed," *Callaloo.*

Chapter Eight

1. White, *Rebel for the Hell of It.*

2. Ugwu, *Let's Get It On;* Lhoman, *Raising Cain;* Elam and Krasner, *African-American Performance and Theatre History.*

3. Boyd, *Am I Black Enough for You?* Cross, *It's Not About a Salary.*

4. Anson, "To Die Like a Gangsta," *Vanity Fair.* In the song "Black Jesus," recorded with the Outlawz in 1999 on the album, *Still I Rise,* Shakur suggests smoking his ashes after he's gone.

5. Banks, *Cloudsplitter;* Olds, *Raising Holy Hell;* Whitehead, *John Henry Days.*

Epilogue

1. Genge, *Urban Legends;* Degh, *Legend and Belief.*

2. Giddins, *Celebrating Bird;* Russell, *Bird Lives!*

3. Gilmore, *Live Fast—Die Young;* Guralnick, *Last Train to Memphis,* and *Careless Love;* Summers, *Goddess;* Giles, *Legend.*

4. Porter, *John Coltrane;* Nisenson, *Ascension;* Redding and Appleby, *Are You Experienced?* McDermott et al., *Hendrix.*

5. Kammen, *Mystic Chords of Memory;* Schwartz, *George Washington,* and *Abraham Lincoln and the Forge of Memory.* Of course in speaking of Tupac's tragic sense of ghetto life, I am playing on Miguel de Unamuno's powerful exploration of the clash between reason and emotion, much like Tupac's, even if with different emphases, in his classic *Tragic Sense of Life.*

BIBLIOGRAPHY

Books

Ackerman, Diane. *Deep Play*. New York: Vintage Books, 2000.

Adjaye, Joseph K., and Andrews, Adrianne R., eds. *Language Rhythm 'N Sound: Black Popular Cultures into the 21st Century*. Pittsburgh: University of Pittsburgh Press, 1997.

Alexander, Amy. *The Farrakhan Factor: African-American Writers on Leadership, Nationhood, and Minister Louis Farrakhan*. New York: Grove Press, 1999.

Alexander, Frank, with Cuda, Heidi S. *Got Your Back: The Life of a Bodyguard in the Hardcore World of Gangster Rap*. New York: St. Martin's Press, 1998.

Angelou, Maya. *I Know Why the Caged Bird Sings*. New York: Bantam Books, 1971.

Bailey, Alicia A. *Serving Humanity*. New York: Lucis, 1987.

Banks, Russell. *Cloudsplitter*. New York: HarperCollins, 1999.

Baraka, Amiri. *Blues People: Negro Music in White America*. New York: Morrow, 1963.

Barrett, Leonard. *The Rastafarians*. Boston: Beacon Press, 1997.

Berger, Phil. *Blood Season: Mike Tyson and the World of Boxing*. Four Walls, Eight Windows, 1996.

Berlin, Ira. *Many Thousands Gone: The First Two Centuries of Slavery in North America*. Cambridge: Harvard University Press, 1998.

Besant, Annie, and Das, Bhagavan, trans. *Bhagavad-Gita*. Madras, India: Theosophical Publishing House, 1979.

Boccaccio, Giovanni. *Decameron*. Edimat, 2000.

Boston Women's Health Book Collective. *New Our Bodies, Ourselves: A Book by and for Women*. New York: Simon & Schuster, 1998.

Boyd, Todd. *Am I Black Enough for You? Popular Culture from the Hood and Beyond*. Bloomington: Indiana University Press, 1997.

Branch, Taylor. *Parting the Waters: America in the King Years, 1954–63*. New York: Simon & Schuster, 1988.

———. *Pillar of Fire: America in the King Years, 1963–65*. New York: Simon & Schuster, 1998.

Bruno de Jesus-Marie, Father. *St. John of the Cross*. New York: Sheed & Ward, 1957.

Butterfield, Fox. *All God's Children: The Boskett Family and the American Tradition of Violence*. New York: Avon Books, 1996.

Carr, Ian. *Miles Davis: The Definitive Biography*. New York: Thunder's Mouth Press, 1999.

Carson, Clayborne. *In Struggle: SNCC and the Black Awakening of the 1960s*. Cambridge: Harvard University Press, 1981.

Cloward, Richard A., and Piven, Frances F. *Regulating the Poor: The Function of Public Welfare*. 2nd edition. New York: Vintage, 1993.

Cone, James. *God of the Oppressed*. Rev. ed. Maryknoll, N.Y.: Orbis Books, 1997.

Creme, Benjamin. *Messages from Maitreya the Christ*. Vol. 1: *Messages 1–100*. St. Pacoima: Tara Press, 1980.

Cross, Brian. *It's Not About a Salary . . . Rap, Race and Resistance in Los Angeles*. New York: Verso, 1993.

Datcher, Michael, and Alexander, Kwame. *Tough Love: Cultural Criticism and Familial Observations of the Life and Death of Tupac Shakur*. Alexandria, Va.: Alexander Publishing Group, 1996.

Davis, Angela. *Angela Davis: An Autobiography*. International Publishers, 1989.

Davis, Miles, and Troupe, Quincy. *Miles: The Autobiography*. New York: Touchstone Books, 1990.

Degh, Linda. *Legend and Belief: Dialectics of a Folklore Genre*. Bloomington: University of Indiana Press, 2001.

De Unamuno, Miguel. *Tragic Sense of Life*. Trans. J. Crawford Flitch. New York: Dover, 1990.

Dewey, John. *John Dewey on Education*. Chicago: University of Chicago Press, 1983.

Dittmer, John. *Local People: The Struggle for Civil Rights in Mississippi*. Urbana: University of Illinois Press, 1994.

DuBois, W. E. B. *Souls of Black Folk*. New York: Penguin Books, 1989.

Duncan, Martha Grace. *Romantic Outlaws, Beloved Prisons: The Unconscious Meanings of Crime and Punishment*. New York: New York University Press, 1996.

Dyczkowski, Mark S. G. *The Doctrine of Vibration: An Analysis of the Doctrines and Practices of Kashmir Shaivism*. State University of New York Press, 1987.

Dyson, Michael Eric. *Reflecting Black: African-American Cultural Criticism*. Minneapolis: University of Minnesota Press, 1993.

_____. *Race Rules: Navigating the Color Line*. Reading, Mass.: Addison-Wesley, 1995.

_____. *Between God and Gangsta Rap: Bearing Witness to Black Culture*. New York: Oxford University Press, 1996.

_____. *I May Not Get There with You: The True Martin Luther King, Jr*. New York: Free Press, 2000.

Essert, Charles Ernest. *Secret Splendor: The Journey Within*. New York: Philosophical Library, 1973.

Fairclough, Adam. *Race and Democracy: The Civil Rights Struggle in Louisiana, 1915-1972*. Athens: University of Georgia Press, 1995.

Fanon, Frantz. *The Wretched of the Earth*. New York: Grove Press, 1986.

Forkos, Heather. *Tupac Shakur (They Died Too Young)*. New York: Chelsea House, 1998.

Foucault, Michel. *Ethics: Subjectivity and Truth: The Essential Works of Foucault,*

1954-1984. Vol. 1. Ed. Paul Rabinow; trans. Robert Hurley et al. New York: New Press, 1997.

Freire, Paulo. *Pedagogy of the Oppressed.* Trans. Myra Bergman Ramos. Continuum Publishing Group, 2000.

Garrow, David. *Bearing the Cross: Martin Luther King, Jr. and the Southern Christian Leadership Conference.* New York: Random House, 1986.

Genge, N. E. *Urban Legends: As-Complete-as-One-Could-Be Guide to Modern Myths.* New York: Three Rivers Press, 2000.

George, Nelson. *Buppies, B-Boys, Baps and Bohos: Notes on Post-Soul Culture.* Boston: Da Capo, Updated and Expanded 2001.

Gibran, Khalil. *Tears and Laughter.* New Jersey: Castle Books, 1993.

Giddings, Paula. *When and Where I Enter: The Impact of Black Women on Race and Sex in America.* New York: Morrow, 1984.

Giddins, Taylor. *Celebrating Bird: The Triumph of Charlier Parker.* Da Capo Press, 1999.

Giles, Fred Lawrence. *Legend: The Life and Death of Marilyn Monroe.* Scarborough House, 1991.

Gilmore, John. *Live Fast—Die Young: My Life with James Dean.* New York: Thunder's Mouth Press, 1998.

Gintis, Herb. *Game Theory Evolving.* Princeton: Princeton University Press, 2000.

Grant, Joan. *Life as Corolla.* Columbus, Ohio: Ariel Press, 1986.

Gratus, Jack. *The Great White Lie: Slavery, Emancipation and Changing Racial Attitudes.* New York: Monthly Review Press, 1973.

Guralnick, Peter. *Last Train to Memphis: The Rise of Elvis Presley.* New York: Little, Brown, 1995.

———. *Careless Love: The Unmaking of Elvis Presley.* New York: Little, Brown , 2000.

Gutierrez, Gustavo. *A Theology of Liberation: History, Politics, Salvation.* Trans. Caridad Inder and John Eagleson. 15th ed. Maryknoll, N.Y.: Orbis Books, 1988.

Harris, William H. *The Harder We Run: Black Workers Since the Civil War.* New York: Oxford University Press, 1982.

Hine, Darlence Clark. *Hine Sight: Black Women and the Re-construction of American History.* Brooklyn, N.Y.: Carlson, 1994.

Hirsch, E. D. *The Dictionary of Cultural Literacy: What Every American Needs to Know.* 2nd ed. Boston: Houghton Mifflin, 1993.

Hobsbawm, Eric. *Primitive Rebels: Studies in Archaic Forms of Social Movements in the 19th and 20th Centuries.* New York: Praeger, 1953.

———. *Bandits.* New York: Delacorte Press, 1963.

Hoffer, Richard. *A Savage Business: The Comeback and Comedown of Mike Tyson.* New York: Simon and Schuster.

Horsley, Richard. *Jesus and the Spiral of Violence: Popular Jewish Resistance in Roman Palestine.* Penn.: Fortress Press, 1992.

Horsley, Richard, with John S. Hanson. *Bandits, Prophets, and Messiahs: Popular Movements in the Time of Jesus.* Trinity Press International, 1999.

James, Darius. *That's Blaxploitation: Roots of the Baadasssss 'Tude (Rated X by an All 'Whyte Jury).* New York: St. Martin's Press, 1995.

Johnson, Charles Bertram. *Songs of My People.* Boston: Cornhill Company, 1918.

Jones, Charles, ed. *The Black Panther Party Revisited.* Baltimore: Black Classic Press, 1998.

Jones, Quincy. *Tupac Shakur, 1971–1996.* New York: Three Rivers Press, 1998.

Kammen, Michael. *Mystic Chords of Memory: The Transformation of Tradition in American Culture.* New York: Knopf, 1991.

Kasher, Stephen. *The Civil Rights Movement: A Photographic History, 1954–1968.* New York: Abbeville Press, 1996.

Kaufmann, Walter, ed. *The Portable Nietzsche.* New York: Viking Press, 1977.

Kelley, Robin D. G. *Yo' Mama's Disfunktional! Fighting the Culture Wars in Urban America.* Boston: Beacon Press, 1997.

Kidron, Michael, and Segal, Ronald, eds. *The New State of the World Atlas.* Part 1. New York: Simon & Schuster, 1984.

Kincaid, Jamaica. *At the Bottom of the River.* New York: Farrar, Straus, and Giroux, 1983.

Kornfield, Jack, and Fronsdal, Gil, eds. *Teachings of the Buddha.* Boston: Shambhala. Distributed by Random House, 1993.

Kozol, Jonathan. *Savage Inequalities: Children in America's Schools.* New York: Crown, 1991.

Krasner, David, and Elam, Harry J., eds. *African-American Performance and Theatre History: A Critical Reader.* New York: Oxford University Press, 2000.

Lasch, Christopher. *The Culture of Narcissism: American Life in an Age of Diminishing Expectations.* Rev. ed. New York: Norton, 1991.

Lee, George L. *Interesting People: Black American History Makers.* London: McFarland, 1989.

Lhoman, W. T., Jr. *Raising Cain: Blackface Performance from Jim Crow to Hip-Hop.* Cambridge: Harvard University Press, 2000.

Light, Alan, and Watson, Margeaux. *Tupac Amaru Shakur, 1971–1996.* New York: Crown, 1997.

Macleod, Jay. *Ain't No Making It: Aspirations and Attainments in a Low-Income Neighborhood.* Boulder: Westview Press, 1995.

Martinez, Gerald; Martinez, Diana; and Chavez, Andres. *What It Is . . . What It Was! The Black Film Explosion of the 70's in Words and Pictures.* New York: Hyperion, 1998.

Massey, Douglas S., and Denton, Nancy A. *American Apartheid and Segregation and the Making of the Underclass.* Cambridge: Harvard University Press, 1993.

McCall, Nathan. *Makes Me Wanna Holler: A Young Black Man in America.* New York: Random House, 1994.

McCann, Justin, ed. *Cloud of Unknowing*. London: Burns and Washbourne, 1936.

McClary, Susan. *Feminine Endings: Music, Gender and Sexuality*. Minneapolis: University of Minnesota Press, 1991.

McDermott, John, et al. *Hendrix: Setting the Record Straight*. New York: Warner Books, 1992.

Mellon, James, ed. *Bullwhip Days: The Slaves Remember*. New York: Weidenfeld & Nicolson, 1988.

Melville, Herman. *Moby Dick; or, The White Whale*. New York: Rinehart & Co., 1949.

Merton, Thomas. *No Man Is an Island*. New York: Harcourt, Brace, 1955.

Morgan, Robin. *Sisterhood Is Powerful: Anthology of Writings from the Women's Liberation Movement*. New York: Random House, 1970.

Morris, Aldon. *Origins of the Civil Rights Movement: Black Communities Organizing for Change*. New York: Free Press, 1984.

Murray, Charles. *Losing Ground: American Social Policy, 1950–1980*. New York: Basic Books, 1995.

Nisenson, Eric. *Ascension: John Coltrane and His Quest*. New York: Da Capo Press, 1995.

Norrell, Robert J. *Reaping the Whirlwind: The Civil Rights Movement in Tuskegee*. New York: Random House, 1992.

Olds, Bruce. *Raising Holy Hell: A Novel*. New York: Penguin, 1997.

Olsen, Jack. *Last Man Standing: The Tragedy and Triumph of Geronimo Pratt*. New York: Doubleday, 2000.

Passman, Donald S. *All You Need to Know About the Music Business*. New York: Prentice Hall, 1991.

Patillo-McCoy, Mary. *Black Picket Fences: Privilege and Peril Among the Black Middle Class*. Chicago: University of Chicago Press, 1999.

Patterson, Orlando. *Rituals of Blood: Consequences of Slavery in Two American Centuries*. New York: Basic Books, 1998.

Pattison, Robert. *The Triumph of Vulgarity: Rock Music in the Mirror of Romanticism*. New York: Oxford University Press, 1997.

Pearson, Hugh. *The Shadow of the Panther: Huey Newton and the Price of Black Power in America*. Reading, Mass.: Addison-Wesley, 1994.

Peck, Ira. *The Life and Words of Martin Luther King, Jr*. New York: Scholastic Book Services, 1968.

Pirsig, Robert. *Zen and the Art of Motorcycle Maintenance*. New York: Morrow, 1974.

Pope, Alexander, trans. *The Odyssey of Homer*. Philadelphia: James Crissy, 1828.

Porter, Lewis. *John Coltrane: His Life and Music*. Ann Arbor: University of Michigan Press, 2000.

Price, Richard. *Clockers*. New York: Harper Perennial Library, 2001.

Puzo, Mario. *The Godfather*. New York: Putnam, 1969.

Redding, Noel, and Appleby, Carl. *Are You Experienced? The Inside Story of the Jimi Hendrix Experience.* New York: Da Capo Press, 1996.

Rickford, Russell John. *Spoken Soul: The Story of Black English.* New York: John Wiley & Sons, 2000.

Roberts, Dorothy. *Killing the Black Body: Race, Reproduction and the Meaning of Liberty.* New York: Pantheon, 1997.

Rosengarten, Theodore. *All God's Dangers: The Life of Nate Shaw.* Rev. ed. New York: Norton, 1999.

Russell, Gary Ross. *Bird Lives! The High Life and Hard Times of Charlie (Yardbird) Parker.* New York: Da Capo Press, 1996.

Salinger, J. D. *Catcher in the Rye.* Boston: Little, Brown, 1951.

Scholem, Gershem. *Kabbalah.* New York: Quadrangle/New York Times Book Company, 1974.

Schwartz, Barry. *George Washington: The Making of an American Symbol.* New York: Free Press, 1987.

———. *Abraham Lincoln and the Forge of National Memory.* Chicago: University of Chicago Press, 2000.

Scott, Cathy. *The Killing of Tupac Shakur.* Las Vegas: Huntington Press, 1997.

Seal, Graham. *The Outlaw Legend: A Cultural Tradition in Britain, America and Australia.* Cambridge: Cambridge University Press, 1996.

Shakur, Assata. *Assata: An Autobiography.* Lawrence Hill, 1988.

Shakur, Sanyika. *Monster: The Autobiography of an L.A. Gang Member.* Reading, Mass.: Addison-Wesley, 1998.

Shakur, Tupac. *The Rose That Grew from Concrete.* New York: Simon & Schuster, 1999.

Sing-Ha, Shri. *Karma-glin-pa. The Tibetan Book of the Dead.* New York: Bantam Books, 1994.

Sleeman, W. H. *Journey Through the Kingdom of Oude, 1849–1850.* 2 vols. South Asia Books, 1995.

———. *Rambles and Recollections of an Indian Official.* 2 vols. South Asia Books, 1995.

Southern, Eileen. *The Music of Black Americans: A History.* New York: Norton, 1983.

Stavig, Ward. *The World of Tupac Amaru: Conflict, Community, and Identity in Colonial Peru.* University of Nebraska Press, 1999.

Stetson, Earlene. *Black Sister: Poetry by Black American Women, 1746 to 1980.* Bloomington: Indiana University Press, 1981.

Styron, William. *Confessions of Nat Turner.* New York: Random House, 1967.

Summer, Anthony. *Goddess: The Secret Lives of Marilyn Monroe.* New York: Macmillan, 1985.

Sun Tzu. *Art of War.* New York: Oxford University Press, 1984.

Sutton-Smith, Brian. *The Ambiguity of Play.* Cambridge: Harvard University Press, 2001.

Teilhard de Chardin, Pierre. *Phenomenon of Man*. New York: Harper, 1959.

Terr, Lenore. *Beyond Love and Work: Why Adults Need to Play*. New York: Scribner, 1999.

Thomas à Kempis. *Imitation of Christ*. London: Burns & Oakes, 1959.

Thurman, Howard. *Jesus and the Disinherited*. Boston: Beacon Press, 1996.

Twain, Mark. *The Prince and the Pauper*. New York: Random House, 1999.

Ugwu, Catherine, ed. *Let's Get It On: The Politics of Black Performance*. Bay Press, 1995.

Underhill, Evelyn. *Mysticism: A Study in the Nature and Development of Man's Spiritual Consciousness*. New York: New American Library, 1955.

Walker, Alice. *In Search of Our Mothers' Gardens: Womanist Prose*. San Diego: Harcourt Brace Jovanovich, 1983.

Watts, Alan. *The Wisdom of Insecurity*. New York: Pantheon, 1951.

White, Armond. *Rebel for the Hell of It: The Life of Tupac Shakur*. New York: Thunder's Mouth Press, 1997.

White, Deborah Gray. *Ar'n't I a Woman? Female Slaves in the Plantation South*. New York: Norton, 1999.

_____. *Too Heavy a Load: Black Women in Defense of Themselves, 1894–1994*. New York: Norton, 1999.

Whitehead, Colson. *John Henry Days*. New York: Doubleday, 2001.

Wilmshurst, W. L. *The Meaning of Masonry*. London: W. Rider & Son, 1923.

Wilson, William Julius. *The Truly Disadvantaged: The Inner City, the Underclass and Public Policy*. Chicago: University of Chicago Press, 1987.

_____. *When Work Disappears: The World of the New Urban Poor*. New York: Knopf, 1996.

Wittgenstein, Ludwig. *Philosophical Investigations: The English Text of the Third Edition*. Trans. G. E. M. Anscombe. 3rd ed. New York: Prentice Hall, 1999.

Wolff, David. *You Send Me: The Life and Times of Sam Cooke*. New York: Quill, 1996.

Wright, Richard. *Native Son*. New York: Harper, 1940.

Journal Articles

Barrett, Lindon. "Dead Men Printed." *Callaloo* 22, 2 (spring 1999).

Fox, Martin. "Expanded Theory Of 'Brady' Material Rebuffed by Judge in Rapper's Appeal." *New York Law Journal,* May 1, 1996, p. 1.

Glickman, Simon. "2Pac." *Contemporary Musicians* 17: 228–231.

Keeling, Kara. "'A Homegrown Revolutionary'? Tupac Shakur and the Legacy of the Black Panther Party." *Black Scholar* 29, 2/3 (summer 1999): 59–63.

Magazine Articles

Alexander, Frank. "The Day the Hip-Hop Died." *Hip-Hop Connection,* October 1998, pp. 16–21.

Anson, Robert Sam. "To Die Like a Gangsta." *Vanity Fair,* March 1997, pp. 244–252.

"Are Rappers Predicting Their Own Deaths?" *Jet,* March 31, 1997, pp. 60–63.

Ashon, Will. "The Six Faces of Tupac Shakur." *Hip-Hop Connection,* May 1996, pp. 40–41.

Baker, Calvin. "Living Dangerously." *People,* September 23, 1996, pp. 75–76.

Baker, Soren. "Music After Death." *The Source,* February 1998, p. 44.

Berman, Eric. "2Pac *Strictly 4 My N.I.G.G.A.Z.*" *The Source,* April 1993, pp. 69–70.

"Bits and Pieces." *The Source,* April 1995, p. 27.

Blount, Erika. "Out on Bail Tupac Gets a Taste of Freedom." *The Source,* December 1995, p. 32.

_____. "Tupac's Trail." *The Source,* November 1995, p. 26.

Braxton, Charlie. "Conspiracy Theory." *The Source,* May 1998, p. 42.

Brown, Ann. "Afeni Shakur Launches Label, Writer Disputes Tupac's Biography." *Rap Sheet,* December 1997-January 1999, p. 32.

Bruck, Connie. "The Takedown of Tupac." *New Yorker,* July 7, 1997, pp. 46–65.

Callahan-Bever, Noah. "The Death of Battle Rap." *The Source,* February 1998, p. 41.

Castro, Peter. "All Eyes on Her." *People,* December 1, 1997, pp. 151–154.

Cook, Dara. "Tupac's Stage Debut." *Rap Sheet,* December 1998, p. 8.

Davis, Eisa. "Trials and Tribulations." *The Source,* January 1994, p. 46.

Dawsey, Darell. "A Eulogy for Tupac." *Essence,* December 1996, p. 38.

Delvin, Mark. "Hip-Hop's Darkest Hour?" *Hip-Hop Connection,* October 1996, p. 7.

Emory, Andrew. "Encyclopaedia Raptannica." *Hip-Hop Connection,* December 1997, p. 27.

_____. "Dead Poets Society." *Hip-Hop Connection,* March 1999, p. 32.

Farley, Christopher John. "From the Driver's Side." *Time,* September 1996, p. 70.

Gambles, Jeff. "Afterthuglife." *The Source,* August 1995, p. 24.

Gilmore, Mikal. "Why Tupac Should Be Heard." *Rolling Stone,* October 31, 1996, pp. 49–51, 84.

Gordon, Allen S. "Tupac Shakur: R U Still Down?" *Rap Pages,* p. 102.

_____. "Tupac: Me Against the World." *The Source,* April 1995, pp. 78–79.

Green, Kim. "War Stories." *The Source,* August 1993, pp. 56, 58–59, 92.

Hamilton, Kendall, and Samuels, Allison. "Double Trouble for 2Pac." *Newsweek,* December 12, 1994, pp. 62–63.

Hampton, Dream. "Hellraiser." *The Source,* September 1994, pp. 80–89.

_____. "Keep Your Head Up." *The Source,* April 1994, p. 19.

Henderson, Cinque. "Split Personality." *New Republic,* October 7, 1996, p. 46.

Herbert, Wray. "The Making of a Hip-Hop Intellectual." *U.S. News and World Report,* 1996.

Hewitt, Bill. "Rapper Sheet." *People,* December 6, 1993, pp.89–90.

"Interscope Splits from Time-Warner! 2Pac Signs to Death Row." *Hip-Hop Connection,* p. 4.

June Joseph. "Tuff Links." *Hip-Hop Connection,* January 1995, pp. 24–27.

Kinnon, Joy Bennett. "Does RAP Have a Future?" *Ebony,* June 1997, p. 76.

Lacayo, Richard. "Shootin' up the Charts." *Time,* November 15, 1993, pp. 81–82.

"Legends." *Rap Pages,* April 1999, p. 118.

Leland, John. "Gangsta Rap and the Culture of Violence." *Newsweek,* November 29, 1993, pp. 60–64.

Lodge, Veronica. "Jackin' Beats." *Rap Pages,* September 1998, pp. 65–68, 71.

———. "Inside Dope." *Rap Pages,* February 1999, pp. 24–25.

Morganthau, Tom. "The New Frontier for Civil Rights." *Newsweek,* November 29, 1993, pp. 65–66.

"Most Influential Rapper." *The Source,* January 1998, p. 169.

"Pac and Biggie." *Rap Pages,* January 1999, p. 27.

Pendleton, Tonya. "Soul for Sale." *Rap Pages,* October 1997, pp. 56–63, 102–103.

Phillips, Chuck. "2PAC's Gospel Truth." *Rolling Stone,* October 28, 1993, p. 22.

Pollack, Phyllis. "Tupac's Dad Gets His Day in Court." *Rap Pages,* March 1998, p. 56.

Powell, Kevin. "The Short Life and Violent Death of Tupac Shakur." *Rolling Stone,* October 31, 1996, pp. 38–46, 49–51.

"Rap Execs Face Police Investigations." *Billboard,* May 1, 1999, pp. 3, 80.

"Rapper Snoop Doggy Dogg to Leave Death Row Records; Fear for His Life." *Jet,* February 2, 1998, p. 15.

Ro, Ronin. "The Whole Nine." *Rap Pages,* May 1997, pp. 49–50, 53–54, 90.

Roberts, Johnnie L. "Grabbing at a Dead Star." *Newsweek,* September 1, 1997, p. 48.

Rogers, Patrick. "Prophecy Fulfilled." *People,* September 30, 1996, pp. 79–80.

Ross, Barbara. "Cop Killed." *The Source,* December 1992, pp. 16–17.

Samuels, Allison. "Who Stole Tupac's Soul?" *Rolling Stone,* June 25, 1998, pp. 23–25.

Samuels, Allison, and Leland, John. "Trouble Man." *Newsweek,* September 23, 1996, pp. 66–69.

Samuels, Allison, and Schoemer, Karen. "Back in the Thug Life Again." *Newsweek,* February 26, 1996, p. 68.

Sandy, Dan. "Reunited." *Hip-Hop Connection,* September 1997, p. 6.

Senna, Danzy, and Smith, Vern E. "The Postures and the Reality." *Newsweek,* November 15, 1993, p. 86.

Solotaroff, Ivan. "Gangsta Life, Gangsta Death." *Esquire,* December 1996, pp. 78–82.

"Still No Arrest." *Time,* December 30, 1996, p. 130.

Strange, Adario. "Real Thug Life." *The Source,* February 1995, p. 19.

Tabu, Hannibal. "Tribute to Tupac Shakur." *Rap Pages,* May 1997, p. 90.

Thigpen, David. "Is Rap to Blame?" *The Source,* December 1998, p. 168.

Tirella, Joseph V. "Police Sweep L.A. in the Wake of Shakur Murder." *Rolling Stone,* November 14, 1996, p. 32.

"Tupac Shakur." *Economist,* December 1996, p. 91.

"Tupac Shakur, R.I.P." *Hip-Hop Connection,* January 1997, p. 60.

"2PAC." *Hip-Hop Connection,* August 1996, p. 35.

"2PAC." *The Source,* January 1994, p. 24.

"2PAC: Unforgiven." *The Source,* November 1993, p. 16.

Van Biema, David. "What Goes Around . . . " *Time,* September 23, 1996, p. 40.

Wazir, Burhan. "Life Before Death." *Hip-Hop Connection,* February 1988, p. 41.

_____. "2Pac 'Me Against The World.'" *Hip-Hop Connection,* May 1995, p. 40.

_____. "Tupac Shakur." *Hip-Hop Connection,* December 1996, pp. 32–33.

_____."Mum's the Word." April 1998, pp. 28–31.

Whitehead, Colson. "An Unforgiving New York Which Urges Self Destruction . . . " *The Source,* March 1992, pp. 47–48.

Wielenga, Dave. "A Free Man on Death Row." *Rolling Stone,* November 30, 1995, p. 42.

_____. "Hip-Hop Nation Shaken by Tupac Shakur Ambush off Las Vegas Strip." *Rolling Stone,* October 17, 1996, p. 40.

Newspaper Articles

"Anti-Rap Crusader Claims That Gangsta Lyrics Ruined Her Sex Life." *Daily Record,* August 5, 1997, p. 13.

"Anti-Rap Crusader Files $10 Million Suit Against Shakur's Estate." *Entertainment Litigation Reporter,* August 30, 1997.

"Arrest Warrant Extended for Rapper Tupac Shakur." *Los Angeles Times,* January 26, 1994, p. 2B.

Barron, James. "Rapper Becomes Victim." *New York Times,* December 1, 1994, p. 3B.

Beale, Lewis. "Tupac Bail Aid Rapped." *New York Daily News,* May 13, 1995, p. 6.

Britt, Donna. "A Little Poetic Justice." *Atlanta Journal and Constitution,* November 8, 1993, p. 9A.

Charen, Mona. "Putting a Muzzle on Gangsta Rap." *Atlanta Journal and Constitution,* May 30, 1995, p. 7A.

Charles, Jeff. "Be Against the World." *Houston Chronicle,* April 9, 1995, p. 6.

"Citing Health, Rapper Misses Court Hearing." *New York Times,* December 6, 1994, p. 3B.

Coleman, Chrisena. "Shakur's Lifestyle Is a Hard Cell Upstate." *New York Daily News,* March 16, 1995, p. 6.

Crowe, Jerry. "Atop the Charts from Behind Bars." *Los Angeles Times,* April 8, 1995, p. 1F.

Danquah, Meri Nana-Ama. "A Rising Chorus." *Los Angeles Times,* January 12, 1995, p. 1E.

Deggans, Eric. "Taking the Gangsta out of Rap." *St. Petersburg Times,* October 15, 1996, p. 1D.

Farber, Jim. "2pac: 'Me Against the World.'" *New York Daily News ,* April 11, 1995, p. 33.

Fried, Rinat, "Tupac v. Shakur." *Recorder,* November 15, 1995, p. 2.

Furse, Jane. "Tupac's Side of the Story." *New York Daily News,* March 1, 1995.

Gelder, Lawrence. "Rapper, Shot and Convicted." *New York Times,* December 3, 1994, p. 26E.

Gladwell, Malcolm. "Shakur Goes Free Pending Appeal." *Washington Post,* October 14, 1995, p. 8D.

Goldsmith, Laura B. "America's Black Man Carries Heavy Burden." *San Francisco Chronicle,* March 1, 1994, p. 17A.

———. "Rapper Tupac Shakur Robbed, Shot in New York." *Washington Post,* December 1, 1994, p. 1A.

Harrington, Richard. "Fro Rap, Some Arresting Developments." *Washington Post,* December 29, 1993, p. 7C.

Hayes, Ted. "Excusing Negative Rap Is Wrong." *Los Angeles Times,* January 21, 1995, p. 5B.

Hays, Tom. "Wounded Rapper Leaves Hospital." Associated Press, December 1, 1994.

Helmore, Edward. "Pop Music." *Independent* (London), December 2, 1994, p. 27.

Himes, Geoffrey. "Classic Funk from Clinton." *Washington Post,* December 31, 1993, p. 12N.

Hochman, Steve. "Pop Eye: 2Pac's Pals Turn Out for Tupac-less Video." *Los Angeles Times,* September 24, 1995, p. 73.

Hopkins, Tracy E. "Critics Rap Gangsta Lyrics for Obscenity, Misogyny." *Washington Post,* July 20, 1994, p. 11C.

Huang, Vivian. "Rap Producer Slain Near Home." *(New York) Daily News,* December 1, 1995, p. 2.

Hunter-Hodge, Karen. "Rap Getting a Bum Rap." *Calgary Herald,* November 13, 1993, p. 5E.

———. "He's a B.I.G. Help to Junior M.A.F.I.A." *(New York) Daily News,* November 19, 1995, p. 39.

Iverson, Esther. "Screen Star Debuted on the Streets." *Record,* July 27, 1993, p. 11B.

———. "The Softer Side of Tupac Shakur." *Los Angeles Times,* July 24, 1993, p. 12F.

James, George. "Rapper Faces Prison Term for Sex Abuse." *New York Times,* February 8, 1995, p. 1B.

Jones, Clarisse. "For a Rapper, Life and Art Converge in Violence." *New York Times,* December 1, 1994, p. 1A.

———. "Trouble Aplenty: Rapper's Life Mirrors Music." *New York Times,* December 4, 1994, p. 2D.

———. "Rapper Slain After Chase in Queens." *New York Times,* December 1, 1995, p. 3B.

Jones, James T. "Rapper's Run-ins with the Police." *USA Today,* November 2, 1993, p. 2D.

———. "Jury Finds Shakur Guilty." *USA Today,* December 2, 1994, p. 2D.

———. "Menace or Martyr?" *USA Today,* March 29, 1994, p. 1D.

Lacharite, Gretchen. "Gangsta Protesters Arrested." *Washington Times,* January 6, 1994, p. 3C.

Larkin, Kevin. "Sexual Abuse Rap Lands Shakur in Holiday Lockup." *Chicago Sun-Times,* December 25, 1994, p. 26.

Lowry, Tom. "Rap on Label." *New York Daily News,* August 1995, p. 32.

———. "Shakur Denies Gang-rape Rumors." *USA Today,* July 11, 1995, p. 2D.

Maull, Samuel. "Art of Anarchy? Gunplay Spurs Rap Debate." November 3, 1993, p. 1D.

———. "Police Have Video That Shows Rapper in Sex Act." Associated Press, November 26, 1993.

McShane, Larry. "Rap the Rap. Walk the Walk." Associated Press, December 24, 1994.

———. "Rapper Tupac Shakur Shot While Jurors Deliberate Sexual Assault Charges." Associated Press, November 30, 1994.

Merida, Kevin. "Lawmaker Using CIA Controversy to Marshal Forces." *Washington Post,* October 25, 1996, p. 16A.

Minton, Torri. "Jury Hears 2 Views of How Rapper's Gun Killed Boy." *San Francisco Chronicle,* November 7, 1994, p. 11A.

———. "Marin City Haunted by Boy's Shooting Wrongful Death Trial to Begin." *San Francisco Chronicle,* November 3, 1994, p. 1A.

Minton, Torri, and Doyle, Jim. "Settlement in Rapper's Trial for Boy's Death." *San Francisco Chronicle,* November 8, 1994, p. 1A.

Morehouse, Macon. "Rapper Accused of Shooting Two Off-Duty Cops." *Atlanta Journal and Constitution,* November 1, 1993, p. 1B.

Murray, Sonia. "Tupac's Mama." *Atlanta Journal and Constitution,* May 28, 1995, p. 1K.

"The NAACP's New Taste for Rap." *Washington Times,* February 11, 1994, p. 22A.

Oliphant, Thomas. "2Pac on the Dole Hits Low Notes." *Boston Globe,* June 4, 1995, p. 87.

Pareles, Jon. "How Real Is 'Realness' in Hip-Hop?" *New York Times,* December 11, 1994, p. 34.

_____. "A Night for Surviving Through Hip-Hop." *New York Times,* March 14, 1995, p. 16C.

Perez-Pena, Richard. "Wounded Rapper Gets Mixed Verdict in Sex-Abuse Case." *New York Times,* December 2, 1994, p. 1A.

Philips, Chuck. "Q & A with Tupac Shakur." *Los Angeles Times,* October 25, 1995, p. 1F.

Pringle, Peter. "Rap Star Accused After Sex Attack." *Independent* (London), November 25, 1993, p. 15.

_____. "Peter Pringle's America: Rapped up in a Violent Life." *Independent* (London), December 5, 1994, p. 15.

Pristin, Terry. "Rap Star Faces Charges." *New York Times,* August 1, 1996, p. 1B.

Proffitt, Steve. "Russell Simons: Defending the Art of Communications Known as Rap." *Los Angeles Times,* August 27, 1995, p. 3M.

"Rap Singer Arrested in a Weapon Inquiry." *New York Times,* May 2, 1994, p. 18A.

"Rap Singer Sentenced to 15 Days in L.A. Jail." United Press International, March 10, 1994.

"Rapper Gets 4 1/2 Years in Sex Case." *Atlanta Journal and Constitution,* February 8, 1995, p. 9B.

"Rapper Settles Suit over Boy's Death." *Phoenix Gazette,* November 9, 1995, p. 2A.

"Rapper Shakur Released on Bail After 8 Months." *Chicago Sun-Times,* October 15, 1995, p. 3.

"Rapper Shakur Sentenced to Prison in Sexual Assaults." *Houston Chronicle,* February 8, 1995, p. 8A.

"Rapper Shakur Shot." *Gazette* (Montreal), December 1, 1994, p. 13C.

"Rapper Shakur to Spend Christmas in Police Custody." *Gazette* (Montreal), December 24, 1994, p. 11C.

"Rapper Shot Five Times." *Calgary Herald,* December 1, 1994, p. 18D.

Raspberry, William. "Blame Those Responsible for Gangsta Rap." *Houston Chronicle,* August 15, 1995, p. 18.

_____. "Passing the Rap." *Washington Post,* August 14, 1995, p. 17A.

Ross, Sonya. "Women's Group Angry over Tupac Shakur Nomination." Associated Press, January 5, 1994.

"Shakur Charged with Possession." *Gazette* (Montreal), May 3, 1994, p. 5B.

"Shakur's Bail Set at 3 Million." *Gazette* (Montreal), December 22, 1994, p. 7C.

Sims, Calvin. "Gangster Rapper: The Lives, the Lyrics." *New York Times,* November 28, 1993, p. 3D.

Singleton, Don. "Bad Time in Joint for Tupac Cover Pot." *New York Daily News,* June 17, 1995, p. 6.

Smothers, Ronald. "Rapper Charged in Shootings of Off-Duty Officers." *New York Times,* November 2, 1993, p. 16A.

Stovall, Natasha. "Town Criers." *Village Voice,* March 18, 1997, p. 42.

Sullivan, Ronald. "Wounded Rapper Jailed at Bellevue After Failing to Post Bond." *New York Times,* December 24, 1994, p. 30.

Tate, Greg. "Above and Beyond Rap's Decibels." *New York Times,* March 6, 1994, p. 1.

Thomas, Wallace. "2Pac Steps Up: Positive Sounds from Troubled Life." *Cleveland Plain Dealer,* May 1, 1995, p. 1E.

"Time Warner Bails Out of Gangsta Rap." *Phoenix Gazette,* September 28, 1995, p. 2A.

"Too-pock Rapper 2Pac Charged with Sex Attack." United Press International, November 19, 1993.

Toure. "Biggie Smalls, Rap's Man of the Year." *New York Times,* December 18, 1994, p. 42.

_____. "The Professional: Tupac Shakur Gives the Performance of His Life." *Village Voice,* December 3, 1994, p. 75.

Violanti, Anthony. "A B.I.G. Deal." *Buffalo News,* April 21, 1995, p. 30.

_____. "Tupac Shakur Takes on a World of Persecution." *Buffalo News,* April 17, 1995, p. 1.

Washington, Jesse. "Source Awards Honor Past and Present Hip-Hop Giants." Associated Press, April 26, 1994.

Watson, Rod. "Violence Is Not New to Entertainment." *Buffalo News,* June 8, 1995, p. 3.

Webb, Gary. "Dark Alliance." *San Jose Mercury News,* August 18–20, 1996, pp. 1A, 10A, and 17A.

Williams, Jeannie. "Another Gun Arrest for Tupac Shakur." *USA Today,* May 2, 1994, p. 2D.

INDEX